Medicine and Empathy in Contemporary British Fiction

Medicine and Empathy in Contemporary British Fiction

An Intervention in Medical Humanities

Anne Whitehead

EDINBURGH
University Press

Edinburgh University Press is one of the leading university presses in the UK. We publish academic books and journals in our selected subject areas across the humanities and social sciences, combining cutting-edge scholarship with high editorial and production values to produce academic works of lasting importance. For more information visit our website: edinburghuniversitypress.com

Edinburgh University Press Ltd
The Tun – Holyrood Road, 12(2f) Jackson's Entry, Edinburgh EH8 8PJ

Typeset in 11/13 Adobe Sabon by
IDSUK (DataConnection) Ltd, and
printed and bound in Great Britain by
CPI Group (UK) Ltd, Croydon CR0 4YY

A CIP record for this book is available from the British Library

ISBN 978 0 7486 8618 6 (hardback)
ISBN 978 0 7486 8619 3 (webready PDF)
ISBN 978 0 7486 8620 9 (epub)

Contents

Acknowledgements

This book could not have been accomplished without the support of Newcastle University. It was completed during a six-month period of internally funded research leave, and I thank my colleagues for relieving me of managerial and teaching responsibilities during this time. I am also indebted to the generous support of a number of colleagues, who have helped me in different ways over the course of writing the book. Particular thanks are extended to Linda Anderson, James Annesley, Kate Chedgzoy, Ruth Connolly, Karen Corrigan, Neill Marshall, Lucy Pearson and Margaret Wilkinson.

Much of the thinking in this book emerges out of ongoing intellectual conversations with a range of colleagues and friends. The book originated in thinking about feminism and affect, and here I have benefited particularly from working with Carolyn Pedwell, whose intellectual and political energy continues to act as a source of inspiration. Through a series of events on feminism, feeling and human rights, I also had the opportunity to develop and sharpen my thinking in dialogue with Sara Ahmed, Ann Cvetkovich, Aminatta Forna, Clare Hemmings, Ranjana Khanna, Madhu Krishnan, Zoe Norridge, Jackie Stacey and Lyndsey Stonebridge.

The second project that has had a significant influence on my thinking for this book is the *Edinburgh Companion to the Critical Medical Humanities*. It has been a genuine pleasure to work on an editorial team with such energy, vision and incisiveness, and I feel privileged to have worked alongside Angela Woods, Sarah Atkinson, Jane Macnaughton and Jennifer Richards. The contributors to the *Companion* have also provided inspiration and stimulation along the way. A particular thank you, too, to Pat Barker for engaging with me in two public conversations, hosted at Newcastle University and at Durham University. All weaknesses, gaps or errors in this book remain, of course, my own.

I have presented material from this book at various conferences and seminars, and I would like to thank colleagues at the University of Ghent, the University of Zurich, the University of Leuven, the University of Lincoln, Edinburgh University, the University of Zaragozza and at the Association of Medical Humanities conference at Aberdeen University, for their thought-provoking questions and responses.

The book would not have been possible without the support of Edinburgh University Press, and I thank Jackie Jones in particular for her initial responsiveness to the project and for her advice. I am also grateful to Patricia Waugh and Sue Vice for such engaged, productive and thoughtful response and feedback.

I extend particular gratitude to a number of friends who have been there throughout: John Bentley, Kate Davies, Marita Grimwood, Catherine Johns, Helen Jones, Rye Mattick, Neelam Srivastava and Rachel Terry. Thank you.

Introduction

Rita Charon, Professor of Clinical Medicine at Columbia University, has played a leading role in creating the movement of narrative medicine, which is centrally concerned with opening up new approaches in medical education, and its core principles are encapsulated in her monograph *Narrative Medicine* (2006). For her, the clinician's task is essentially one of narrative interpretation: the practitioner is required to listen attentively to a complex and multi-faceted narrative, told in the patient's case history, in bodily symptoms, and in medical and laboratory test results, all of which need to come together into the formulation of a diagnosis and treatment plan. The aim of medical education should therefore be to aid the development of narrative capabilities, which are defined by Charon as: 'recognizing, absorbing, interpreting, and being moved by the stories of illness' (2006: 4). Moreover, for Charon, narrative should not only be read by the trainee practitioner, but also written by her, in the form of a Parallel Chart that records what her patient endures. This, Charon explains, allows the medical student to '*enter* the worlds of [her] patients, if only imaginatively, and to see and interpret these worlds from the patients' point of view' (2006: 9; italics in original). For Charon, then, narrative – whether read or written – is of value to medicine because it is productive of empathetic engagement with the patient. Her work, which has proved highly influential in the field of the medical humanities, comprises a compelling story about the literary, which is seen to be essentially humanising, equipping students with 'compassion' (2006: 8).

Narrative medicine is, as cultural critic Stuart Murray has observed, 'a vital foundational part of critical medical humanities' (2016: 628). Together with the work of Arthur Kleinman (1988) and Arthur W. Frank (1995), Charon has foregrounded the patient experience of illness, and the practitioner's response to it, as central in countering the effects of an increasingly impersonal, fragmented and bureaucratised biomedicine.[1] Nevertheless, the work of Charon and others in the mainstream medical humanities is problematic at a number of levels: in its restriction of medicine to the individualised clinical encounter; in its loose and under-theorised understanding of empathy; and in its representation and positioning of literature, not least as a transparent vehicle for conveying the 'truth' of another's experience. This monograph provides a critical intervention into the medical humanities that addresses each of these points. In the chapters that follow, I argue not only that the clinical encounter itself needs to be situated within a broader, and more politicised, understanding of how power and resource flows through medical institutions, but also that too narrow a focus on the patient–practitioner relation distracts attention from other important sites and domains of medicine. I provide a strong conceptual underpinning for the discussion of empathy, drawing on phenomenological philosophy and on feminist affect theory to emphasise an account of empathy that does not claim to know or to understand the other, but remains alert to her distance and her difference. Through a series of readings in contemporary British novels that engage with ideas of medicine and empathy, I position the literary both as a strategic intervention into current debates on empathy and its meanings, and as expressing a discernible scepticism regarding empathy's limits that runs directly counter to the humanising impulse of the mainstream medical humanities. I also examine literature's propensity towards probing our difficulties in understanding others, and even our lack of care in the face of their pain and suffering.[2]

Rethinking 'medicine'

In order to engage critically with the mainstream medical humanities, Angela Woods and I have recently characterised its 'primal scene' as the clinical encounter between the doctor and the patient that unfolds the diagnosis of cancer (Whitehead and Woods 2016: 2). Asking why this scene has taken on such prominence in the medical humanities, we argue that it is because it both speaks to and encapsulates the three 'Es' that have shaped and defined the field: 'ethics (medical ethics and bioethics), education (medical, but also increasingly health) and experience (particularly qualities of illness experience)' (2016: 3). In what follows, I will briefly discuss each of these categories in turn, before moving on to think about how a critical medical humanities approach might differently frame and define the concept of the medical, and outlining how this monograph has in turn understood and positioned the term 'medicine'.

The medical humanities emerged out of the disciplinary field of medical ethics. Medical ethics, and more recently, bioethics, focuses on health issues in which moral values are open to question; thus, 'end-of-life care and decision making, and reproductive medicine', have been areas of particular interest and concern (Whitehead and Woods 2016: 3). It is no surprise, then, that the scene of the cancer diagnosis, which potentially invokes complex questions of terminal care and decision making, should have become so foundational in and to the medical humanities. Medical ethics is also invested in effective communication within the healthcare setting, and we can again discern a clear line of influence to the 'primal scene', in which the conveying of the cancer diagnosis raises attendant concerns of clear and compassionate communication. Medical ethics turned to the narrative ethics represented by Charon, using the patient's story to illustrate moral dilemmas and to aid in developing more thoughtful responses to them. In so doing, medical ethics, like narrative medicine itself, approaches the story from an investigatory point of view, expecting it to yield a solution or decision, whether that be an ethically appropriate course of action or a clinical diagnosis. For critic Karla F. C. Holloway, this not only runs counter to the impetus of the literary itself, which offers 'incoherent, messy solutions (if there are solutions at all)', but also artificially abstracts the patient's story, which 'fails to give constitutive weight to the cultural and historical context of that experience' (2011: xvii). Medical ethics, like narrative medicine, tends to view the patient outside the complex social, cultural and political landscapes that are constitutive of her identity.

In its attention to an effective communication between practitioner and patient, the 'primal scene' of the medical humanities is also concerned with our second 'E': education. In a claim that is often reiterated, physician Howard Spiro has argued that the primacy accorded in medical training to dissection, basic science and medical imaging, followed by the exhausting rituals of residency, has a cumulatively objectifying effect: 'Students begin their medical education with a cargo of empathy, but we teach them to see themselves as "experts", to fix what is damaged, and to "rule out" disease in their field' (1993c: 9). Spiro's reference to 'disease' invokes a binary of 'illness' and 'disease' that was central to first-wave medical humanities, with disease aligned with scientific knowledge and data, and illness denoting the patient's subjective experience. In order to shift the balance of clinical treatment towards the latter, medical educators asked whether empathy was a skill that could be taught, and narrative emerged as the solution. For Spiro, empathy represents a resource that can 'grow' through the practice of reading: 'to read great works of fiction is to widen experience readily, to find our patients in the stories of the masters' (1993b: 5). Not only does Spiro set up here a model of empathy that is something that one has, lacks and can accrue, but he also grounds reading in 'the masters', implying a select canon of literary works that can foster the development of empathy. Reflective writing has also been seen as a vehicle through which medical students can understand patient experience. Literary critic Rebecca E. Garden has noted, however, that the distinction between empathy and appropriation seems particularly indistinct in this context:

> What part, if any, of a narrative that is written *as if it were* the patient's perspective accurately represents the patient's point of view if the narrative is written by a medical professional? What measures, if any, are taken to ensure that the narrative is written in collaboration with the patient and is not simply a practitioner's projection and appropriation of the patient's life-story, another kind of mastery of discourse over which the professional assumes authority? . . . How do such exercises in empathy represent the patient's difference or (if that is possible within the institutional discipline of medicine) a counter-gaze? (2007: 555; italics in original)

Although Garden confines her critique to the Parallel Chart, the same concerns could also be raised in relation to reading: how can we know if the doctor's narrative interpretation maps accurately on to the patient experience, or is reflective of her own feelings and concerns?

This brings us to the third 'E' of the medical humanities: Experience. Enumerating the advantages of an empathetic mode of clinical communication, psychiatrist Jodi Halpern has noted that it encourages fuller disclosure of the illness experience, which leads to more effective diagnosis and treatment. Taking us back to our 'primal scene', she also observes that it 'helps patients process emotionally difficult information, such as hearing a cancer diagnosis' (2001: 94), which can in turn facilitate improved decision making. Yet, Garden notes that here, too, there are discernible hazards. If patient and practitioner are abstracted from their social and cultural backgrounds, we can fail to account for 'the way that recognizing the patient as like oneself or seeing the patient as "other" factors into . . . empathy' (2007: 555). At the same time, there is a contrary risk that knowing something of a patient's culture and beliefs is seen to equate to 'knowing a particular person's experience of illness' (2007: 555); there is a need to work closely and carefully with patients themselves to ensure effective understanding and health care. More than this, Garden cautions that it is essential that practitioners remain mindful that clinical empathy is 'ultimately a component of the medical technology and knowledge with which physicians manage patients' (2007: 562). This latter point is power-fully reinforced by cultural scientist Rebecca Hester, who notes of cultural competence training and expertise that it is precisely a man-agement tool: 'cultural competence . . . is not only about knowing the patient more and better, but also about being able to use that cultural knowledge "effectively" to persuade the patient to do what the physi-cian wants him or her to do' (2016: 553). Here, the impetus towards equalising doctor–patient relations blurs into the more troubling ter-rain of ensuring patient compliance, indicating that empathy can tend towards the disciplinary as well as the compassionate.

The three 'Es' afford us valuable insight into the priorities, and the problems, of first-wave medical humanities. The field pays partic-ular attention both to clinical medicine and to medical education. Its primary concern is with effective doctor–patient interaction, and it displays a marked tendency at once to individualise and to decontex-tualise this relation. A more critical approach would be cognisant of the complex ways in which gender, class, race, sexuality and debility can play out in and through the clinical encounter, as well as inter-rogating its cultural, historical and institutional setting (Whitehead and Woods 2016: 2). It would also entail an awareness of empa-thy's implication in discourses and practices of management. Woods and I have also indicated that a critical medical humanities approach might usefully widen the horizon of our gaze, to take in more than the doctor and the patient in isolation. Within the clinical setting, we might thus usefully ask:

> What else . . . is in the room, and with what forms or modes of agency might it be associated? How might we account for non-human objects and presences, for belief systems, and even for the diagnosis itself – what, for example, is its history, or its status as a performative act? (Whitehead and Woods 2016: 2)

We would thus pose different questions of the clinical encounter than have characterised the medical humanities to date. We might also productively expand the definition of 'medicine' itself, moving beyond the fixation of the mainstream medical humanities on clini-cal medicine and medical training. Thus, there are a diverse range of scenes and sites that are also important to our understanding of health and illness, and that would benefit from our critical engagement and attention (Whitehead and Woods 2016: 2). How might the medical humanities relate to medical research, for example, with its primary setting of the laboratory? What kinds of scenes are opened up to view if the medical is placed within a historical or a non-Western setting? And at a time when medical knowledge circulates across public spheres, how might we think about the literary text itself as a site for the negotiation and the contestation of medical ideas and meaning?

In what follows, I do not turn away from a focus on the clinical encounter, which necessarily remains a central focus for the medical humanities, but I do ask different questions of it. My interpretative focus is not on the individualised care relation, but rather on how it is situated within and inflected by the workings of biomedical power. In Chapter 2, I read Pat Barker's *Life Class* (2007), which depicts the nursing experience of Paul Tarrant as a First World War orderly, to address the importance of the institutional context in assessing the relation of care. Chapter 3 focuses on Ian McEwan's *Saturday* (2005), a novel that famously centres on neurosurgeon Henry Perowne's treatment of Baxter, a violent intruder into his home. Here, I ask how medical and scientific knowledge is produced, and what role the humanities might play in shaping and constituting such knowledge. Chapter 4 investigates Aminatta Forna's *The Memory of Love* (2010), a novel that speaks powerfully to the global disparities in standards and practices of medical care. I argue that, through a mode of descriptive realism, the novel opens up to view the unfamiliar clinical scenes and settings in hospitals in Sierra Leone, as well as depicting the political and economic conditions that underpin such a chronic lack of resource. My readings are also attentive to the agency of non-human objects and presences; thus, I argue, for example, that the medical glove takes on powerful, if distinct, symbolic resonance in the novels of Barker and Forna.

The monograph opens and closes by discussing works of fiction that do not depict the relation between doctor and patient; in selecting a canon of literary works for this book, I have deliberately extended 'medicine' beyond the clinical encounter, foregrounding two novels that do not feature a doctor, either as protagonist or as character. Chapter 1 reads Mark Haddon's *The Curious Incident of the Dog in the Night-Time* (2003) to open up the idea of medicine to the site of the diagnosis, looking at autism and Asperger syndrome as diagnostic classifications to which empathy, or more precisely, its lack or absence, is seen to be central. I analyse the constitutive role of history and culture in the construction of the medical diagnosis. In Chapter 5, I analyse Kazuo Ishiguro's dystopian fictional treatment of the new forms of life created under biocapitalism in *Never Let Me Go* (2005). I return to the complex inter-relation of individual and institution in the care relation, asking what effect the commercialisation of feeling might have on relations of care. I also address our ambivalent affective relation to the liminal modes of life produced out of the bioscientific technologies and processes of the research laboratory, drawing on social theorist Nikolas Rose's concept of the 'politics of life' (2007), to ask what happens to care when it is placed at the service of a market economy of supply and demand. I thus intervene into the medical humanities by opening up the idea of 'medicine' to social, cultural and political analysis, as well as to the possibility that cultural knowledges might play a constitutive role in medical discourse and practice. I also expand the field of settings, domains and agencies that constitute 'medicine' beyond those that have dominated the medical humanities to date.

Theorising empathy

Woods and I identified a fourth and final 'E' that characterised first-wave medical humanities: Empathy (Whitehead and Woods 2016: 5). Subtending the other three 'Es', empathy signifies in first-wave medical humanities the humanising compassion that is increasingly absent from, and a 'cure all for[,] an increasingly mechanical medicine', through the production of 'more empathic' practitioners (Bishop 2008: 15). This monograph is firmly committed to the belief that empathy remains relevant to the medical humanities; however, it calls into question the value that was accorded to empathy in first-wave medical humanities. I move beyond the prevailing sense that empathy is necessarily positive; an attribute that needs to be cultivated, and that can heal the deficiencies of contemporary biomedicine. As such, empathy becomes a goal or an end point in and of itself. The problem with this approach, as cultural theorist Carolyn Pedwell has aptly noted, is that:

> [empathy's] naming can represent a conceptual stoppage in conversation or analysis. Thus, the most pressing questions tend to be less, 'what is empathy?', 'what does it do?', or 'what are its risks?', but rather the more automatic refrain of 'how can we cultivate it?' (2014: x)

In the chapters that follow, I seek to pursue precisely these 'pressing questions' in the context of the medical humanities, providing an account of empathy that is critical, robust and that offers a rigorous theoretical underpinning for a medical humanities approach.

Garden has observed that, in spite of the broad consensus in first-wave medical humanities that empathy needs to be taught and practised, 'there is not yet consistency and clarity in the medical literature about what empathy is and how it works' (2007: 552). To some extent, this is entirely understandable: empathy currently represents a ubiquitous topic, and its dispersal across a wide variety of disciplines and discourses strains any singular notion or definition, so that we might perhaps more accurately speak of empath*ies*. Without dismissing the volatility and the instability of the category, I nevertheless aim in the opening chapters of this volume to respond to the question, 'what is empathy?', at least as it might productively – if necessarily provisionally – be answered for the medical humanities. This involves, on the one hand, engaging critically with the major areas of debate on empathy in the sciences and in the humanities: respectively, neuroscience and autism research, and the newly emergent field of human-rights studies. In so doing, I argue that mainstream medical humanities has displayed a noticeable insularity, and has not sufficiently addressed its own relation to these fields of study: the concerns of medical education have thus been largely divorced from developments in medical research, while medical humanities has engaged narrowly with medical ethics and bioethics, without looking to wider critical debates on literature, reading and ethics. At the same time, I also turn to the philosophical tradition of phenomenology, which has a long and distinguished tradition of intellectual engagement with the concept of empathy. Here, I locate a definition of empathy that is responsive to the problem of appropriation, and that takes account of an embodied mind and subjectivity.

Chapters 1 and 2 survey current approaches to empathy in the neurosciences – with particular attention to autism research – and in human-rights discourses. Common to both fields is the refrain that empathy is somehow lacking or deficient; in autism, the empathetic facility is seen to be impaired, while in human-rights scholarship, 'we' are not sufficiently empathetic towards the suffering of distant others. It is also notable that empathy is positioned as the attribute of the individual subject, and the ability to make good its perceived deficit is the primary goal or outcome of the research. For the neurocognitive scientist, this outcome might be achieved through the localisation of empathy to identifiable patterns and areas of brain activity, while human-rights scholarship places its faith in narrative; reading more books about more kinds of marginalised subjects will enable 'us' to cultivate more empathetic feelings for them. While neuroscience produces various models of empathy, locating it as variously innate and learned, and higher- and lower-level functioning, human-rights approaches gravitate towards the model of perspective taking that also dominates first-wave medical humanities. In addressing the question 'what is empathy?', both approaches are nevertheless characterised by the kind of conceptual blockage to which Pedwell refers, falling back on the idea of empathy as an attribute that needs to be cultivated. It is also, implicitly or explicitly, the attribute by and through which 'we' want to define ourselves; certain borders, or lines of demarcation, are at work here, so that empathy marks out the difference between illness and health, and the distinction between those who are nearby and those who are far away, whether geographically, socially or culturally.

I accordingly turn to phenomenology, and to more recent scholarship in neo-phenomenology, to articulate an alternative model for what empathy is. In locating empathy, phenomenology attends to the world that we share. In engaging with others, we encounter them as intentional beings, whose feelings and states of mind are expressed through bodily action and gesture. Phenomenological approaches thus work at the intersection between mind and body, and between inner and outer.[3] Further, phenomenologist Edith Stein's (1891–1942) pioneering study, *On the Problem of Empathy* (1989) carefully elaborates how our interactions with lived others give the other person to us as the locus of *her own* agency and experience, offering an expansive model of engagement that enables us to open out to how others see the world.[4] Such an understanding of empathy, that highlights difference and otherness, is particularly suggestive for the medical humanities, because it can potentially speak with sensitivity about how we engage with those affected by severe mental-health conditions. Drawing on philosopher Matthew Ratcliffe's notion of radical empathy (2012), I accordingly extend Stein's account to outline a model of empathy that can encompass how we relate *differently and variously* to our world in common. Tracing a line from Stein to contemporary neo-phenomenology, I thus produce a definition of empathy that both leads out to the other, rather than reverting back to the self, and that accounts for how we encounter and engage with (cognitive, as well as other forms of) difference.

In asking what empathy does, I turn to another rich strand of thought, namely feminist affect theory.[5] I am particularly interested to tease out the ways in which empathy is differentially felt and mobilised across various geographical, cultural and social positions; again, my focus is not so much on what binds us together, our supposed common humanity, but rather on empathy's relation to, and production of, modes and practices of distinction. Feminist theorist Clare Hemmings has noted that affect does not travel freely, but tends to follow already defined lines and routes of power. Further, it speaks not so much of oneness or unity between subjects, as of what separates them: 'only for certain subjects can affect be thought of as attaching in an open way; others are so over-associated with affect that they themselves are the object of affective transfer' (2005: 561). Hemmings's words chime with Sara Ahmed's (2004) emphasis on emotion as that which 'sticks' to certain subjects and in certain places, which are indicative of sites of tension. We can thus consider empathy as a form of travelling affect that identifies, and enables us to critique, existing hierarchies and sites of privilege. Such an approach is productive in reading *The Memory of Love*: here, Forna's depiction of British psychiatrist Adrian Lockheart's humanitarian work in Sierra Leone is closely engaged with how, and with what effects, empathy attaches itself to certain subjects and not to others. Forna also questions whether, for the object of empathy, such 'affective transfer' is welcomed or desired; for Adrian's patient, Agnes, his interest in her serves to expose her to further danger, without alleviating her impossible situation. The idea of travelling affect is also suggestive in relation to *Saturday*; here, McEwan's restriction of empathy's flow or circulation to the Perowne family speaks of the novel's conservatism, and a demarcation of boundaries that are at once social, cultural and biological. At the same time, empathy can, through new encounters, find alternative routes and trajectories that underpin change and transformation. My reading of Forna thus suggests that the transnational mobility that she puts in play can potentially lead in surprising and unexpected new directions.

In addition to asking what empathy does, feminist theory is engaged with the further question: who does the work of empathy? Empathy is defined as a competency within the contemporary neoliberal economy, and is measured in terms of its market value. Training in empathy is accordingly associated with the production of profitable affective capital. The question of empathy as competency was recently addressed in the medical context by essayist Leslie Jamison, in her best-selling *The Empathy Exams* (2014). Speaking from the perspective of a medical actor, who takes on the role of a patient in order to train medical students in effective clinical communication, Jamison highlighted the fine line between empathy and performance when compassion enters the marketplace:

Checklist item 31 is generally acknowledged as the most important: 'Voiced empathy for my situation/problem'. We are instructed about the importance of this first word, *voiced*. It's not enough for someone to have a sympathetic manner or use a caring tone. The students have to say the right words to get credit for compassion. (2014: 3; italics in original)[6]

Jamison captures here the strange 'mechanics' of empathy, once it has been rendered as emotional labour (2014: 18), although she notably does not extend beyond the individualised clinical relation to broader social and political critique.[7] In Chapter 5, I argue that *Never Let Me Go* does engage in precisely such analysis, casting the labour of the clones as carers both as a form of affective labour that is utterly instrumentalised by the marketplace, and as a study in the feelings that emerge when emotion and agency are entirely subsumed under capitalism. In Kathy H.'s unsettling narrative tone, as well as in the artwork produced by the clones, Ishiguro challenges us to respond affectively to an oddly mechanical sensibility, which, I argue, is also that of our own attenuated feelings.

Turning to the question of empathy's risks, feminist affect theory has taken a leading role in highlighting that social emotions such as empathy and compassion can act as distractions or diversions from social and political change. Thus, the drama of affective transformation in the empathising subject can too readily become a goal or an end point. In the context of the medical humanities, this concern takes on particular resonance, as the doctor's empathetic feeling for the patient can too easily take centre stage, effacing both the patient's own perspective and the social, cultural, political and structural dimensions of illness and care.[8] Perhaps unsurprisingly, then, the novels studied in this monograph are engaged, variously, with the tensions between affective transformation and broader political change, and the risk that the former might either obscure or replace the latter. In McEwan's *Saturday*, Henry Perowne's dramatic conversion to the value of poetry – in the staging of Victorian poet Matthew Arnold's (1822–88) ability to save the day – combined with his subsequent life-saving operation on Baxter, mute broader political events, in the form of the London protest march against the Iraq war. The high drama of individual feeling displaces attention from the bigger political questions that are at stake on that particular Saturday in February. In Forna's *The Memory of Love*, the problem is explicitly articulated in surgeon Kai Manderley's critical assessment of British and American aid workers – including Adrian himself – for being more interested in their own affective journey than in the social and economic realities of life in Sierra Leone. In Ishiguro's *Never Let Me Go*, the affective labour of care is deliberately instrumentalised to divert the clones' attention from broader structural inequality and exploitation. In complex and ambivalent ways, these works of fiction not only mobilise empathy, but also indicate the hazards of reading too immersively, of becoming overly invested in an identificatory relationship with Perowne, Adrian or Kathy H. In staging empathy's risks, the novels thus potentially implicate the reader within the very problem that they bring to light.

Summarising the status of empathy in the medical humanities, Garden has noted:

> theories of empathy that emphasize interpersonal relations should not obscure the larger social contexts that determine illness and disability, beginning with inequities in access to and quality of health care based on ethnicity, class, gender, and sexual/affectional orientation. These problems compel rather than discourage the development of sophisticated paradigms of empathy as a means of reframing the discussion of ethics in medical education and clinical practice. (2007: 564)

My treatment of empathy in this monograph builds on Garden's clarion call for a more sophisticated, as well as a more politicised, conceptualisation of the category. Moving beyond the individualised doctor–patient relation, and the question of how empathy can best be cultivated, I ask rather what empathy does, as well as who, in turn, does the labour of empathy, attending closely to the issues of difference and inequality that emerge, and to the risks and challenges of utilising empathy as a critical framework. Unlike Garden, however, I do not only locate the significance of such a project in the domains of 'medical education and clinical practice'; as discussed in the previous section, a more critical medical humanities not only reframes the kinds of questions that we might ask in relation to the clinical scene, but also expands our conception of medicine itself to include a more diverse range of practices and settings.

Re-situating fiction

In positioning narrative as the vehicle to cultivating empathy, first-wave medical humanities has focused particularly on patient accounts of illness. Spiro notes that: '[t]he anecdotes of pathography tell the narrative of what patients feel and suffer in their bodies' (1993c: 12).

Fiction, too, though, can also act as a valuable medium for generating empathy. Spiro thus continues: 'to take a current example, John Updike . . . can teach us much about what it is like to have a heart attack or to be a lover with psoriasis' (1993c: 13). Spiro's model of reading is premised on an understanding of empathy as 'feeling one with'; narrative is positioned as a transparent mode of access to another's subjective experience. It acts as a window onto another's feelings, which in turn leads to an understanding of her situation: 'what it is like to have a heart attack or to be a lover with psoriasis'. Knowing through empathy is thus seen to equate to 'truth' or 'reality', but the 'truth' of the other's situation is notably limited to her individual subjectivity, which is, in turn, abstracted from the very relations of power that play such a constitutive role in forming subjectivity itself. In what follows, I re-orient fiction's relation to empathy, arguing that it is a site in and through which empathy is not only felt and imagined, but also negotiated and contested. Neither does contemporary fiction lead to knowledge or understanding of another; it is more often concerned with the difficulties and deficiencies in our intersubjective encounters, and with their disturbance by the effects of power, and it is fascinated, too, by how, when, and why we fail to care for one another.

The emphasis of mainstream medical humanities on the idea that reading literature makes us more empathetic has broad cultural resonance. This belief has been advocated by politicians – most notably former President Barack Obama – historians, philosophers and arts-funding organisations.[9] The widespread popularity of book groups is founded on empathetic modes of reading, and the selection of novels that lend themselves readily to character identification,[10] while the Shared Reading movement has recently gained considerable traction by promulgating the idea that collectively reading literature aloud creates strong empathetic bonds and has discernible health benefits.[11] In this volume, I discuss the claims of cognitive-literary studies scholar Lisa Zunshine (2003, 2006) that reading fiction provides a mental workout for those areas of the brain that are associated with Theory of Mind, an influential model of empathy in the neurosciences. Claims for reading's ability to enhance empathy are thus given a scientific grounding and evidence base. I also examine the arguments of key human-rights scholars and activists, such as Lynn Hunt (2007) and Martha Nussbaum (2010), that reading fiction was not only foundational to the inception of the human-rights movement, but also provides an essential underpinning for current democratic societies, values and governance. Common across all of these approaches is the belief that novel reading leads to, or results in, a defined outcome – namely, the enhancement of the empathetic sensibility – and that it is therefore an activity that is morally virtuous and/or beneficial for the health (both individual and societal). Reading is cast as an immersive, serious and potentially strenuous activity – no reward without labour – and there is no space for fiction to be regarded as playful, subversive, superficial or even frivolous.

Although the term 'empathy' originated in late-nineteenth-century aesthetic theory, the belief that literature enhances our feelings for others can be traced back to earlier, eighteenth-century debates on sympathy. Philosophers such as David Hume (1711–76) in *A Treatise of Human Nature* (1978) and Adam Smith (1723–90) in his *Theory of Moral Sentiments* (1976) elaborated a vocabulary of feeling that still holds resonance for us today. Hume's sympathy represents a form of emotional contagion, the intellectual legacy of which is recognisable in contemporary theories of lower-level empathy, connected to the activity of mirror neurons. Thus, Hume writes suggestively: 'the minds of men are mirrors to one another not only because they reflect each other's emotion, but also because these rays of passion, sentiments, and opinions may often be reverberated' (1978: 365). For Smith, too, sympathy has a discernible physical basis, and his attention is particularly caught by the phenomenon that we would refer to today as motor mimicry:

> When we see a stroke aimed, and just ready to fall upon the leg or arm of another person, we naturally shrink and draw back our own leg or our own arm; and when it does fall, we feel it in some measure, and are hurt by it as well as the sufferer. (1976: 10)

Sympathy, then, has a strong physical basis, but for both Smith and Hume, the imagination also plays a significant role. For Hume, the initial physical response activates the mind: 'when I perceive the *causes* of any emotion, my mind is convey'd to the effects, and is actuated with a like emotion' (1978: 576; italics in original). For Smith, imaginative perspective taking enables us to make sense of another's physical expression:

> *by the imagination* we place ourselves in his situation, we enter as it were into his body, and become in some measure the same person with him, and thence form some idea of his sensations, and even feel something which, although weaker in degree, is not altogether unlike them. (1976: 9; my italics)

It is this imaginative aspect that lent itself to the idea that reading literature could enhance sympathy, although for Smith there remained an important distinction between novel reading and actual experience. Garden thus explains that, for Smith, '[r]eaders, simply by closing the book, are always in control of calibrating the degree of distance and the intensity of engagement' (2007: 564). In spite of this reservation, the eighteenth-century novel of sensibility, which placed particular emphasis on dramatic scenes of compassion and pity, was avidly consumed by a middle-class readership, in the expectation that, by engaging imaginatively with the lives and feelings of characters of a different gender and/or class, one might develop a more sympathetic sensibility. Eighteenth-century sympathy, like today's empathy, was also linked to social action; if the reader feels for the other's suffering, then she is more likely to seek to alleviate it. As for Nussbaum, so for Hume and Smith, sympathy makes us good and virtuous citizens, and is of social as well as individual benefit.

The attractions of such an account of reading are evident. Not only does it elevate novel reading beyond the merely pleasurable into a personal and civic virtue; it also provides a response to criticisms that literature, and the arts more broadly, do not have a measurable purpose, use or value. Nevertheless, there are hazards here of instrumentalising literature, and of harnessing it too readily to social, educational and political agendas. There is, too, a danger, as literary critic Nicholas Dames has pointed out, that novel-reading falls into a 'profile of . . . withdrawal, retreat, and even sanctified self-communion, an antidote to the assault of stimuli presented by modern, media-rich existence' (2007: 7). Dames has his eye here on the kinds of novels that empathetic readers are supposed to engage with, and on the ways in which they are expected to read them. Nussbaum has been a particularly influential proponent of the ethics of sympathetic reading, and she has positioned the Victorian novel as a central site for engaged and responsible reading. It is, Dames notes, the length of these works of fiction, 'particularly their prolonged duration and descriptive fullness', that is seen to provide the complexity and depth required to exercise the sympathetic imagination (2007: 17).[12] The consumption of the Victorian novel takes the form of a concentrated, sustained and immersive attention that both generates and trains us in the reflective yet sympathetic cognition that, for Nussbaum, is the ultimate goal of reading. Dames's central argument is that Nussbaum's model of novel reading is historically misleading: the Victorian consumer of fiction was influenced by a physiology of reading that focused on the very qualities of distraction and inattention that she positions the nineteenth-century novel as a bulwark against.[13] We might further observe, however, that Nussbaum produces a selection of edifying literary works that strongly privileges realist and canonical texts.[14] Like Spiro's identification of 'the masters' (1993b: 5), there is a discernible conservatism and elitism at play in the identification of the *right kind* of reading for empathy's cultivation, which excludes from consideration more middlebrow and popular fictional works.

The novels that constitute the focus of this monograph comprise the contemporary middlebrow. They are written by authors whose work circulates prominently across prize culture and reading group alike, and who feature regularly in the culture pages of the *Guardian*. Their novels have been successfully adapted into television, film and theatre works, which have garnered high audience figures and enthusiastic critical reviews. Suzanne Keen has noted of the reader of the contemporary middlebrow:

> Attention to the interests of the middlebrow reader, who populates the book clubs and buys most of the fiction sold in the United States and Great Britain, suggests that she seeks empathetic reading experiences. I propose that novels inviting empathy do better in the marketplace (perhaps because they get better word-of-mouth recommendations) and that empathetic reading habits make up a core element of middlebrow readers' self-image. (2007: 104)

It is certainly the case that the works of fiction collected together in this book can be seen to 'invi[te] empathy' in the way that Keen suggests: Haddon and Ishiguro write from the first-person perspectives of Christopher Boone and Kathy H. respectively; McEwan presents *Saturday* entirely from Perowne's point of view; and although Barker and Forna utilise a mobile narrative perspective, they prioritise the viewpoints of Paul Tarrant and Adrian Lockheart over those of the other characters. It is my contention, however, that the writers studied in this monograph are highly invested in the question of empathy and its limits, and in probing critically questions of ethics, distance and difference. Empathetic feeling is mobilised, but it is also complicated, problematised and interrogated, sometimes through debates on art and literature within the novel itself.[15] My readings do not primarily focus on the reader's affective relation to specific characters, a hermeneutic strategy that risks reinforcing the individualising tendencies of first-wave medical humanities, but ask instead how, and with what effects, empathy is defined by and circulates within the work, and what its limits and its limitations might be.[16]

The body of fiction that forms the focus of this book is comprised of contemporary British novels. In critiquing mainstream medical humanities, Claire Hooker and Estelle Noonan have argued that, in a field which is achieving global reach, its textual canon is notably restricted to a narrow and conservative range of Anglo-American and European literary works. Even in medical humanities courses taught in Asia, for example, the authors aver: '[w]hat often emerged was a quasi-Western canon of medical humanities (in history, philosophy, literature, and art) in which the diversity, sophistication and richness of different cultural traditions was uncomfortably marginalised' (2011: 79). Paradoxically, in a field that had emerged precisely in order to make certain kinds of difference visible – those, as Hooker and Noonan identify, that 'are produced within contexts of illness and/or disability' (2011: 79) – there has been a marked tendency to overlook other forms of marginalisation, which are tied to social, cultural and geopolitical factors. One obvious solution to the problem is to open up the canon of works studied in medical-humanities curricula: 'one can increase and diversify one's use of non-Western creative works in the classroom, engaging in cross-cultural comparison where appropriate' (2011: 83). Yet, for Hooker and Noonan this does not quite do the trick, because it fails to address the assumption that reading such texts will deliver the 'truth' of the illness experience in such contexts. We are returned again to the emphasis in first-wave medical humanities on the individual subjectivity, rather than on broader structural questions:

> Because of the tendency within the medical humanities to approach difference within . . . the contexts of 'appreciative' and 'receptive' encounters – devoted to 'drawing close', 'connecting with', 'bearing witness' or 'active listening', 'experience' can frequently disguise itself as empirical fact. Consequently, difference can become reified, dissolving into the uniquely denatured and decontextualized perspective of the individual patient. (2011: 82)

It is not sufficient, then, simply to add more texts by marginalised voices onto a medical-humanities reading list, although the diversification of curricula is clearly desirable. We also need to develop more critical, and more political, analytic encounters with difference. For Hooker and Noonan, such a project would also encompass challenging and complicating the vocabulary of 'the West' and 'the rest', because the field of the medical humanities 'unwittingly tends to reproduce such troubling locations as the "Western" and the "Oriental"' (2011: 80).

The inclusion in this monograph of the transnational or 'world' writers Aminatta Forna and Kazuo Ishiguro complicates any straight-forward notion of the 'British' novel; in our current globalised economy, the conceptual framework of a 'national' literature is increasingly, and productively, strained and challenged. Not only do Forna and Ishiguro, with their respective Sierra Leonean-Scottish and Anglo-Japanese heritages, speak of a complex pattern of migration and mobility that refuses easy or simple categorisation, but their fictions also lead the way in articulating more politicised encounters with difference that underscore medicine's own implication in the categories and structures of exclusion. In Chapter 4, I examine Forna's critique of the neocolonial dimensions of global humanitarian medicine, and of the funding awarded to projects that are of interest to Anglo-American concerns at the expense of more localised diseases and health problems. Chapter 5 considers Ishiguro's close attention in *Never Let Me Go* to the complex intersections between different forms of marginalisation, so that a line is traced across the othering effects of biological, racial and economic difference. More than this, I argue, Ishiguro's unusual temporal setting implicates his dystopian world as one that very easily might have been, had the major developments in biomedical research taken place a few decades earlier and coincided with the exclusionary racial ideologies of post-war Britain. Like Forna, Ishiguro is insistent that medicine does not only encounter difference, but is also productive of its own exclusions and exceptions. In this sense, the fiction of these writers is engaged both with complicity and with a structural failure of care.

If *The Memory of Love* and *Never Let Me Go* gesture towards the category of world fiction, another important genre represented in the monograph is the 'phenomenological' or 'syndrome' novel. Connected to the rise of interest in phenomenology across a range of disciplines, and also to the influential neo-phenomenological work of philosophers such as Dan Zahavi and Shaun Gallagher, the phenomenological novel opens up a fictional exploration of human embodiment, consciousness and intersubjectivity, that is closely informed by developments in neuroscience. It is particularly interested in the subjectivities produced by cognitive damage or difference, which often become emblematic of a broader estrangement, which might be social or that can speak of a disconnection from the 'self' produced by new technologies and modes of sociality. These works of fiction do not individualise the protagonist, but depict her as an intentional agent in the shared world that the novel depicts; she both acts and is acted upon, and she is complexly intertwined with the agency and intention of other characters. Chapter 1 examines *The Curious Incident of the Dog in the Night-Time*, often claimed as the originator of the genre, assessing the novel's depiction of Christopher not as a vehicle for understanding the autistic mind, but rather as a reflection on the social and political fragmentation of a post-Thatcher Britain. In Chapter 3, *Saturday* offers, through Perowne's neurosurgical perspective, a series of reflections on the mystery and the wonder of his own and others' embodied consciousness. I discuss McEwan's treatment of cognitive damage, in the form of Baxter's Huntington's disease and Perowne's mother, Lily's, Alzheimer's, arguing that *Saturday* articulates a complex and ambivalent language of the biological, as that which at once binds us inexorably together, and that can also open up glimpses of alterity and difference.

In re-situating fiction for a critical medical humanities, this monograph refuses its positionality as a window onto another's experiential truth. Literature is both more unpredictable and less instrumental than this model can encapsulate. In the eloquent words of literary critic Ann Jurecic: 'Empathy is not salvation; it's not certainty or knowledge; and it blurs boundaries in ways that can be both generative and destructive' (2011: 22). Following Suzanne Keen (2007), I also contend that fiction has more *agency* than mainstream medical humanities has allowed: the contemporary novel is deeply engaged with the politics of empathy, as well as with its ambiguous effects, and it is highly self-conscious about fiction's own long, complex and ambivalent relationship to the sympathetic imagination. My intervention recasts literature's role in and for the medical humanities from that of a 'supportive friend' (Whitehead and Woods 2016: 2) to a relationship that is at once less benign and more critical. At the same time, I also reposition empathy in relation to literature, seeking, as Woods and I have expressed it elsewhere: '[to] move beyond the assumption that all affect and feeling are found in the arts and humanities, and all hard-nosed pragmatism in the biomedical sciences' (Whitehead and Woods 2016: 5). As we will see, there is much to learn in the novels under discussion in this book, not only about 'pragmatism', but also about affective distance, and the limitations and failures of care.

Overview

Chapter 1 addresses the cognitive neurosciences as a key site for the current interest in empathy, highlighting in particular the importance of best-selling popular science publications. If the field has played a defining role in the value and currency accorded to empathy, it has also focused on empathy as an individual attribute, and one that operates according to a model of lack or gain. The field of autism research has been particularly high-profile, and has produced the diagnostic category of autism in relation to empathy's impairment. I draw on the influential philosopher of science, Ian Hacking, to open up the question of how medical knowledge is produced and circulated, and to emphasise the inter-relation of scientific research and cultural narrative in the construction of the medical classification or diagnosis. Turning to Haddon's *The Curious Incident of the Dog in the Night-Time*, I argue that a critical reading of the novel can enable us to identify the cultural ideologies and investments that underpin our fascination with autism. I also draw on phenomenology to move away from the prevailing critical tendency to celebrate our 'shared humanity' with Christopher, and to articulate a more radical model of empathy based in the recognition of human difference and diversity.

In Chapter 2, I move on to the second major area of activity in relation to empathy: human-rights studies. I argue that this field of study is closely aligned with first-wave medical humanities, both in its emphasis on empathy as perspective taking, and in its belief that reading fiction is productive of empathy.[17] Engaging critically with these liberal-humanist approaches, I draw on phenomenology and feminist affect theory to advance an account of empathy that is not only other-directed, but that is also cognisant of its own implication in structures of power and privilege. I read Barker's *Life Class* in dialogue with American cultural theorist Susan Sontag's *Regarding the Pain of Others* (2003) to elaborate an account of the response to another's pain that is not only an act of compassionate human witness, but that is also aware of its implication in, and complicity with, the anonymity and indifference of the institution. More than this, I emphasise the importance of positionality: the clinical encounter thus looks very different according to the vantage point that one occupies, and how one's gaze is constituted by gender, race, class, sexuality and debility. This chapter indicates that ethics remains a primary concern in and for the medical humanities, but seeks both to expand the frame beyond the specific disciplinary concerns of medical ethics and bioethics, and to produce a more politicised, and a more entangled, understanding of the term.

If Chapters 1 and 2 address the construction of empathy in the sciences and the humanities respectively, Chapter 3 asks how we might productively think through the question of interdisciplinarity in and for the medical humanities. Des Fitzgerald and

Felicity Callard have recently pointed to the subordinate role of the humanities in mainstream medical humanities, arguing that:

> scholars have begun to worry that the success of the medical humanities is tied up with being *useful* to biomedicine, that the medical humanities has been able to establish itself only by appearing as the domain of pleasant (but more or less inconsequential) helpmeets – lurking hopefully, poetry books in hand, at the edges of the clinical encounter's 'primal scene'. This is, we know, a caricature; still, it is not without its truth. (2016: 36; italics in original)

In the British context, I argue, the question of the literature–science relationship is particularly long and fraught, extending back through the mid-twentieth-century 'two cultures' debate between C. P. Snow (1905–80) and F. R. Leavis (1895–1978), to the late-nineteenth-century clash between titans T. H. Huxley (1825–95) and Matthew Arnold. In reviewing these debates, I argue that the question of disciplinary value is inextricably tied to issues of class. Further, extending my discussion to the contemporary 'third culture' movement, I argue that a non-partisan imagining of interdisciplinarity remains elusive, tied as the matter inevitably is to issues of institutional power and resource. My reading of McEwan's *Saturday* examines the novel's engagement with the literature–science debate, suggesting that McEwan, too, finds it difficult to articulate a persuasive connection between the disciplinary domains, without either ceding the ground to science or becoming mired in class politics. Nevertheless, I suggest, a more positive model of interdisciplinarity potentially opens up in McEwan's representation of Lily's Alzheimer's disease, whereby a more modest emphasis on what science and literature do not know, and are unable to grasp or to understand, provides the possible basis for a more productive movement forward.

Chapter 4 turns to the question of how empathy circulates, and where it 'sticks', within a global or transnational context, arguing that it is inextricable from structural and material relations of power. I begin by focusing on current debates about medical migration; specifically, claims that the movement of medical personnel from sub-Saharan Africa to the global north has resulted in a health crisis in their own countries of origin. Identifying that, by individualising the problem, such arguments efface important political, social and economic factors, I indicate that Forna's *The Memory of Love* offers a complex historical account of Sierra Leone's medical 'crisis', through a narrative that is set not only in the present day, but that also extends back to the period immediately after decolonisation. Forna's detailed representation of medical care in Sierra Leone is grounded in, and expressive of, a deep concern for the uneven global economics of medical resource. The material circulation of knowledge, goods and personnel is, in turn, indissociable from the affective circulation of empathy, and I draw on critical human-rights scholarship to analyse the significance of Adrian's acts of empathetic *mis*recognition, in relation to his patients in Sierra Leone. I close by suggesting that the past can, nevertheless, move us forward in unexpected ways, and, through the novel's depiction of activist Julius Kamara, I indicate that the decolonisation era offers a model not only of political disappointment, but also of a vision of possibility that might still offer future hope.

Chapter 5 considers the relation of empathy to the questions of exchange, value and commodification that are centrally at stake in our contemporary biocapitalist regime. Under what Rose has termed 'the politics of life' (2007), life itself has become a commodity, susceptible to market exchange and value, and we need to pay careful, critical attention to what this means for our modes of governance and for the relations of care that they both embody and perform. Reading Ishiguro's *Never Let Me Go* as a complex, uneasy meditation on these issues, I use Sianne Ngai's evocative discussion of 'ugly feelings' (2005) to open up the question of what emotions are produced and circulated when affect is co-opted by and for the capitalist marketplace. I then turn to examine Ishiguro's relation to biopolitics, arguing that, like Forna, he deploys a complex temporality to foreground the politics of the might-have-been. However, if Forna's unrealised history represents a utopian vision of possibility for Africa's global position, Ishiguro's is the dystopian vision of a racialised biocommercialism, that is not our own present – *Never Let Me Go* is a fiction – but that nevertheless haunts the margins of our cultural imaginary. The chapter closes by addressing Ishiguro's critique of art as expressive of our inner humanity, and productive of a humanising compassion. Disconnecting art and literature from humanist thought and sentiment, Ishiguro leaves us with the challenge of what an inhuman empathy, which is responsive both to the mechanical and to the superficial, might look like.

I end this book by offering some concluding reflections on the importance of moving beyond the binary thinking that has characterised the medical humanities to date. In particular, I indicate the relevance of rethinking the significance accorded to 'the human' in the medical humanities. The 'humanity' of the patient has been opposed to the dehumanising practices of biomedicine, and the 'humanising' potential and capacity of the humanities has been harnessed to champion a more compassionate medical regime. Following on from where Ishiguro has led us, a more critical approach would take up the question of literature's inhuman aspects, as well as engaging with contemporary fiction's own critical interrogation of humanity's limits and boundaries. It would think through the relationship between 'the human' and 'the citizen'; both Forna and Ishiguro have indicated that 'health citizenship' is a vulnerable concept in a context in which health represents a marketable form of capital, and in which access to that market is highly differentiated in social, economic and global terms. It would confront us with the question of human difference that plays as a constant refrain through this volume's discussion of empathy; how, then, might empathy be responsive to, and account for, human diversity and alterity? Finally, the medical humanities might look to the posthuman, drawing in and on the vibrant debates currently taking place in animal studies, environmental studies, new materialism and posthuman theory itself, to address critically the ways in which medicine continually produces, reinforces and challenges the boundaries between human and non-human, as well as to open up new and different ways to imagine care, empathy and relationality in the context of 'non-' and 'post-' human others.

Notes

1. For a fuller account of the development of mainstream medical humanities, see Anne Whitehead (2014).
2. In interrogating the notions of the 'medical', 'empathy' and 'narrative' that lie at the heart of first-wave medical humanities, this volume builds on my previous research in the critical medical humanities; see, in particular, Whitehead et al. (2016).
3. It is, however, worth noting Will Viney's caution that phenomenology can still be read as producing and policing the borders of identity, distinguishing between 'a human inner and a non-human outer' (2016: 115).
4. Although I have modelled my account of empathy on a genealogy of thought extending back to female philosopher Edith Stein, this is not to discount alternative intellectual trajectories. In particular, literary scholar Carolyn Burdett is excavating a fascinating and suggestive body of work by another female pioneer of empathy: British writer, Vernon Lee (1856–1935). See Burdett (2011).
5. For a fuller account of feminist theory and the question of affect, see Pedwell and Whitehead (2012).
6. For further discussion of empathy as a skill, in the context of the recommendations made by the Francis Report (2013) into failings of care at the Mid Staffordshire National Health Service Trust, see Smajdor (2013).
7. We might ask of Jamison's essay, for example, how the labour of the medical actor is valued relative to that of the doctor. Who performs the labour in each case, and with what implications? Jamison does

nevertheless usefully probe the question of empathy as 'invasive' rather than 'intimate', and reflects on the symptoms of her medical role or persona, 'Stephanie Phillips', as a means of protecting her 'privacy' under the clinical gaze (2014: 18, 6).

8. I am thinking here, for example, of the work of physician-writer Rafael Campo, whose work has occupied a position of particular prominence in first-wave medical humanities. See Campo (1997).

9. The most recent iteration of the potential of the arts to bridge an 'empathy gap' comes from the former Chair of Arts Council England, Peter Bazalgette (2017).

10. Literary critic Suzanne Keen has usefully warned against placing too much interpretative weight on discussions of fiction that take place in public settings, such as reading groups, however, because the 'cultural valorisation' of reader empathy might place pressure on readers 'to respond acceptably to a fictional character' (2007: 78).

11. For further discussion, see Longden et al. (2015).

12. Lisa Zunshine, in contrast, privileges modernist literature and detective fiction in the canon of cognitive-literary studies, because their complex layers of embedded narration and experimentation with our mind-reading abilities lend themselves to the exercise of Theory of Mind. For more extended discussion, see Chapter 1.

13. As discussed in Chapter 2, nineteenth-century novelist George Eliot is of particular importance to Nussbaum. Dames produces a physiological reading of Eliot's *Daniel Deronda* (1876) that positions the novel as a study in 'how the consumption of art over extended time periods takes place, with what possibilities and what sacrifices' (2007: 125). He views the novel as an aesthetic experiment, inspired by the music of composer Richard Wagner (1813–83), in an extended reading practice that alternates between attention and distraction.

14. For a more extended discussion of Nussbaum and canonicity, see Chapter 2.

15. In the following chapters, I will discuss the representation of art in Barker and Ishiguro, as well as McEwan's engagement with literature and music in *Saturday*.

16. Although I have not taken a reader-response approach in this monograph, recent work in the field of narratology has been characterised by the development of sophisticated analytic tools, that would offer a rigorous underpinning for critical interpretations of readerly empathy. See, in particular, Fludernik (1996); Herman (2002, 2011); and Palmer (2008).

17. My critique of human-rights studies does not include recent, critical developments in the field, represented by scholars such as Lyndsey Stonebridge and Joseph R. Slaughter. For a more extended discussion of their work, see Chapter 4.

Chapter 1

Empathy and Mind

Introduction

The recent surge of interest in empathy both within the academy and in broader cultural debate can arguably be ascribed to two key developments: first, the engagement of science with empathy across various fields including neuropsychiatry, neurocognition and primatology, accompanied by a number of best-selling popular science publications;[1] and second, the claims made by the burgeoning human-rights field for the relation between empathy and ethics, particularly as this is shaped through interaction with the literary, artistic or cultural text. The first two chapters of this monograph focus on each of these developments in turn, first setting out the claims made for or about empathy by the sciences and human-rights proponents respectively, asking what in particular is at stake for them in reifying the term, and then moving on to think critically about what the respective accounts of empathy occlude or omit. In broad terms, the two chapters open up to critical interrogation the claims made on and about empathy by the sciences and the humanities; my aim in so doing is not to set the two in opposition, but rather to make evident the disciplinary investments in this highly contested concept, which raises in turn the question of whether we can in fact talk about 'empathy' as a singular term at all, or whether we are rather engaged with a number of different, but intersecting, empath*ies*. What the scientific and humanities approaches to empathy do share is an emphasis on empathy as inherently positive, and therefore to be cultivated and nurtured. Whether it is seen to be deficient in the autistic subject, or lacking in the public response to humanitarian crisis, empathy is what one has or what one lacks, and it is by implication located within the individual self who understands, or fails to understand, the feelings of others. These chapters will open up to debate where and how empathy is located, moving towards the approach taken by feminist cultural theorists Sara Ahmed (2004, 2010) and Lauren Berlant (2004a, 2008, 2011), whose work on affect takes as its underlying premise that 'feelings do not reside in subjects or objects, but are produced as effects of circulation' (Ahmed 2004: 8). This model of empathy as a form of travelling affect will provide the basis for discussion in later chapters of this volume.

Scientific research on empathy has focused on developing our understanding of how we understand and access the thoughts and feelings of others; what, in other words, is the mechanism underpinning our intersubjective relations? Two key developments have produced a marked increase in scientific interest in and research on empathy: first, the emergence of brain-imaging technologies, such as functional magnetic resonance imaging (fMRI) and positron emission tomography (PET), which produce images of the functioning of the brain as it is engaged in a particular task or activity; and second, the significant rise in diagnoses of autism and Asperger syndrome, which is medically designated in terms of a deficit in, or difficulties with, empathy, alongside impairments in language acquisition and use, and in imaginative interests and behaviours. Across scientific research on empathy, as well as on autistic disorders more specifically, the impetus is towards locating a biological or neurological foundation for empathy, and various regions of the brain have been advanced as being key to our intersubjective facilities. It is worth noting from the outset, however, that while this is the current scientific foundation for thinking about empathy, and while it has driven a number of research centres and projects, the results presently leave many core questions unanswered. Even within the scientific community both empathy and autism are radically unstable and highly contested terms. Of empathy, phenomenologist Dan Zahavi has recently noted that:

> there is still no clear consensus about what precisely it is. Is empathy a question of sharing another's feelings, or caring about another, or being emotionally affected by another's experiences though not necessarily experiencing the same experiences? Is it a question of imagining oneself in another's situation, of imagining being another in that other's situation, or simply of making inferences about another's mental states? (2014: 129)

While these might seem somewhat fine-grained, if not fussy, distinctions, these differences do matter, and the responses to the questions posed can produce very different theories of the location and functioning of empathy in the brain. Stuart Murray summarises the current state of autism research as follows:

> We don't know what causes autism. For all that neurology continues to help us understand how the brain is the site of the condition, we don't know fully which brain areas are responsible for the ways in which those with autism process their experiences of the world. Equally, despite advances in genetics, we have no real idea which genes are those connected to autism. (2012: 2)

Murray goes on to caution that, for all its insights, medical thinking in this area is '*necessarily* speculative' (2012: 3; italics in original) and therefore subject to its own biases and blind spots. Part of the work of this chapter will, accordingly, be to identify what might be missing or overlooked in the predominant scientific accounts both of empathy and of autism.

As outlined in the Introduction, first-wave medical humanities has been especially invested in empathy as the relation between two individuals, namely the doctor and the patient in the clinical encounter. Empathy, or its lack, has been located in the individual, specifically the medical practitioner, and the primary question has been how a perceived empathy deficit might be addressed or reversed. A significant shift that is enacted in this chapter is in locating empathy, not in the context of clinical practice, but rather in the context of medical research: if empathy can be identified anywhere in what follows, it is in the brain scans and images that emerge from the research laboratory. Thus, although empathy is still perceived by the medical sciences as inhering in the individual and in terms of deficit, this chapter opens up to view an institutional setting that has largely been excluded from first-wave medical humanities, especially where the question of empathy is at stake. In the first section of the chapter, I will survey the scientific research on empathy and autism emerging out of cognitive psychology, examining how the different schools of thought have evidenced their claims through the neurosciences. I will also consider the response of disability studies to this neurocognitive research. The following section turns to phenomenology, which has seen something of a resurgence in response to the neurosciences. I draw on phenomenology to identify a theory of empathy that is located, not in the individual subject, but rather in the

world that we share; the move from the individual to the social
that phenomenology enacts gestures in turn towards the feminist
cultural theory approaches to empathy that will underpin the late
chapters of this volume.[2]

This chapter's engagement with autism also locates empathy
in the medical context of diagnosis. Here, too, we are engaged
with an aspect of medicine that has not garnered particular attention from the mainstream medical humanities. What, then, does it
mean to focus on empathy, or more precisely, on its perceived deficiency, through the lens of the diagnostic act itself? Ian Hacking's
work on autism provides a productive starting point for responding to this question. He distinguishes between two categories of
diagnostic disorder: 'indifferent kinds' are conditions with no
awareness of being measured, and which accordingly cannot be
affected by the classification; 'interactive kinds' of disorder, on the
other hand, are involved in what Hacking terms a 'looping effect',
whereby the very acts of classification and diagnosis can influence
their behaviour, which in turn changes the classification. Hacking
identifies autism as both 'indifferent', through its neurological and
physiological aspects, and 'interactive', in that the responses of
those diagnosed, their families and carers, and the culture more
broadly, to the label of autism can alter the diagnostic classification. The point here, and Hacking is explicit about this, is not to
become caught in a debate over whether autism should be located
as a biological or a cultural phenomenon; it is always already both.
Rather, Hacking calls attention to the *dynamic* nature of those
diagnostic categories that are 'interactive'; through the 'looping
effect' created by the ways in which scientific research and cultural
narratives continually and necessarily rub up against each other,
the categories themselves are in a process of constant change and
evolution (1999: 114–22). This is not to say that the symptoms of
those diagnosed under these classifications are in any way unreal
or inauthentic; rather, the flex and the flux of these categories indicates the inevitable confluence of biological and cultural factors in
gathering together certain symptoms into a specific diagnostic classification. Medical sociologist Jonathan M. Metzl has been particularly trenchant in arguing that psychiatry 'would . . . benefit from
more ongoing, engaged, political analysis of the ways in which
cultural forces impact diagnostic categories' (2009: 205).[3] Focusing the gaze on the diagnostic aspect of medicine thus entails that
we approach diagnosis with a critical awareness of the cultural,

historical, political and social undercurrents that inform the construction of classifications.

The final section of this chapter locates autism in the products of popular culture, looking specifically at Mark Haddon's best-selling novel *The Curious Incident of the Dog in the Night-Time* (2003). This work of fiction is narrated by 15-year-old Christopher Boone, whose narrative voice and characterisation correspond closely to the diagnostic classification of Asperger syndrome, although the diagnostic category is not mentioned explicitly in the narrative.[4] My reading is attentive to Hacking's caution against approaches to autism texts that focus on the supposed imaginative and narrative journey 'inside' the autistic mind (2009: 1469). I position Haddon's fiction as a key forerunner of a genre that literary critic Patricia Waugh has recently defined as the 'syndrome novel' (Waugh 2013). I am interested, first, in Waugh's association of the syndrome novel with the resurgence of phenomenology, such that fiction becomes a vehicle for exploring the preoccupations of feeling, mind, body and intersubjectivity with which phenomenology is concerned; a vehicle that is, moreover, singularly well equipped to explore these questions, in and through its creation of a world. Focusing on the neo-phenomenological aspects of the novel draws attention not to Christopher's mind, his individual interiority or subjectivity, but rather to his interactions as an intentional agent with other intentional agents in the shared world that the novel creates. Haddon establishes his narrative as a mystery to be solved; Christopher's detections lead to the discovery that, like him, the other characters – and indeed the broader society – in the novel experience themselves to be atomised, fragmented and modularised. In the novel's depiction, autism is at once a distinct and recognisable condition affecting Christopher and his family, and also a figure for the contemporary condition; it symbolises the pathology of late-capitalist modernity. I suggest that a critical reading of Haddon's fiction can accordingly help to reveal the cultural and political investments that underpin our fascination with autism. Read against the grain, the novel's very success as a 'humanising' representation of the condition can illuminate what mainstream depictions of autism celebrate, and what they choose to omit. Returning to Hacking's point that medical and popular definitions of disorders inevitably develop in relation to each other, the literary analysis performed in this chapter can thus begin to identify some of the cultural ideologies that both inform and underpin the act of medical classification and diagnosis.

Locating empathy

In this section, I will trace and review the key models through which the cognitive sciences have described and understood the workings of empathy, namely Theory of Mind and simulation theory. Each of these models constructs empathy differently, underlining the instability of the term, and the variable sense of how empathy functions leads in turn to different accounts of where in the brain it is located. What these models share, however, is a drive towards the visual; through brain-imaging technologies, the hidden workings of the mind are both mapped and evidenced through activity that we can observe in the brain. This propulsion is symptomatic of biomedical culture more broadly, which displays a strong bias towards the visual, especially in relation to what is counted or valued as modes of evidence. Neuro-cognitive theories of empathy have dominated research into autism; the promise that they hold is that if difficulties with empathy can be identified in specific brain patterns and locations, then treatment and cure might become possible. Neurocognitive approaches to autism have, however, also attracted criticism from disability-studies scholars and activists, for whom the diagnostic classification of autism is located as a social construction that is stigmatising in its effects. Disability-studies scholars argue that, by identifying autism in terms of empathy deficit, the neurosciences fail to recognise difference and fall into the ideological trap of reinforcing stereotypes of neurotypicality. More than this, if biomedical culture treats autism as an individual pathology, disability studies position autism rather as an identity, the shared culture of a social group. The close of this section will review disability-studies approaches to empathy and autism, arguing that for all of their opposition to the neurosciences, they have in common a bias towards the visual, such that disability studies has tended to prioritise visible physical disabilities at the expense of cognitive, intellectual and neurological disabilities, including autism (Osteen 2008b: 3–4).

The dominant conceptual model in discussions of empathy and autism has been that of Theory of Mind. This is largely due to the influential work of Simon Baron-Cohen, Professor of Developmental Psychopathology at Cambridge University and Director of the University's Autism Research Centre. In a now seminal article, Baron-Cohen, Alan M. Leslie and Uta Frith argued that autistic people suffer from an impaired Theory of Mind and accordingly cannot understand 'that other people know, want, feel, or believe things' (1985: 38). This inability to read or interpret other minds was described, variously, as 'circumscribed cognitive failure', 'cognitive dysfunction', 'cognitive deficit' (1985: 44) and a 'striking poverty' (1985: 38). As disability scholar Melanie Yergeau (2013) has identified, the full weight of the lack or deficiency model of autism can be seen in operation here. Baron-Cohen's subsequent publication *Mindblindness: An Essay on Autism and Theory of Mind* (1995) garnered widespread popular support for this understanding both of empathy and of autism. According to the Theory of Mind model, our understanding of others is inferential in nature; because mental states are not directly observable, they must be interpreted or postulated and are therefore mediated through a theoretical framework. In the model of theory theory, to which Baron-Cohen subscribes, this involves an appeal to folk psychology, which offers us a common-sense explanation of why people do what they do; in predicting another's future actions, for example, we reason from our knowledge of their past and present behaviour and circumstances. Following the standard view, children develop a Theory of Mind at around the age of four years old.[5] Thus, as phenomenologists Shaun Gallagher and Dan Zahavi note, a direct implication of theory theory seems to be that 'young children will lack any understanding of self and others during the first three to four years of life'. Nevertheless, they observe, Baron-Cohen concedes that 'various mechanisms . . . might be regarded as precursors to a theory of mind' (2012: 195), meaning that children can understand something of the psychological states of others at an early stage. Theory theory establishes a conceptual basis for autism as a developmental disorder that becomes diagnosable in children at the point at which the mechanisms underpinning Theory of Mind would normally become established. For Baron-Cohen, the deficiency in Theory of Mind is innate and hard-wired into the brain from birth; for other researchers, it can be acquired through social interaction and development. Across both approaches, however, autism emerges as a childhood condition that results from a dysfunction in the development of Theory of Mind. In discussing the mutual influence of the biological and the cultural later in this chapter, I will return to the ideological implications of the close association between autism and the child, which acts as a recurring trope or motif of autism research.

Although Baron-Cohen developed his theories prior to the rise of neuro-imaging technologies, his more recent research has sought to map Theory of Mind onto specific anatomical areas of the brain. He has paid particular attention to the amygdala, within the limbic system, which is associated in functional terms with the emotions and sociability; thus, fMRI scans have linked patterns of activity in this region to facial recognition and interpretation. Autism scholar Majia Holmer Nadesan aptly observes:

> Those neuropsychologists [like Baron-Cohen] that believe that the Theory of Mind is innate often point to fMRI research on abnormal patterns of activity in the amygdala of autistic patients, thereby localizing the development of the Theory of Mind at least partially in that brain component. (2005: 121)

A notable challenge to this approach has emerged from researchers on autism who focus not on empathy and its deficit, but rather on the autistic person's difficulties in planning and in coping with novelty (Houston and Frith 2000). Here, emphasis on Theory of Mind is replaced by attention to the mind's 'executive functions', the purported impairment of which is linked to the autistic person's propensity towards inflexibility and fixed routines.[6] Under this model, Nadesan notes, a different area of the brain comes to the fore: '[t]he theory of executive functions appeals to those cognitive researchers who seek to link their cognitive models with the brain's frontal lobes and/or cerebellum, typically cited as the source of executive function operations' (2005: 121). Here, then, the differing location of autism in the brain is connected to the focus on different aspects of autistic symptomatology. In what follows, however, I will indicate that different theories of empathy itself also produce contrasting accounts of how and where it manifests at the level of measurable brain activity.

The main opposition to theory theory from within the Theory of Mind model is known as simulation theory. As in theory theory, simulation theory posits that our understanding of others' minds is produced through a process of inference, but rather than a theoretical stance, it recognises that we ourselves have minds that we can use to illuminate our knowledge of the thoughts and feelings of others; it argues that we turn to our own emotional and cognitive resources in our processes of mentalisation. Thus, philosopher Alvin I. Goldman (2006) has suggested that we 'simulate' in our own minds the minds of others; placing ourselves in their position, we use our own imagined responses to frame our understanding of what the other person will think, feel or decide. According to this model, then, empathy becomes a mode of perspective taking. This has led to criticism on the grounds of our capacity genuinely to step into another person's shoes. Gallagher and Zahavi have thus questioned:

one might ask whether it is really legitimate to cast our experiences of others in terms of a first-person imaginative exercise. When we project ourselves imaginatively into the perspective of the other, when we put ourselves into his or her shoes, will we then really attain an understanding of the other, or will we merely be reiterating ourselves? (2012: 197)

For Gallagher and Zahavi, then, simulation theory raises the question of whether empathy is truly other-directed in its intentionality, or rather a veiled or disguised form of self-referentiality. In spite of these reservations, simulation theory has offered an influential alternative to theory theory explanations of empathy deficit in autism; according to this approach, intersubjective difficulties are based in cognitive problems with or impairments in perspective taking. Philosophers Amy Coplan and Peter Goldie have observed that its empirical evidence base is less robust than for theory theory, as it has tended to look not towards neuro-imaging, but to draw instead on 'substantial work in developmental and empirical psychology' (2011: XXXIV).

Theory theory and simulation theory produce different accounts of empathy, but both assume that it is, inherently, a process of theorising about others, and that it involves higher-level cognitive processes. Significant questions have been raised, however, as to whether our intersubjective relations are, in fact, most accurately described through processes of theorisation. Are we involved at such a conscious level when we interact with others, or are we operating at a more basic, non-conscious level of functioning? Might empathy, in other words, be located not in higher-level cognitive processes, but in lower-level aspects of our mental lives? As outlined above, simulation theory has accounted for empathy in terms of higher-level processes, but it has also significantly expanded to encompass empathy as a lower-level activity. The main impetus behind this development was the 'discovery' in the early 1990s of mirror neurons by Giacomo Rizzolatti and his research team at the University of Parma.[7] The researchers found that a special class of neurons in the ventral premotor area of the macaque brain, which came to be known as mirror neurons, were activated not only when the monkey was performing a particular task, but also when it observed another monkey performing the same type of action. The macaques were thus seen to mirror each other at a neural level; the neurons seemed to enable them to understand and to recognise other monkeys' actions. Brain-imaging experiments on humans using fMRI suggested that the regions of the inferior frontal lobe cortex and the superior parietal lobe are active both when a person performs an action and when s/he sees it performed by others, leading to claims that these areas of the human brain contain mirror neurons. From there, a number of researchers independently claimed that the mirror neuron system provides the basis for human empathy. Primatologists Stephanie Preston and Frans de Waal (2002) used the mirror neuron to advance an evolutionary account of human empathy, arguing for an integrated function that operated across individuals, species and stages of development. Psychiatrist Marco Iacobini influentially claimed that mirror neurons form the foundation of empathy and that they solve the problem of how we understand other minds:

> Mirror neurons undoubtedly provide, for the first time in history, a plausible neurophysiological explanation for complex forms of social cognition and interaction. By helping us to recognize the actions of other people, mirror neurons also help us to recognize and understand the deepest motives behind those actions, the intentions of other individuals. (2008: 5–6)

In claiming mirror neurons as the foundation for empathy, these researchers were also effectively redefining empathy itself: no longer a process of theorising about others, it had become a form of feeling what others feel. On this account, based in ideas of mimicry and contagion that also speak to eighteenth-century philosophical accounts of sympathy, empathy does not involve knowing about the other, or about their mental state, but rather is conceived of as a sharing of the mental state in question. According to this new research, we are evolutionarily and neurologically adapted to respond to others at an implicit, non-conscious and motor level. Nikolas Rose and Joelle M. Abi Rached note that such arguments have led to the emergence of ideas of the 'social brain', which they describe as 'a way of thinking about the human brain as specialized for sociality through the built-in capacity to understand the beliefs and intentions of others' (2013: 147).

Such developments have not been without attendant controversies. While espousing a biological account of empathy, neurophilosopher Patricia Churchland (2011) has expressed significant reservations about the sweeping claims made for mirror neurons as the basis for intersubjectivity. She argues that the model of simulating observed actions has unresolved philosophical issues, and that in neuroscientific terms, the individual neuron is not a sufficiently complex mechanism to underpin and support explanations of empathy. Her notes of caution typify other responses, which are summarised by Rose and Abi-Rached as follows:

> Critics argued that the claims made [for mirror neurons] were philosophically, conceptually, and empirically problematic and that there was little or no evidence that these mirror neurons actually could achieve the effects claimed for them – of understanding the intentions from observing actions or appearances of others, especially when it came to complex interpretations of social behaviour or the communicative acts of others – and indeed that there was actually rather little evidence for the existence of mirror neurons in humans. (2013: 147)

A particular sticking point identified by Rose and Abi-Rached is the move from the original claims of imitation and simulation to identifying mirror neurons with the capacity to grasp the intention behind an action. Gallagher and Zahavi also pick up on this key development in mirror-neuron research, pointing out that mirror activation processes do seem appropriately to describe 'a direct perception of the other's actions', but extend less comfortably to broader claims for an implicit, non-conscious function of empathetic resonance with that other person (2012: 199).

Scientific approaches to empathy thus take the form of a dynamic, contested and rapidly evolving area of research activity, with the broad impetus to define a biological foundation for empathy. Such is the volatility of the term empathy within the various fields of scientific enquiry that it has led Zahavi to question 'whether it would not be best to simply drop the term', focusing instead on the 'more general field of social cognition' (2014: 141). If empathy as a term enables us to focus on the issues specific to our knowledge of others, our brief survey has revealed that this knowledge can be self- or other-directed, conscious or innate, hard-wired or acquired, and located in a range of neural regions and functions. Across all of these approaches, however, is a common belief that we can see the mind in the brain; that if we are to learn more about empathy, then the neurosciences become key to unlocking its secrets. Thus, in conceptualising empathy in the twenty-first century, we must recognise that, in the words of Jo Winning, it is 'always-already mediated by bio-medical culture, its technologies, its paradigms, and its practices' (2016: 328). This is not to say, however, that we are entirely confined by the dominant logics of biomedicine, even as we are necessarily entangled within them. Winning identifies two potential modes of critical intervention. First, bearing in mind the predominance of visuality in biomedical culture – its 'drive towards the twinned processes of observation and measurement' – Winning suggests that one task would be 'to restore biomedicine to a more holistic sense of the human body'. Second, recognising that 'the technologies of biomedical imaging are . . . often placed in the service of other cultural concerns', she indicates that a further task would be to identify and analyse the cultural ideologies and investments that are at stake (2016: 329). In the following section, I draw on phenomenology to offer an account of empathy that is grounded in a more 'holistic' conception of the embodied mind, and in the final section I will undertake a cultural analysis of autism, through a reading of Haddon's novel.

It would, however, be a disservice to move into a critical engagement, both with neuroscientific accounts of empathy and with autism research without first acknowledging the significant work already achieved in these areas by disability scholarship and activism. Disability studies has made a significant contribution to autism research by critiquing the biomedical understanding of autism as producing and reinforcing the stereotypes of neurotypicality. If cognitive neuroscientists designate those with autism as 'mindblind', disability activists argue that autistic minds can illuminate the limitations of 'normal' empathy and cognition. More than this, as Ralph James Savarese and Lisa Zunshine point out, the irony of the neurotypical observer designating autistic empathy in terms of deficit 'is that it is the neurotypical observer who is "mindblind" (i.e. incapable of reading the other person's mind) yet the label of mindblindness or an "impaired" theory of mind is firmly attached to the individual exhibiting the unconventional behaviour' (2014: 22). The neurodiversity movement has indicated that Theory of Mind focuses only on the ability to read human minds, thereby excluding the understanding that some autists display in relation to animal minds, as well as a marked cognitive and emotional connection to objects.[8] Viewed in the context of neurodiversity, those with autism take on the identity of a minority population whose subjectivity needs to be taken into account. While this rights-based research has made a significant impact in relation to destigmatising the condition, it tends to base its claims on those with high-functioning autism and so risks its own 'blindness' regarding the heterogeneity within autism itself, such that the diagnostic spectrum encompasses a broad and diverse range of behaviours and cognitive states.[9]

Disability-studies research also understands disability to be socially constructed rather than biologically given, and as such it is interested in the kinds of conditions that are considered disabling, and how these vary over time, place and context, as well as the shifting meanings that are attached to them. The diagnostic category of autism first emerged in the post-war period, with the pioneering research on children of Hans Asperger (1906–80) at Vienna University and Leo Kanner (1894–1981) at Johns Hopkins University Hospital. Nadesan notes that the emergence of autism as a diagnostic classification in the early 1940s can be understood culturally in terms of the 'matrix of professional and parental practices marking the cultural and economic transition to the twentieth century' (2005: 19). Certainly, we can note the close association between autism and the child that is also evident in neurocognitive approaches. In the 1960s and 1970s, autism was classified in the *Diagnostic and Statistical Manual* (*DSM*) under the criteria for childhood schizophrenia. It first appeared as a separate diagnostic category in the third edition of the *DSM* (1980) and Asperger syndrome was added to the fourth edition (1994). In the fifth edition of the *DSM* (2013), Asperger's as a separate diagnostic category was removed and merged into autism spectrum disorder. Here, then, the boundaries of autism shift from one edition of the *DSM* to the next, illustrating the instability of the diagnostic classification. Reflecting on the dynamic qualities of autism, Nadesan has observed that: 'perhaps autism is not a *thing* but is a nominal category useful for grouping heterogeneous people all sharing communication practices deviating significantly from the expectations of normalcy. These communication practices are becoming, increasingly, standardized, codified, and widely distributed' (2005: 9; italics in original). Nadesan's emphasis on the cultural dissemination of autistic symptomatology gestures towards Hacking's notion of 'interactivity'; that the act of classification can affect and change the very category that it is describing. The neurodiversity movement adds to this that the category of autism is constructed, in part, by autistic people themselves; the term encompasses the shared culture that is produced by those who are either medically categorised or self-identify with the diagnostic category.[10] Mark Osteen has nevertheless indicated that disability studies has, in emphasising the cultural, often excluded more physical modes of explanation: 'disability studies has concentrated so heavily on the sociocultural construction of disability that it has largely ignored the physical realities on which its discipline is founded' (2008b: 2). In the terms offered by Hacking, disability studies has attended to the 'interactive' aspects of the autism classification, arguably at the expense of its more 'indifferent' elements.

Disability studies has offered a vital counterweight to the biomedical objectification of disabled people. It has contributed to autism research the politics of neurodiversity and a sociocultural analysis of the diagnostic category. I want to close, however, by returning to the motif of the visual. Disability studies has offered a compelling critique of the blindness, or more accurately, the restricted vision, of Theory of Mind research, which fails to enquire as to *whose* mind is being designated as deficient, and with what effects. In so doing, however, disability studies also enacts its own restricted vision in failing to ask *whose* autistic mind is being reified as a model, and how that might impact on those who are at the lower-functioning end of the autistic spectrum. Disability studies has also tended to concentrate its attention on visible physical disabilities, in part reflecting the origins and history of the movement, and in part because these disabilities – in and through their very visibility – lend themselves more readily to awareness and fundraising campaigns. Osteen accordingly remarks: 'disability scholarship has ignored cognitive, intellectual, or neurological disabilities, thereby excluding the intellectually disabled just as mainstream society has done' (2008b: 3). Although the neurodiversity movement has to some extent countered this trend, Osteen's observation nevertheless indicates that disability studies can be seen to share aspects not only of the blindness or restriction of vision of which it accuses biomedicine, but also of the propulsion of the biomedical towards what is visible and hence both observable and measurable.

Phenomenology and empathy

The philosophical tradition of phenomenology has long been engaged with the question of intersubjectivity.[11] This section turns to phenomenology as an alternative strand of thinking on empathy, and argues that its analyses can be mapped on to, and have at times been explicitly claimed by, contemporary neurocognitive research. Thus, I trace in what follows phenomenology's engagement with higher-level and lower-level modes of empathy, with empathy as self- or other-directed, and with empathy as reflective or unconscious. More than this, I suggest that phenomenology can move current debates in neurocognition forward in productive ways. Returning to the question of where empathy is located, I discuss phenomenology's attention not to the mind but rather to the world that we share. I also pull through from the previous section the question of visibility; if neurocognitive approaches to empathy have assumed that our thoughts and emotions are hidden in the mind, phenomenology indicates rather that, in engaging with others, we encounter them as lived bodies with whom we interact in a meaningful context or shared situation. As such, we experience others as intentional beings, whose feelings or states of mind are expressed through their bodily actions and gestures. Phenomenology thus shares with lower-level simulation theory the belief that we experience others' states of mind in direct and unmediated ways; however, it departs from the latter in highlighting that we experience the feelings and emotions of others *as theirs*, and not as our own; we are not, in other words, dealing with a form of inner mimicry or contagion. Furthermore, the very fact that we are engaged with others as embodied and *expressive* agents means that there is no need, in most of our interactions, for us to employ theoretical frames or inferences in order to access others' thoughts and feelings; in distinction from Theory of Mind, phenomenology indicates that we typically operate at a more intuitive level in our face-to-face encounters with others, turning to cognitive modes of interpretation only when a more implicit mode of functioning proves inadequate.

It is instructive to begin a survey of phenomenological accounts of empathy with reference to the work of German philosopher Theodor Lipps (1851–1914); in the late nineteenth century, he provided an influential psychological theory of empathy against or in opposition to which phenomenologists defined their own understanding of the term. The word empathy, in German *Einfühlung* or 'feeling into', was coined by German philosopher Robert Vischer (1847–1914), who used it in his doctoral dissertation 'On the Optical Sense of Form: A Contribution to Aesthetics' (1994). Lipps subsequently took up and promoted the term, particularly in his volume *Raumästhetik* (1966), to argue that the aesthetic appreciation of a work of art results from the projection of oneself into the object of perception. While Lipps conceived of empathy primarily as an experience of the mind, his emphasis on feeling oneself into the object also entailed that empathy had a physiological aspect or dimension; in watching a dancer, for example, the observer would come to an aesthetic appreciation of the performance through an unconscious motor imitation of the movements observed. Lipps also emphasised that, through the mechanism of projection, what one encounters in the aesthetic object is, in the end, oneself. Lipps was the first to discuss empathy in relation to intersubjectivity, extending the term from the field of aesthetics into that of psychology, and here he placed particular emphasis on empathy as a feeling of oneness with the mind of the other, achieved through inner imitation. Perhaps unsurprisingly, proponents of lower-level simulation theory have demonstrated particular interest in Lipps's theories; for Zahavi, 'simulationists, such as Iacobini and [Vittorio] Gallese have explicitly referred to and endorsed Lipps' idea that empathy involves a form of inner imitation' (2014: 131). Higher-level simulationists such as Goldman (2006: 11) have also turned to Lipps's ideas for support, finding in his model of 'feeling into' the other's mind a structural similarity to perspective taking; both approaches also have in common the ultimate re-inscription of the self, rather than an attitude directed towards the other.

Phenomenologists directed criticism at Lipps's claims that empathy's foundation lay in inner imitation. Of particular significance for my purposes is the work of Edith Stein, a doctoral student of Edmund Husserl (1859–1938). Her dissertation *On the Problem of Empathy* was the first work exclusively devoted to examining empathy as the descriptive term for intersubjective human relations. Distinctive to Stein's account, and in explicit rebuttal of Lipps's claims, is the conviction that empathy is concerned with 'foreign consciousness'; it is a form of other-directed intentionality (1989: 12).[12] Stein thus avers of encountering another's feelings of distress: 'It is not felt as my own distress, nor as a remembered distress, let alone simply as an imagined distress. No, it is throughout given to me as the other's distress, as a distress lived through by the other' (Stein 1989: 10). Central to Stein's understanding of empathy is the distinction between 'primordial' experience, which refers to one's own experiences in the present ('my own distress') and 'non-primordial experience', which encompasses memory ('a remembered distress') and fantasy ('an imagined distress'). For Lipps, empathy counts as a primordial experience; his emphasis on oneness entails that one feels *as one's own* the other's observed distress. Stein concedes that empathy, taking place in the present, is concurrent with primordial experience, but for her it is not itself primordial:

> The subject of the empathized experience . . . is not the subject empathizing, but another . . . These subjects are separate and not joined together . . . by a consciousness of sameness or a continuity of experience. This other subject is primordial although I do not experience it as primordial. (Stein 1989: 10–11)

Taking the example of perceived joy, Stein elaborates: 'while I am living in the other's joy, I do not feel primordial joy. It does not issue live from my "I"' (1989: 11). Stein's argument addresses itself directly to Lipps's understanding of empathy as shared feeling; it also, however, speaks productively to contemporary mirror-neuron research, which – in its claims for a shared mental state between subject and observer – also collapses the distinction between primordial and non-primordial experience.

Stein's view of empathy is underpinned by the recognition that the body of the other is experienced directly as *a person*, an intentional being that is actively engaged in and with the world. Stein explains as follows:

> This individual is not given as a physical body, but as a sensitive, living body belonging to an 'I', an 'I' that senses, thinks, feels and wills. The living body of this 'I' not only fits into my phenomenal world but is itself the centre of orientation of such a phenomenal world. It faces this world and communicates with me. (1989: 5)

Stein's observation directs attention to our experiencing of a different subjectivity in our encounter with the other. Because the other is also an 'I', our experiential access to her mind is necessarily partial and limited. This limitation is not, however, regarded by Stein to be a shortcoming of empathy, but rather is identified as its very value and purpose; it gives the other person to us as a locus of agency and experience. In so doing, empathy holds the potential to act as 'an important aid to self evaluation' (Stein 1989: 116). In encountering others, we continually rub up against new 'centres of orientation' that have the capacity to open up different perspectives on the world, and also on ourselves; Stein remarks that in our everyday interactions, we accordingly 'run into ranges of value closed to us' (Stein 1989: 154). For Stein, then, feeling ourselves into the non-primordial images that exist in other minds can enable us to know and evaluate ourselves more effectively, as well as to appreciate that our own experiences differ in various ways from those of others.

Stein's analysis of intersubjectivity also takes us back to the question of visibility; for her, we are not seeking to access the mind of the other, but are focused rather on their meaningful and observable bodily actions. Matthew Ratcliffe thus observes that, for Stein, 'experience and expression are inextricable' (2012: 475). Feeling contains an inherent surplus or excess, which demands to be expended through bodily gesture and movement: 'Feeling in its pure essence is not something complete in itself. As it were, it is loaded with an energy which must be unloaded' (Stein 1989: 51). Such an approach significantly confounds any distinction between mind and body; we are envisioned by Stein to function as minded bodies, or as embodied minds. By extension, Stein's model can also shed light on the implicit Cartesianism of Theory of Mind approaches, which are predicated on the belief that the observable behaviour of others is meaningless, and that it therefore requires an intellectually derived attribution of psychological meaning. Reinforcing Stein's point, Zahavi and Josef Parnas accordingly assert against Theory of Mind: 'On the contrary, in the face-to-face encounter, we are neither confronted with a mere body, nor with a hidden psyche, but with a unified whole' (2003: 65). At the same time, Stein does not exclude from her account of empathy more theoretical processes of understanding others; she postulates a multi-level account of empathy, which encompasses more intuitive and more cognitive elements. How we respond to others thus becomes bound up with the context of any particular encounter, and may be influenced by such factors as the situation or environment in which we find ourselves, or how much experience we can assume to be shared. For Stein, then, a pre-reflective mode of empathy both underpins and exists alongside more complex, theory-constituted modes. This is notably different from theory theory approaches, which postulate that intuitive, non-theoretical modes of understanding constitute the basis of young children's intersubjectivity, to be superseded by the development of Theory of Mind (Baron-Cohen 2000: 1251). Shaun Gallagher usefully reinforces the phenomenological understanding that a more basic form of intersubjectivity provides the lasting foundation for our empathetic relations:

> Primary, embodied subjectivity is not primary simply in developmental terms. Rather it remains primary across all face-to-face intersubjective experiences, and it subtends the occasional and secondary intersubjective practices of explaining or predicting what other people believe, desire or intend in the practice of their own minds. (2001: 91)

The concern here, then, is that intersubjective processes should not be reduced to theoretical models; for Stein and contemporary neo-phenomenologists, the pre-reflective remains a central component of empathy, combined with an attitude of openness to others, a willingness to recognise and engage with their different experiences of and perspectives on the world that we share.

Stein's careful elaboration of empathy offers an account that is, above all, other-oriented. Summarising her intellectual contribution, literary critic Meghan Marie Hammond concludes: 'Stein [is] interested in empathy as a cognitive process through which we can understand how other people see the world' (2014: 150). In the context of autism, this trajectory of thought is suggestive. Adopting a Theory of Mind approach, whether based in reasoning from what we already know or simulating based on our own experience, it is easy to conclude that we cannot empathise with the autistic mind because it is too radically different from our own. Understood as 'fellow feeling', empathy thus reaches its limit when the other person is affected by autism. Stein's work, though, offers us a way to reorient the debate; for her, empathy does not amount to or describe that feeling of oneness with the other that was so central to Lipps, but rather an appreciation that the other's experience of, and orientation towards, the world differs from my own. More than this, Stein emphasises that we do not, indeed cannot, understand the other's experience, which will be fully present only to herself. Building on Stein's philosophy, Ratcliffe has defined a model of 'radical empathy' that helps us to think through intersubjectivity in the context of serious mental-health conditions, such as schizophrenia, severe depression or autism. For Ratcliffe, empathy describes a mode of engaging with the other that 'involves suspending the usual assumption that both parties share the same modal space' (2012: 483). Radical empathy begins from the premise that interacting with another makes me *feel* a certain way, which, Ratcliffe explains, can 'incorporate a degree of experiential insight into what that world is like' (2012: 489). At the same time, it remains cognisant that this presentation, this feeling, is inherently incomplete; that it differs from how the *other* experiences her world. Difference thus becomes inscribed into this model of empathy both at the level of the other's experience of the world, and at the level of *my* experience of that experience as I engage in interaction with her. Ratcliffe's model, like Stein's, also usefully shifts attention from the individual subject(ivity) to the important role that is played in intersubjectivity by how we relate, variously, to our world in common; in understanding others, then, we are not getting into their minds, but rather attending to the world that we share with them.[13]

Phenomenology thus offers an account of empathy that, in its other-directedness, is responsive to difference; like the neurodiversity movement, it is attentive to the possibility of a range of modes of experiencing the world. The following section turns to analyse the literary representation of autism in Haddon's *The Curious Incident*.

Pulling together the phenomenological account of empathy with Waugh's definition of the neo-phenomenological novel, I propose to approach the work of fiction, not as a narrative vehicle for accessing the autistic mind and subjectivity of Christopher, but rather by asking how Christopher is oriented towards the imagined world of the novel, and how that orientation relates to or differs from that of the other characters. How might these modes of relation be inflected, in turn, by the characteristics of that world that is shared in the novel?

Narrating autism

In 2003, Mark Haddon's *The Curious Incident of the Dog in the Night-Time* became an unexpected marketing phenomenon. Bridging the genres of detective fiction, coming-of-age story and autistic memoir, and published simultaneously as both children's and adult fiction, the work truly exemplified the literary genre that critic Rachel Falconer has termed the 'crossover novel' (2008).[14] Upon publication, *The Curious Incident* immediately went to the top of the adult bestseller list, and children's sales figures were also very high. It won the 2003 Whitbread Award for Best Novel, as well as the overall prize for Book of the Year. It was also longlisted for the Booker Prize and Falconer records that 'the Chair of Judges, John Carey, publicly criticised his fellow judges for failing to select it for the short list' (2008: 96). At a time when autistic autobiographies were also enjoying considerable marketing success, the novel was widely lauded for its remarkable insight into the autistic mind, and for helping to humanise and destigmatise the condition. Haddon's work was, in other words, regarded as a remarkable feat of imaginative empathy, which fostered, in turn, an empathetic response for Christopher – and by extension for other autistic people – from the reader.[15] My own reading offers a more critical approach to the intersection of autism and empathy in the novel. Reading the work first as a *Bildungsroman*, I analyse the figure of the autistic child, which has run as a *leitmotif* throughout this chapter. If the novel is framed as a developmental coming-of-age story, especially important to the children's literature market, I ask how and in what ways Christopher matures in the course of the novel. I then turn to consider the novel as a detective fiction, which is more closely aligned with the adult reader's market, turning to Lisa Zunshine's (2006) influential idea that our pleasure in reading detective fiction derives from exercising Theory of Mind. If this is the case, then what are the implications of Christopher as a detective-narrator who, by his own account, does not have a Theory of Mind? I close the section by approaching *The Curious Incident* as a syndrome novel, asking how the neo-phenomenological elements of this genre might potentially reposition questions of empathy and autism in the novel, enabling us to focus less on Christopher's mind than on the fictional world that he both inhabits and shares with other characters.

A useful point of departure for thinking about the representation of autism in British fiction is Stuart Murray's discussion of the 'contemporary sentimental' (2006). In spite, or perhaps because of, the cultural prevalence of narratives of autism, Murray argues that many fictions tend to reproduce a narrow range of stereotypes of the condition, to position the autistic character as a vehicle for growth and change in others – particularly adult male characters – and to locate agency elsewhere in the narrative. In particular, Murray points to the figure of the savant as characteristic of this mode of representation. Its continual reproduction misunderstands the nature of autism, because savant skills are uncommon in the autistic population. Furthermore, the function of the savant figure is to provide a narrative opportunity for modifying or transforming character relations; in so doing, it implies that growth or development is associated with the non-autistic population, while savantism itself constitutes the main worth and interest of the autistic character. In a subsequent study of autistic representations, Murray also identified the figure of the child to be integral to fictions of autism, noting of its ubiquity: 'Again and again in contemporary cultural narratives it is the child who carries the weight of what we wish to say about the condition, and it is through a focus on children that autism is being increasingly understood' (2008: 139).[16] The child figure can readily be mapped on to the defining features of the 'contemporary sentimental': from the pioneering research of Kanner and Asperger on, autism has been associated predominantly with the child, at the expense of the adult autist population, so that it conforms to a narrow or stereotyped version of autism.

In Murray's view, *The Curious Incident* largely evades the dominant tropes of the 'contemporary sentimental'. While noting that savantism is particularly associated in the popular imagination with mathematics and memory skills, both of which are characteristic of Christopher, Murray concludes that: 'for all his skills . . . , Christopher . . . is not a savant' (2008: 88). Equally, Murray asserts that Haddon's creation of Christopher resists either a more metaphorical treatment of autism, or sidelining the character to secondary status within the story; as protagonist and narrator, Christopher asserts and insists upon his own narrative identity. If Haddon is necessarily entangled in the figures of contemporary autism representation, Murray thus argues that the novel nevertheless avoids misrepresentation:

> Haddon creates Christopher to resonate with the public's general awareness of what autism is and how it works . . . This is, of course, a very delicate balancing act. Overstressing the stereotypical elements would tip the novel into the kind of exploitation that Haddon clearly wishes to avoid; yet to make Christopher work as a character, he needs to be recognizable enough to a readership that has only the passing relationship with autism that comes with the general cultural (mis)representation of the condition. (2008: 48)

In spite of Murray's defence of Haddon, however, there are elements of the novel that do seem to tip its representation of autism towards, rather than away from, more stereotyped versions. Christopher's mathematical prowess reinforces the notion that savantism is a characteristic of 'the autistic mind'. Autist critic Gyasi Burks-Abbott accordingly concludes, in the opposite vein to Murray, that '[a] monolithic view of autism is evident in the choices made in constructing the character Christopher' (2008: 291). Likewise, considering *The Curious Incident* as a *Bildung*, it is doubtful whether Christopher evidences any genuine growth or development over the course of the novel. In one sense, we can trace a fairly conventional path of progress through the narrative: his parents' divorce occasions the 'curious incident' of the dog stabbed to death with a pitchfork with which the novel opens, and this sets Christopher on his journey of discovery. He not only solves the mystery of the dog's murder; in so doing, he also confronts his fears, undertaking what is for him the epic voyage from Swindon to London, and at the novel's close he successfully navigates the rite of passage of his Maths Advanced Level examination. In concluding his story, Christopher neatly sums up:

> I will get a First Class Honours Degree and I will become a scientist. And I know I can do this because I went to London on my own, and because I solved the mystery of Who Killed Wellington? and I found my mother and I was brave and I wrote a book and that means I can do anything. (2003: 268)

Cutting across these remarkable achievements, however, is the child-ish tone of the narrative voice, which remains consistent from begin-ning to end of the novel and indicates that Christopher has not developed in any meaningful way at all. James Berger has likewise analysed Christopher's preference for spatial over temporal frame-works in the novel, suggesting that his ideal existence would be in a world of unchanging physical objects. Here, too, Berger suggests, is a narrative resistance to the forward trajectory of the *Bildung*: 'It would be a world of routine and habit, of problems or puzzles that need to be solved, but not of personal growth or of life-changing decisions' (2008: 275–6). Even Murray concedes that, if personal maturation is achieved in *The Curious Incident*, it can most readily be located in Christopher's father, Ed. In the course of the novel, he has to confront the consequences of his decision to tell Christopher that his mother had died, rather than that she had left to start a new life in London with another man, as well as establish a different basis for the relationship with his son. We are returned here, then, to the genre of the 'contemporary sentimental', in which the relation-ship with the autistic child leads to an adult learning process, in and through which ideas of male responsibility and agency are negotiated (Murray 2006: 33).

If the interpretative lens of the *Bildung* leads back to the 'con-temporary sentimental', indicating that *The Curious Incident* does rely on and reproduce cultural stereotypes of autism, how might a reading of the novel be differently inflected if we turn to the genre of detective fiction? In her influential study, *Why We Read Fiction* (2006), Lisa Zunshine's argument that our enjoyment derives from exercising Theory of Mind finds particular support in the genre of detective fiction.[17] Combining literary criticism and cognitive psy-chology, Zunshine contends that writers of fiction experiment in a range of ways with our mind-reading abilities, requiring of us that we exercise our capacity to account for behaviour in terms of ascribed thoughts, feelings, beliefs and desires, as we watch characters read – and often misread – one another's intentions. Of the detective-fiction genre specifically, Zunshine avers:

> I suggest that detective stories 'work out' in a particularly focused fashion our ability to store representations under advisement and to re-evaluate their truth-value once more information comes in. They push this ability to its furthest limits, first, by explicitly requiring us to store a lot of information under a very strong advisement – that

is, to 'suspect *everybody*' – for as long as we can possibly take it and, then, as the story comes to an end, to readjust drastically much of what we have been surmising in the process of reading it. (2006: 123–4; italics in original)

According to Zunshine's account, in reading detective fiction we distrust or disbelieve nearly every character that we encounter until the very close of the novel, so that we can determine and weigh up their motives in relation to the crime committed, and make our own inferences about their guilt or innocence in the case before the detective discloses the 'true' criminal and motive. By extension, the detective is positioned as a character who possesses a remarkable aptitude for Theory of Mind; a capacity to read and evaluate a number of different behaviours at once, and to ascribe motive from the smallest, most apparently insignificant, behavioural detail.

It might, then, come as a surprise that there is a growing popular acceptance of the idea that autistic individuals make good detectives. Uta Frith has argued that most of the detectives from the 'golden age' of detective fiction, including Christopher's literary hero, Sherlock Holmes, were 'on the spectrum' (2003: 154). Recalling Murray's account of the 'contemporary sentimental', such a statement can be seen to be underpinned by a narrow view of autistic characteristics, specifically an advanced capacity for memory and observation, and a deep interest in a restricted number of topics. It might nevertheless be argued that, in spite of its stereotyping qualities, the detective-fiction genre offers a potential recognition and celebration of neurodiversity, in according value to the cognitive skills of the detective. In *The Curious Incident*, Christopher certainly shares Holmes's impressive memory and attention to detail; by his own admission, however, he completely lacks a Theory of Mind. Literary critic Michelle Resene (2016) has observed in this context that Christopher is unable to tell lies, or to understand why others might be motivated to do so. Moreover, confronted by a number of possible suspects for the murder of Wellington, and required to identify and evaluate a range of different motives, Christopher becomes anxious and frightened. Pushed to his limit, and unable to understand why his father might have lied to him about his mother's departure, Christopher closes down entirely and enters a state of physical and mental paralysis. Lacking Theory of Mind also entails that Christopher does not, in fact, solve the mystery of Wellington's death through his own investigations; the answer is given to him through his father's confession, although the reader has already pieced the clues together. For Resene, Haddon's positioning of Christopher as both a bad detective and the bad narrator of a detective story establishes a narrative dynamic in which the reader occupies a superior position to the protagonist. Once again, Christopher is deprived of narrative agency or development.

Read through the lens of detective fiction, then, *The Curious Incident* is not a celebration of neurodiversity but an affirmation of the neurotypical perspective, positioning autism in terms of lack or deficit. Resene regards the novel as 'a retrograde step' in young-adult fiction's treatment of disability, noting:

> If Christopher is unable to fill the detective role due to his intellectual disability, then that can lead readers to assume that he – and therefore the real child or teenager with autism – is somehow intellectually inferior to the neurotypical reader. (2016: 82)

In *The Curious Incident*, Christopher's deficit in mindreading – in Baron-Cohen's terms, his 'mindblindness' – accordingly needs to be compensated by the reader's aptitude. Here, then, we are back full circle to the arguments surveyed in the Introduction for fiction reading as beneficial to, if not productive of, empathy.[19] Ann Jurecic has noted of Zunshine in particular that her claims for fiction as a form of exercise or 'work out' for Theory of Mind mark a return to 'the humanist educators who teach literature because it stimulates empathy' (2011: 23). Viewed in this light, Zunshine's cognitive-literary approach effectively puts old wine into new bottles. Reading *The Curious Incident* as a detective-fiction story places the hermeneutic emphasis on mindreading skills, and so positions empathy as that which Christopher lacks and the reader possesses.[20] In my final approach to the novel, I therefore turn to the category of syndrome fiction, to ask how a neo-phenomenological reading might reorient the discussion towards a less cognitive and character-based mode of interpretation.

In describing *The Curious Incident*, Murray has positioned the novel as the beginning of 'syndrome publishing' (2006: 33). Literary critic Stephen J. Burn has identified as central to the 'syndrome novel' a mode of narration that reflects neurological damage or dysfunction, such that the ordinary world, the world shared by the characters, is defamiliarised or rendered strange: 'the disordered mind reformulates the complex world so that its basic axioms, rather than its elaborate superstructure, are brought back to the centre of the novel's circle of experience' (2013: 43). The purpose of this exercise in cognitive estrangement is, Burn contends, to 'probe . . . the root conditions of modernity' (2013: 43). Waugh adds to this that, in syndrome fiction, the syndrome itself becomes the target of defamiliarisation. For her, the contemporary is defined by the naturalisation of the syndrome, which entails that the biomedical paradigm reduces the 'self' to a series of neural connections, and its breakdown to a mechanical fault. The syndrome novel acts as a reminder that this notion of the self is actually a construct of our own time, and that it does not map on to lived experience. Waugh thus avers: 'In the end, the importance of the neo-phenomenological or syndrome novel is that in an age when the biomedical and neo-corporate threaten to name and incorporate what we are, it both keeps alive and explores the threats to the complexity and contradictoriness of felt selfhood' (2013: 31). In analysing *The Curious Incident* as a syndrome novel, I follow two particular lines of enquiry. First, I ask what the defamiliarisation enacted through Christopher's narration might reveal about autism as syndrome. How does Christopher's perspective on his world make us see it afresh, and what might that new vantage point reveal about the contemporary condition?[21] Second, I turn to phenomenology's potential to open up an appreciation that the other's experience of the world differs from my own. Can a neo-phenomenological reading of *The Curious Incident* draw on the cognitive estrangement of the syndrome novel to facilitate a mode of empathy that is based not on *feeling into* or *feeling with* Christopher, but rather on the registration of, and respect for, his difference?

The world that Christopher shares with the other characters of the novel is that of early-twenty-first-century suburban Swindon. His investigation of Wellington's murder leads him to interview the neighbours on his street, both to gather more information and to build up a list of possible suspects. Although the neighbours are friendly and helpful, they evidently do not know each other. Living in detached houses, they, like Christopher, form fragments of a nuclear family unit and there is no evidence in the novel of more extended relational networks. Berger summarises: 'Haddon portrays Swindon as exemplary of a post-Thatcher England characterized by vibrant high-tech industries co-existing with declining social services and education, rising unemployment and homelessness. It seems to lack social networks and civic, community, and class organizations' (2008: 280). For Berger, this is an environment characterised by 'a pervasive social autism', such that Christopher – and, by extension, autism itself – becomes the figure for a broader social disconnection (2008: 280). In the hands of other writers, such a portrait of a specifically post-Thatcher collapse of working-class community structures would take on the function of political critique.[22] Haddon, however, subordinates the political and economic causes of social isolation to the neurological, privileging the idea of an autistic spectrum that implicates us all as modified versions of Christopher. Berger thus concludes: 'the social and political conditions depicted in this novel become secondary to . . . our neurology. The ideology of neurology trumps traditional ideology critique' (2008: 285).

The syndrome novel's privileging of the neurological renders it an inherently conservative genre, one that represents, but that does not seek to change or transform, the status quo.[23] Returning to Waugh's definition of the genre, however, a more positive reading might be advanced by locating autism, rather than the social world through which it is explored, as the target of defamiliarisation. The 'social autism' represented in the novel accordingly becomes a means for Haddon to identify the ideological investments that underpin our current fascination with the condition; a cultural preoccupation that feeds back into the medical classification and diagnosis through the 'looping effect' that Hacking has described. In this sense, the novel enacts its own dynamic of 'interactivity' or 'looping' through which autism represents at once both neurological phenomenon and broader social disconnection. Haddon's unsettling of autism as neurological syndrome through its simultaneous representation as social fragmentation brings into view the late-modern cultural anxieties about loss of community that inform popular definitions of autism, and that constitute one of the cultural undercurrents that underpin the construction of the diagnostic classification.

In my preceding discussion of phenomenology, I focused on its capacity to be other-directed, to engage with the other's view of the world as different from my own. In the context of mental-health conditions, Ratcliffe expanded on this aspect of the phenomenological to formulate the notion of 'radical empathy', a mode of engaging with the other that can feel something of their mode of inhabiting the world, while also recognising that this presentation is partial and indicative; it cannot encompass their reality. The narrative genre of syndrome fiction, based on a form of cognitive difference, opens up a neo-phenomenological mode of reading, focused, in *The Curious Incident*, on how Christopher's orientation to the world differs from that of other characters. The other narrative perspective that we hear first-hand in the novel, and not mediated through Christopher, is that of his mother.[24] As Christopher reads through the letters that she has sent from London, and that his father has hidden away without opening, a narrative voice breaks in to the novel that contrasts powerfully with that of Christopher in its emotional directness. Contained in the letters is the story of everyday human fallibility: a mother's struggle to cope with the emotional demands of a young autistic son; her feelings of isolation within the family unit; and the comfort offered by her neighbour's husband, Mr Shears, with whom she eventually leaves to begin a new life in London. Berger notes that these letters reveal 'an extreme instance of another cognitive and emotional mode of being' (2008: 281). Christopher is unable to deal with the affective complexity and intensity of the letters, which results in a state of temporary collapse.

Introduced to Christopher's mother through her letters, we subsequently meet her when she unexpectedly finds Christopher sitting on her doorstep in London, having successfully navigated the perilous journey by train from Swindon. She is reunited with her son, having received no response from him since she had left the family home:

> And Mother put her arms around me and said, 'Christopher, Christopher, Christopher'.
> And I pushed her away because she was grasping me and I didn't like it, and I pushed really hard and I fell over.
> And Mr Shears said, 'What the hell is going on?'
> And Mother said, 'I'm so sorry, Christopher, I forgot'.
> And I was lying on the ground and Mother held up her right hand and spread her fingers out in a fan so that I could touch her fingers. (2003: 233)

Berger's analysis of Christopher's reunion with his mother, which he regards as 'the emotional climax of the novel' (2008: 282), focuses on her response to the news that Christopher's father had claimed that she had died. Hearing of this, Christopher's mother is at first silent, and then makes a long wailing sound. In spite of the similarity of this response to some of Christopher's own emotional outbursts, he is unable to connect with it, exhibiting, in Berger's words, 'a failure of empathy' (2008: 282). Here, then, we are returned to the have/have not model of empathy, which again positions Christopher in terms of lack or deficit.

My reading holds attention on the moment of encounter between mother and son. Here, we witness the instinctive reaction of Christopher's mother to her child, reaching out to hold him to her. At the same time, Christopher's response recalls the behaviour that we know from his mother's letters she found so difficult to cope with in the past. There is, then, a strong narrative impulse towards 'feeling with' Christopher's mother in this scene, as her emotional reactions are readily identifiable. Falconer notes, however, that this affective propulsion towards Christopher's mother is complicated by our having for so long seen the world from Christopher's point of view; from his perspective, the close physical contact offered by his mother represents a threatening dissolution of boundaries. Here, then, a form of double vision is at work, requiring us to hold in balance two different orientations towards the world. Further, Falconer suggests that Haddon's representation of this climatic moment unsettles the reader's accustomed viewpoint: 'the reader is estranged from his or herself as s/he empathetically sees how distasteful this empathetic blurring of identities must appear to Christopher himself' (2008: 107). Through cognitive difference, the everyday is seen anew, and we are given an important insight into what it feels like to be Christopher, without having to experience oneness with him or to claim full understanding. Empathy, in this sense, leads out towards the other rather than back towards the self. In closing, I turn to the gesture of touching fingers that the Boone family has improvised as a mode of physical communication, and that we see enacted at various points in the novel in key moments of tenderness, distress or crisis. Here is a vocabulary of touch that reaches across the different needs and perspectives of Christopher and his parents, without negating the validity of either party. I suggest that this form of contact – one that engages with the other while remaining mindful of its own boundaries and limitations – acts as a moving encapsulation of the radical mode of empathy that has been a focus of this chapter and that, at its most productive, Haddon's novel has the potential to convey.

Conclusion

This chapter has identified the cognitive neurosciences as a key driver for current empathy research, even if their account of what empathy is and where it is located remains highly volatile, unstable and contested. I have surveyed the distinct but overlapping fields of cognitive psychology and autism research, identifying across them both a common materialistic impulse that seeks to define its findings in relation to specific areas and functions of the brain. A materialistic turn is also evident in the cultural production of the contemporary novel; the genre of syndrome fiction likewise looks to biological and neurological factors to account for the self, arguably to the detriment of social and political critique. More positively, the syndrome novel can act as a powerful vehicle of estrangement, requiring us to encounter and think through modes of cognitive difference, and acting as a reminder that the syndrome as a mode of self-definition is a construct of our own times. Poised between a somaticism that defines and determines its characters, and a resistance to such biological reductionism, the syndrome novel can be seen as emblematic of the tensions and contradictions that characterise what Rose has termed 'the politics of life itself' (2007).[25] The chapter has also identified phenomenology as an important tradition of philosophical engagement with the question of empathy. Tracing a trajectory of thought extending from Stein into contemporary neo-phenomenology, I have excavated a model of empathy that is directed towards the other, and that investigates how we encounter and engage with difference. In summarising the condition of autism, Murray has suggestively written:

> as an example of the *diversity* of humankind, it possesses the ability to offer a critique of those lazy assertions of, and appeals to, a 'shared humanity', to replace that strand of humanist thought that in its totalizing ideologies created the disabled subject, and to counter it with a radical notion of human difference and potential. (2012: 104; italics in original)

My neo-phenomenological reading of *The Curious Incident* resonates with this definition of autism, departing from the prevailing tendency to laud our 'shared humanity' with Christopher, and identifying instead a 'radical' notion of empathy, based in the recognition and celebration of human difference and diversity.

Notes

1. See, for example, Simon Baron-Cohen (1995, 2003, 2008, 2011) and Frans de Waal (2005, 2009).
2. Feminist cultural theory work on affect has its own basis in phenomenological thought; see, in particular, Sara Ahmed (2006).
3. Metzl's own work on the structural, cultural and historical underpinnings of and investments in medical diagnosis has focused on schizophrenia and has illuminated the ways in which racial ideologies have become written into the diagnostic classification; see, in particular, Jonathan M. Metzl (2009). More recently, Metzl has turned a critical lens onto the instruments of medical diagnosis, in the form of brain-imaging technologies, and argued that they too 'emerg[e] within a

racialised legacy of image production both within and outside of medicine in the U.S.' (Andrews and Metzl 2016: 243).

4. Asperger syndrome is categorised as a developmental disorder, which is characterised by significant difficulty in social interaction, including empathy, accompanied by restricted and repetitive patterns of behaviour. It is a mild autism spectrum disorder and overlaps with high-functioning autism. Although Haddon mentions neither autism nor Asperger's in the novel, the cover of the adult edition originally included a quotation from eminent neurologist Oliver Sacks that explicitly named the condition of Asperger's. This was removed from subsequent editions.

5. Research into the development of mindreading or Theory of Mind in young children has been dominated by the 'false belief test', developed by philosophers Heinz Wimmer and Joseph Perner (1983). Hacking observes of recent research into the autistic child: 'A single ingenious experiment originally suggested by philosophers has spawned an experimental industry. That is often the case in psychology, where new experimental ideas are as hard to invent as deep mathematical proofs or truly new magic tricks' (1999: 115).

6. 'Executive functions' are a set of cognitive processes that are necessary for the cognitive control of behaviours, selecting and monitoring those behaviours that are appropriate to achieve a chosen aim or goal. They include attention, inhibition, memory, flexibility, problem solving and planning, and their functioning is associated with the prefrontal cortex.

7. In Theory of Mind approaches to empathy – theory theory and simulation theory – we have been operating in terms of a dynamic that Nadesan has described as a '*top-down explanation*', in that it works from the specific cognitive problem or theoretical approach to locate it within a specific brain area or function. In shifting focus to a model of the simulation theory associated with lower-level functioning, it is notable that we have moved to what Nadesan terms a '*bottom-up explanation*' (2005: 115, italics in original), which takes its starting point in the observable brain pattern or function and then seeks to define the cognitive theory that might account for or explain it.

8. The publishing phenomenon of autistic memoir or auti-biography has been influential in voicing autistic experience and provides an important underpinning for research and activism on neurodiversity. Temple Grandin (2006; Grandin and Johnson 2006) has provided a powerful example of the autistic mind in relation to animals, while Tito Mukhopadhyay (2000) focuses on capturing non-verbal and sensory modes of cognition and interaction.

9. Low-functioning autism provides an example of the challenges posed by severe mental-health conditions to the disability-rights movement, as discussed by feminist philosopher Eva Feder Kittay (2001). Such conditions are designated by Kittay as 'liberalism's limit case' (2001:

559); the disability-rights movement relies on the model of feminist- and gay-rights activism and invokes a concept of political participation based on having a voice. The lower-functioning autist, however, relies on advocacy, and so 'falls outside the conventional understandings of the relationship between equals within liberalism' (2001: 562).

10. The development of autistic communities is a recent phenomenon, emerging as the first generation of children to be diagnosed in large numbers with the disorder are reaching adulthood, and significantly aided by online interaction and communication platforms.

11. It is worth registering at the outset of this discussion that empathy comprises a contested and unstable term within phenomenology itself, and that my analysis draws on a particular strand of thought running from Husserl through Stein and picked up in contemporary neo-phenomenological philosophy.

12. Carolyn Pedwell rightly picks up on Stein's deployment of the word 'foreign', noting:

> From the perspective of late liberalism and its postcolonial bio-politics, Stein's use of the term 'foreign' is suggestive, connoting both those materials and forces understood to be outside the fleshy boundaries of the individual human body and those (frequently racialised and sexualised) bodies and practices excluded from the 'we' of the nation. (2014: 9)

Here, then, phenomenology is productive of boundaries that mark out the distinction between various categories of self/other.

13. Dan Zahavi and Josef Parnas provide an illustration of a 'radical theory' approach to autism, postulating from Temple Grandin's description of her experience that, in some cases at least, the world is experienced as a difficulty in engaging pre-reflective or implicit modes of social interaction, which can lead in turn to a compensatory reliance on Theory of Mind techniques for understanding others (2003: 67). This is a radically different account from that espoused by the proponents of theory theory.

14. Haddon wrote *The Curious Incident* with an adult audience in mind, but his literary agent thought the novel better suited to the children's market. Sent out simultaneously to children's publisher David Fickling and adult publisher Jonathan Cape, the manuscript was accepted by both and the publishers decided to produce and market a dual edition (Falconer 2008: 96).

15. Such a reading was encouraged by the quotation from Ian McEwan on the front cover of *The Curious Incident*: 'Mark Haddon's portrayal of an emotionally dissociated mind is a superb achievement. He is a wise and bleakly funny writer with rare gifts of empathy' (Haddon 2003: front cover).

16. Murray specifies further that

> it is the figure of the boy who, more than any other, speaks to us in the present about what autism might be . . . In fictional narratives that depict autism, boys predominate; their autism, their masculinity, and their youth combine to form the contemporary autistic character. (2008: 140)

    This is particularly striking given that the most celebrated autism autobiographies are by adult women, including Temple Grandin and Dawn Prince. In the British context, Murray has also indicated that the association of autism with the child was reinforced in the early 2000s by media attention to health concerns about an alleged link between the Measles, Mumps and Rubella (MMR) vaccination and autism.

17. Zunshine bases her work closely on Simon Baron-Cohen's account of Theory of Mind; see, for example, Zunshine 2006: 4–9.

18. *The Curious Incident* effectively excludes autistic people from reading fiction. For a similar argument, see Zunshine: 'Fiction presents a challenge to people with autism because in many ways it calls for the same kind of mind-reading as is necessary in regular human communication – that is, the inference of the mental state from the behaviour' (2003: 273). The case is notably made by reading both autism and fiction through the lens of Theory of Mind.

19. For a reading of *The Curious Incident* from a narrative-medicine perspective, see Wooden (2011).

20. It is notable that Resene's more favourable reading of autism in Siobhan Dowd's *The London Eye Mystery* (2007) shifts focus from the narrator's cognitive processes of detection to the material evidence of the clues; in so doing, narrative agency is given to the detective-narrator who has the same information as the reader throughout the novel (Resene 2016: 88–94).

21. See Falconer's (2008) reading of *The Curious Incident* for an analysis of Haddon's effective use of the child's viewpoint to reinforce the notion of seeing anew. Although this interpretation may seem to return to the 'contemporary sentimental', Falconer persuasively contends that Haddon's self-conscious use of the device would resist such a positioning.

22. For a discussion of how British novelists Pat Barker and James Kelman have pushed the representation of the post-Thatcher breakdown of working-class community, both formally and in terms of political critique, see Head 2002: 68–9.

23. I will return to this question of the inherent conservatism of the syndrome- or neuro-novel in my discussion of Ian McEwan's *Saturday* in Chapter 3 of this volume.

24. Haddon's representation of Christopher's mother has been discussed in the context of early research on autism, most notably that of Austrian-born child psychologist Bruno Bettelheim (1903–90), which influentially located its cause in the infant's early relationship with the mother. Literary critic Sheryl Stevenson thus observes: 'Haddon's realistic portrait may sound the death knell of the refrigerator mother, even if this cultural archetype is one of those phantasms that Woolf observes are "far harder to kill . . . than a reality"' (2008: 197).

25. Rose's account of the 'politics of life itself' also offers a more positive reading of the biopolitical than this chapter has provided, and one that is suggestive in the context of autism. For Rose, the identification with biologically defined forms of identity holds the dangers of reductionism and the rejection of more social modes of explanation, but it equally provides access to an influential discourse of human-rights and identity politics that offers new opportunities for claiming value and recognition. In this light, the syndrome novel might be positioned not as depoliticising, but rather as engaging in a new mode of identity politics.

Chapter 2

Empathy and Ethics

Introduction

In the previous chapter, I focused on the recent surge of scientific interest in empathy emerging out of the related areas of autism research and cognitive neuroscience. Giving rise to widespread popular interest in, and awareness of, the relation between empathy and mind, scientific research has particularly emphasised the Theory of Mind model of empathy and, through mirror-neuron research, lower-level simulation theory. This chapter turns to a second key impetus behind the current cultural preoccupation with empathy, namely the rapid growth of interest in human-rights discourses in the early years of the twenty-first century. Gaining momentum after the terrorist attacks of 11 September 2001, human-rights scholarship has sought to trace and analyse changing understandings and practices of war, imprisonment and torture, drawing on conceptual approaches developed over the previous decade in trauma studies, postcolonial studies, feminist studies, and Holocaust and genocide studies.[1] In contrast to the scientific work on empathy, human rights approaches have highlighted the higher-level simulation, or perspective-taking, model of empathy. This focus accords with the investment of human-rights scholarship in the capacity of the novel to stimulate the process of stepping imaginatively into another person's shoes, and this mode of engagement is, in turn, seen to underpin the very possibility of a democratic, humanitarian society. The first section of this chapter will review key claims made by human-rights academics and activists for the empathy-building qualities of fiction, focusing in particular on historian Lynn Hunt and philosopher Martha Nussbaum. I will then move on to the critical response to such claims that have arisen from feminist affect studies, before closing with a return to Stein's other-directed model of empathy, which I position as a promising framework for the ethically grounded work of a human-rights scholarship and politics.

The second section of this chapter provides a feminist underpinning for an other-directed approach to empathy by looking at the responses of two women writers to the rhetoric of humanitarian aid campaigns. Sara Ahmed opens *The Cultural Politics of Emotion* (2004) with a close and attentive reading of a Christian Aid charity letter on landmines. Although Ahmed does not explicitly reference Virginia Woolf, her analysis inescapably brings to mind the famous passage from *Three Guineas* (1977), in which Woolf addresses her response to receiving anti-Fascist campaign photographs relating to the Spanish Civil War; a genealogy of feminist thought is thus implicitly claimed or established. Both writers probe and unsettle the complex intersections between reading, feeling, and altruistic action, calling into question the liberal-humanist attitudes upon which the rhetoric of humanitarian campaigns is founded. This discussion forms the basis for my pairing in the third chapter section of two further feminist writers, who cast a critical gaze on the notion of art as an essential good and as productive of justice and humanity: American philosopher Susan Sontag and British novelist Pat Barker. Reading across Sontag's *Regarding the Pain of Others* (2003) and Barker's *Life Class* (2007), I argue that both works emphasise a mode of empathy that distinguishes the empathiser from the object of empathy, and in so doing enables a critical appreciation of the social and political inequalities and hierarchies that structure and underpin the relationship.[2] In looking at another's suffering, my gaze is always already positioned in certain ways; for Sontag and for Barker, a critical mode of empathy would be cognisant of its own implication in structures of power and privilege, as well as of its potential to tip over into more problematic modes of voyeurism and appropriation.

The final section of the chapter continues to hold its gaze on where and when the scene of empathy is situated, and with what effects. Looking specifically at Barker's fictional exploration of what it means to look at, and to represent artistically, the suffering of war, I focus on the significance of the military-medical institution as a setting for the intimate and sustained encounter with another's pain. Whether based in the Belgian front-line hospitals of the First World War, or in the pioneering facial surgery unit of Harold Gillies at Queen Mary's Hospital in Sidcup, Kent, the military-medical institution places particular pressures and demands on the empathetic gaze, which complicates a humanising or transcendent vision of art.[3] What is left in its place is more modest, and more compromised, in its achievements; it is an artistic practice that emerges not from fellow feeling, but from its recognition and recording of a pain that it does not, and indeed cannot, claim to know as its own. In witnessing the effects of war, Barker suggests, art and empathy are not irrelevant, but the insights that they offer are, necessarily, both limited and contingent.

Together, the first two chapters of this monograph identify key factors that can help us to understand why empathy has come to matter so much in and for the medical humanities, indicating the broader cultural and intellectual trajectories that have influenced the field. In turning to contemporary cognitive psychology and neuroscience, as well as to current human-rights scholarship, I suggest that the medical humanities should not be considered in isolation, and that its positioning and understanding of empathy speaks to broader claims made about empathy from across the sciences and the arts and humanities. This chapter also initiates the project of politicising empathy, a line of thought that will extend across the remainder of the chapters in this volume. Expanding on Stein's description of empathy's capacity to open up to us different perspectives on the world, I consider the question of *positionality* in the intersubjective relation: what difference does it make to our understanding of the empathetic encounter if we ask where and when it takes place, as well as between whom? What questions of power and privilege are thereby introduced into the frame? In turning to the military-medical institution as a key site for the empathetic encounter in Barker's fiction, I further indicate that these difficult and troubling questions of influence, if not potential violence, in the empathetic relation are perceived by Barker to be institutional and systemic, rather than individual, in nature.[4] Moving between individual stories of pain and suffering and institutional responses to them, Barker brings into view the gendered and classed underpinnings of healthcare systems. More than this, she reflects on art's implication in – if not complicity with – institutional structures, as well as attending to the troubled, and troubling, relation between violence, aesthetics and beauty, in the artistic representation of pain.[5]

Cultivating empathy

The twenty-first century has seen a significant surge of interest in the relation between literature and human rights, with the genre of the novel accorded particular status and attention. Lynn Hunt's *Inventing Human Rights* (2007) posits a cause-and-effect relation between human rights and literature, making the case that modern human rights could only be formulated at the historical moment of the French and American Revolutions because of the empathetic responses produced in and through the novel form: '[n]ew kinds of reading . . . created new experiences (empathy), which in turn made possible new social and political concepts (human rights)' (2007: 33). Hunt argues that the brief flourishing of the epistolary novel between the 1760s and the 1780s coincided precisely with the birth of human rights, and fostered in readers a capacity to empathise with others across traditional social and economic boundaries.[6] It was, Hunt avers, only when middle-class readers experienced identification with ordinary characters, and learned to think of them as like themselves in some fundamental fashion, that human rights could take on true density and meaning.

Hunt makes a specific historical argument for yoking together the novel and human rights; in doing so, she makes two particular claims about empathy, which resonate across scholarship on fiction as productive of empathy. First, Hunt believes that empathy can be trained and cultivated: 'empathy [was a] skill that could be learned' (2007: 29). Here, then, we are returned to the have/have not model of empathy, according to which eighteenth-century readers increase their stock of empathy, which can, in turn, be invested in the collective human-rights project. Second, empathy is understood on the model of perspective taking; it is based in the endeavour of feeling oneself imaginatively into the inner lives of fictional characters. In Chapter 1, I argued that a hazard of this mode of empathy is that – whether it entails imagining oneself as the other in a given situation, or extrapolating out from how one would oneself respond to a particular set of circumstances – it tends to refer back to the self rather than being truly other-directed. It should come as no surprise, then, to find that Hunt's primary focus is on the benefits *to the reader* of engaging with fiction, in its stimulation of new forms of imaginative engagement with others that enable participation in humanitarian discourse. The other predominantly figures as the beneficiary of human-rights initiatives; her own perspective – not least, her feelings on being designated as the object of empathetic feeling or humanitarian action – remains opaque and underexplored.

For Martha Nussbaum, too, literature helps to train or cultivate the imagination in ways that will help to sustain a more compassionate society. In *Not For Profit* (2010), she addresses the erosion in education programmes of arts and humanities curricula, both in America and beyond, in favour of factual knowledge and logic alone.

Driven by the agenda of a global capitalist system, which accords value to training that can underpin a competitive market economy, such a logic fails to take into account those skills that are crucial for the health of a democracy: namely, the ability to think critically; the capacity to think beyond the local, and to approach problems as a global citizen; and the ability to imagine empathetically the predicament of another person (2010: 7).[7] Again, empathy equates to perspective taking: 'the ability to think about what it might be like to be in the shoes of a person different from oneself, to be an intelligent reader of that person's story, and to understand the emotions and wishes and desires that someone so placed might have' (2010: 95).[8] In distinction from Hunt, however, Nussbaum does not regard novel reading *per se* to be an inherent good. Neither empathy nor reading is, for Nussbaum, moral in and of itself, although it can lead to moral action. Rather, for empathy to be productive of democratic values, reading must be directed towards those works of fiction that cultivate sympathy towards others who are at a distance. Nussbaum is thus interested not only in positioning the novel as the foundation of a democratic education, but also in selecting a canon of fiction that is appropriate to the task. In *Cultivating Humanity* (1997), she prescribes a list of recommended reading that is strongly oriented towards the realist and the canonical, and that includes Henry James, George Eliot and Charles Dickens. Nussbaum also articulates her belief that empathy is inculcated through reading in early childhood (1997: 90). In promoting the liberal-humanist education, Nussbaum thus places her faith, as Suzanne Keen has aptly noted, in 'the right kind of novel reading' (2007: xviii).

In harnessing fiction to the human-rights agenda, Hunt and Nussbaum articulate a vision that seems eminently laudable, and that is seductive in a climate of austerity in which literature is required to define and to defend its social use and value. We might, though, productively ask a number of questions. Are the liberal-humanist values that are extolled here as self-evident as they are claimed to be? How can we know what the affective responses of eighteenth-century readers actually were to the novels that they read? And, as Helen Small has astutely enquired: What are the potential implications of positioning global capitalism as the enemy of democracy, rather than alternative political systems or ideologies (2013: 127)? Of particular interest for this volume is the relation between reading, empathy and altruistic action.[9] Keen has placed particular pressure on this aspect of claims for empathy's social value, pointing to a scarcity of tangible evidence that readerly empathy translates into greater altruism in everyday behaviour. While not contesting that empathy forms a significant aspect of the reader's engagement with fiction, Keen nevertheless resists its co-option into civic goals and agendas. Her objection is based partly on the distinction between identifying with fictional characters and feeling for real others in the world: 'I wonder whether the expenditure of shared feeling on fictional characters might not waste what little attention we have for others on non-existent entities, or at best reveal that addicted readers are endowed with empathetic dispositions' (2007: xxv).[10] Further, she opposes the predictability that approaches such as Hunt's or Nussbaum's would impute to the affective responses of readers, identifying the novel's effects as being more 'unruly', less uniform and homogenous, than they take into account (2007: 68). More than this, Keen points in contemporary fiction to the author's *purposeful* invocation or withholding of empathy, her deliberate exploration of its ambiguous effects. For Keen, then, a crucial aspect of empathy that is overlooked in narrative empathy approaches is 'that novelists actively participate in the debate about the uses and perils of empathy' (2007: xxiv). Drawing on Keen's attention to the *strategic* uses of empathy in contemporary fiction, this chapter will examine Barker's authorial practice of entering into dialogue with prominent cultural critics and thinkers to debate empathy's somewhat dubious merits.

Particularly strong objections to the notion of readerly empathy have arisen from feminist affect theory. Here, the driving force behind the argument is that empathy is an expression of existing political structures; fellow feeling, in other words, can mask, conceal and even enact problematic dynamics and histories of power, influence and appropriation. In analysing empathy, we should therefore remain attentive to the ways in which it maps on to and potentially reinforces hierarchies of privilege that are already in place. Lauren Berlant has emerged as an especially trenchant critic of what she terms the social emotions, which encompass empathy and its cognate terms: sympathy, compassion and pity. Of particular concern to Berlant is the dramatic intensity that is inevitably attached to the transformative moment of compassionate recognition. While this emotional experience, and the feeling of solidarity that it enables, is necessary for political and humanitarian movements to thrive, there is also a danger that the feeling becomes an end in and of itself, rather than mobilising or leading to action. In its theatricality, compassion can obscure a lack of material or political change, providing 'a means for making minor structural adjustments seem like major events' (2011: 182).

For Berlant, compassion is also inherently bound up with privilege: the sufferer is by definition somewhere else, not where we are, and the compassionate subject has a resource that can alleviate their suffering. At the heart of the compassionate relation is the question of how to respond *appropriately* to the observed distress of the other. Berlant believes that fiction does train us in exercising compassion, but for her this is in a more troubling and complicitous mode than by cultivating a more capacious emotional engagement with others. Rather, fiction instructs us in 'not caring', in not recognising the claim on us to act on another's behalf:

> Repeatedly, we witness someone's desire not to connect, sympathize, or recognize an obligation to the sufferer; to refuse engagement with the scene or to minimize its effects; to misread it conveniently; to snuff or drown it out with pedantically shaped phrases or carefully designed apartheids; not to rescue or help; to go on blithely without conscience; to feel bad for the sufferers, but only so that they will go away quickly. (2004b: 9)

We might be tempted here to return to Nussbaum's stipulation that we engage in the right *kind* of reading, but Berlant effectively blocks this route by placing George Eliot – who occupies a central place in Nussbaum's canon – at the heart of her analysis.[11] It is not, then, that Berlant is simply reading the wrong novels. Rather, for Berlant, fiction instructs us in the exercise of compassion by showing us how to moderate feeling with judgement and objectivity; in a global economy of suffering, we learn how to balance the claims of the other against alternative demands upon us, and even refuse them altogether.

A key literary text for thinking through the intersections between narrative, empathy and political action is Harriet Beecher Stowe's *Uncle Tom's Cabin, or Life Among the Lowly* (1852); the novel stands, as literary critic Kathleen Woodward has remarked, as 'the ur-text of the liberal narrative of compassion' (2004: 62). Widely credited with a decisive role in the abolition of slavery, the novel's eliciting of the reader's empathetic identification with the suffering character (mediated through, and instructed by, the medium of another character) is seen to inspire conversion to the abolitionist cause. Witnessing individual pain inaugurates feeling, which leads in turn to an understanding of the causes of suffering, and then to action against injustice. In 'Poor Eliza' (1998), Berlant advanced a powerful critique of liberal-humanist approaches to *Uncle Tom's Cabin*. Reading the novel as sentimental literature, she identified in the genre an ideology of 'true feeling' that 'cannot admit the non-universality of pain'. Identification with the suffering character does not enlarge the range of feeling, but rather offers the illusion that, through feeling, it is possible to transcend structural problems, such as racism and sexism. By witnessing, consuming and identifying with pain, the reader experiences an affective self-transformation that can replace or distract from the requirement for suffering to be 'soothed politically'. This renders empathy a private and 'passive' mode of engagement that weakens the imperative for public political action (1998: 641).

Berlant's analysis cautions against the false consolation of a feeling that mistakes itself for more significant social change, and reminds us that, all too often, empathetic identification elides both distance and difference. Further, she reminds us of the inherent privilege of the reader as compassionate subject, and of the complicity of the novel in structural inequalities. However, her analysis downplays Jacobs's own awareness of the hazards of compassion as an anti-slavery tool. In her reading of *Uncle Tom's Cabin*, Elizabeth Spelman (1997) has paid careful attention to Jacobs's insertion of outrage, instead of tears, as the appropriate response to suffering. Jacobs, in other words, actively and strategically reworks the tropes of the sentimental, to emphasise the importance of judging, and acting against, the institution of slavery. In this sense, Jacobs is already cognisant of, and narratively pre-empting, the short-circuiting of empathy in individual feeling, for which Berlant holds the novel to account.

Berlant closes 'Poor Eliza' by positing a genre of 'postsentimental' fiction, which withholds empathy and so refuses to give its characters or its readers 'too-quick gratification over the none-too-brief knowledge of pain' (1998: 665). Toni Morrison's *Beloved* (1987) is seen to be exemplary of this genre, not least in its evoking and reworking of key scenes and elements from *Uncle Tom's Cabin*.[12] Berlant's reading captures *Beloved*'s powerful disruption and complication of empathy; at its centre is Sethe, who has brutally murdered her baby daughter, and we watch as the other characters circle around what she has done, seeing if they can come to their own terms with her action and all of the suffering and humiliation that lies behind it. Jurecic rightly indicates, however, that Morrison is as interested in empathy's 'possibility and necessity' as in its limits. She accordingly resists Berlant's categorisation of *Beloved* in the distinct genre of the postsentimental, arguing rather that the novel is 'part of a continuing cultural conversation about empathy' (2011: 18). Jurecic's reading of *Beloved* gestures towards the importance of engaging with fiction *on its own terms.* Complicated and contradictory, fiction opens up to view the inner life of another without claiming understanding, and it also unfolds in and across time, requiring of us that we take our time, rather than coming to any quick or easy judgement:

> Morrison does not allow us to feel that we know Sethe. But her reimagining of Margaret Garner's story is itself an empathic act, and the fiction she creates invites readers to experience the interplay of connection, distance, and difference, knowing that their understanding will always be incomplete and imperfect . . . This [is an] exercise of empathy [that is] thoughtful, reflective, slow, and aware of distance and constraints. (2011: 19)

Here, then, the novel offers a sustained, extended and other-directed mode of attention; an emotional, intellectual and aesthetic form of engagement that dwells in uncertainty, and that contemplates the difficulties of knowing and responding to others. This is an approach that is more modest in its claims than Nussbaum or Hunt, or – looking back to Chapter 1 – than Zunshine, because it does not insist that reading can demonstrably change either thoughts or behaviour.

In concluding her essay, Jurecic positions Morrison's *Beloved* as a counterexample to those approaches to narrative empathy that insist on its social utility, arguing as follows:

> the lived complexity of empathy cannot be reduced to an outcome to be assessed, a feeling to be argued out of, or a neurological response . . . [E]mpathy is instead an inexhaustible subject for the practices of contemplation, exploration, and creation. Literature matters . . . not because it changes our brains, hearts, souls, or political convictions, but because the practice of reading literature slows thought down. (2011: 24)

My reading of *Life Class* later in this chapter will argue that, for Barker too, empathy is about taking one's time, exemplified in the slow and concentrated attention to another that is enacted in the artistic practices of life drawing and of portraiture, and that is taught in the life-drawing class.[13] Returning to Nussbaum, then, it is not that reading offers a quick-fix solution to waning democratic values; rather, we might – with Jurecic – productively ask whether our institutions are willing to make time for the thoughtful, creative, complex and often time-consuming practices that are embedded in work across the arts and humanities (2011: 24).

In closing this section, I return briefly to phenomenologist Edith Stein, whose work on empathy I introduced in Chapter 1. I have established that Stein's account of empathy is other-directed, and therefore already oriented towards an ethical approach. I have also outlined that Stein's model of empathy is multi-level; the mode according to which it operates will, to a large extent, be responsive to context and circumstance. Stein distinguishes between three distinct phases of empathy, while also noting that people do not always go through all of the stages. She thus elaborates a model that passes successively through: '(1) the emergence of the experience, (2) the fulfilling explication, and (3) the comprehensive objectification of the explained experience' (1989: 10). In the first phase, which corresponds most closely to perception, I see you in distress and encounter you initially as an object whom I observe. The second stage corresponds most closely to Lipps's understanding and is more closely allied to experience, as I orientate myself towards you and feel myself seized by something of your emotion; for Stein, however, this feeling is non-primordial and can only be defined as empathy if the subject of the experience remains the other person.[14] Stein does acknowledge that our intuition of the other's feelings in the second stage of empathy will be influenced by such experiential factors as '[a]ge, sex, occupation, station, nationality, [and] generation'. When confronted by another person, she explains, '[h]ow much of his experiential structure I can bring to my fulfilling intuition depends on my own structure' (1989: 115). Such differences as class, gender and nationality do not, however, mean that we cannot empathise with those who are unlike us; rather, empathy is precisely what allow us to overcome these limitations, not by giving us access to or understanding of the other's experience, but by showing us that their perspective on the world is different from our own.

The other's distinct perspective is registered at the third stage of empathy, which is described by Stein as one of 'objectification' (1989: 10). After I have encountered the other's experience, I return to myself and the experience enters my consciousness as an object (Stein makes the correspondence with perception once again). This stage is important for Stein, not only because it locates empathy as a cognitive process, but also because it integrates into our consciousness world-views that are different from our own, and so can change or re-orient us. Again, because there remains a clear distinction between self and other, I am not necessarily making the other's view my own, but placing it alongside mine and thereby registering that the same world can be differently viewed. Given that the empathetic process is context-dependent, I would be most likely to enter into the third stage of empathy in those situations when the other is not like me; when my experiential structure does not readily map on to that of the person whose distress I observe, so that I cannot intuitively account for their emotion. Stein's multi-phased model of empathy runs deliberately counter to explanatory models based on the spontaneity of emotional response; there is, in Stein, a narrative element to empathy, such that the process unfolds in and across time. Particularly when the other is more distant from us, empathy for Stein, too, becomes a matter of taking time, of slowing down to engage contemplatively with the world from a different vantage point, and potentially to be transformed in the process.

This section has introduced a liberal-humanist version of empathy that has been dominant in literature and human-rights scholarship, and that can readily be mapped on to the conceptual approach of narrative medicine, outlined in the Introduction: it shares narrative medicine's belief that fiction can train the reader to be empathetic, and it is primarily interested in the benefits accrued to the reader of an enhanced capacity for perspective taking and compassion. The criticisms levelled at the liberal-humanist approach also pertain to narrative medicine. Emphasis on the empathetic connection, or the moment of compassionate recognition, in the clinical encounter can distract from structural inequalities, which are not limited to the hierarchical relation already in place between clinician and patient, but also encompass considerations of gender, class, sexuality, race and disability. Further, the primacy accorded to empathy in and by narrative medicine can itself be read as an over-investment in the individualised relation between practitioner and patient, which in turn obscures broader structural and institutional perspectives.

This section has also indicated that, in harnessing the novel to the human-rights agenda, critics such as Nussbaum and Hunt are providing influential accounts of how and why reading matters. Their emphasis on the social use and value of fiction, its training in skills of perspective taking that in turn underpin democratic and humanitarian citizenship, resonate in narrative medicine's belief that novel reading equips doctors better to understand the patient perspective, which contributes in turn to a more effective healthcare system. I have indicated that such arguments place considerable pressure both on the novel and on reading. I suggest that an alternative approach to how and why fiction matters can be located in its narrative temporality: the novel requires us to take our time, and to engage in a slow and extended unfolding of the relation with the other. In a healthcare context in which time is, quite literally, of the essence, not only in the pressure on the time that can be accorded to the clinical appointment, but also in the time of waiting – be that for referral or treatment, or in the waiting room itself – that emblematises contemporary healthcare delivery in Britain, the question of empathy and temporality seems to constitute a productive site of engagement for future work in the medical humanities.[15]

Reading humanitarian campaigns

Sara Ahmed opens the first chapter of *The Cultural Politics of Emotion* with a quotation from a Christian Aid charity campaign letter, dated 9 June 2003, on the subject of landmines. Her extended analysis of this letter engages with the question of how humanitarian discourse evokes and circulates the pain of others, positioning it as that which demands a response from an 'us' that is broadly defined as the Western subject. Noting that the word 'landmines' acts in the letter as a means of representing the pain of others, in its ability to evoke in the reader images of devastation to the human body that are familiar from media coverage, Ahmed observes that the landmine is quickly transformed from the sign to 'the "agent" behind the injuries'. The campaign letter thus states: 'Landmines are causing pain and suffering all around the world' (2004: 20). It is not that Ahmed seeks to dispute this claim, and declare it as an untruth; rather, it represents a selective version of the truth that effectively *depoliticises* the pain that is the subject of attention, by obscuring from view the human agency behind the laying of the landmine; an act undertaken with the deliberate intention to inflict harm on another person. In calling attention to the suffering body that has been damaged by the landmine, the letter thus distracts from other bodies; namely, those that perform the labour of laying the weapons. Behind these bodies, in turn, stand complex, entangled and extended political histories of war and conflict.

   If the object of the reader's attention is the landmine victim, the focus of the letter itself is, Ahmed contends, firmly on the feelings of the reader, who is already a supporter of Christian Aid and has made previous donations to the charity. The letter surmises of her affective response to the effect of landmines globally: 'it probably makes you feel angry or saddened' (2004: 20). The other's pain is thus transformed into the reader's emotion, which means that she enters into an affective relationship with the other, experiencing negative feelings that will motivate her to make the other, and herself, feel better through the act of further donation. However, the conversion of the other's pain into the reader's emotion is also an act of appropriation that distracts attention from the suffering body of the other onto how the reader feels in response to the pain that she imagines. Premised on a connection between the other's pain and the reader's sadness, or, more precisely, the conversion of the former into the latter, the letter locates the act of charitable giving in the assumption that the other's pain can be known and understood by the reader, eclipsing the other's difference and distance.

The letter proceeds to relate a number of success stories that have resulted from the money that has already been donated to the cause. Its focus, however, is not primarily on how the donations have ameliorated the pain of others, but rather on how the narratives of recovery will change the reader's feelings from the negative emotions of anger and sadness to a more positive affective state: 'I hope you feel a sense of empowerment' (2004: 20). The removal of the other's pain acts as a narrative vehicle for the reader to feel better about herself. The stories of individual pain also become a means of positioning the reader as part of a community of actors who, together, can effect change; the reader, along with the other donators to the charity who are the recipients of the letter ('your regular support'), is aligned with a globalised network of institutions that co-operate to maximise the impact of the donations in removing landmines and treating those who have been exposed to them ('Christian Aid is working with partners across the globe') (2004: 20). Returning to Berlant, the letter can be read as an exercise in overcoming the short-circuiting of feeling in tears ('sadness'), rather than in the altruistic action of giving. Berlant also acts as a reminder that affective self-transformation can replace broader structural change; does charitable donation, in this case, potentially replace, or substitute for, government or state action on the landmine issue?

For Ahmed, too, empathy depoliticises by individualising the response to landmines, and thereby concealing longer, more complicitous, political and economic relations between giver and recipient:

> The transformation of generosity into a character trait involves fetishism: it forgets . . . prior relations of debt accrued over time. In this case, the West gives to others only insofar as it has forgotten what the West has already taken in its very *capacity* to give in the first place. In the Christian Aid letter, feelings of pain and suffering, which are in part effects of socio-economic relations of violence and poverty, are assumed to be alleviated by the very generosity that is

enabled by such socio-economic relations. So the West takes, then it gives, *and in the moment of giving repeats as well as conceals the taking.* (2004: 22; italics in original)

Stories of pain as they circulate in charitable discourses involve complex relations of power. Empathy can reinforce the very histories of subordination and exploitation that are responsible for the suffering to which it responds. A more ethical sociality of pain would be cognisant of how the empathiser is positioned in relation to the other; her complicity in the historical and political inequalities that have marked, if not caused, the other's suffering. The other is also accorded no agency in the letter; she is fixed in place as the one who has pain, and whose suffering demands the resource that the recipient has at her disposal. A more ethical response would direct attention towards the other as other, so that I would, in the words of Ahmed, 'act about that which I cannot know, rather than act only insofar as I know' (2004: 31).

Ahmed's feminist analysis of the humanitarian campaign letter opens her monograph with more than a nod to Virginia Woolf's famous discussion of her own affective response as the recipient of anti-Fascist campaign propaganda in the Spanish Civil War. Woolf's analysis appears in her polemical essay *Three Guineas*, which takes as its main thesis the argument that war is a man's game. 'Scarcely a human being in the course of history', she declares, 'has fallen to a woman's rifle' (1977: 13). If the killing machine has a gender, and that gender is male, then for Woolf women should turn away from it. Historian Daniel Pick has accordingly noted a strain of essentialism running through *Three Guineas*, observing: 'It is possible to read Woolf, at least at certain points of the essay, as endorsing a stark biological dichotomy between men and women, in their respective relations to war and fascism' (1993: 3). My focus is on Woolf's discussion of what it means to look, in the winter of 1936–7, at photographs of the effects on the civilian population of the fighting in the Spanish Civil War. Addressing an imagined male interlocutor, who also looks at and responds to the photographs of suffering, Woolf questions 'whether when we look at the same photographs we feel the same things' (1977: 20). Her discussion of humanitarian discourse thus adds to Ahmed's not only the effects of visual culture – here, the photographs – on the response to another's pain, but also an interrogation of the 'we' that is the imagined Western subject. At stake for Woolf is whether, in spite of gender differences in the approach to war, men and women are brought together in common condemnation of the kinds of atrocities that the photographs depict.

In responding to the question that she has posed, Woolf initially appears to affirm that men and women are united in a 'we' of solidarity, in opposition to the atrocities of war:

> Those photographs are not an argument; they are simply a crude statement of fact addressed to the eye. But the eye is connected to the brain; the brain with the nervous system. That system sends its messages in a flash through every past memory and present feeling. When we look at these photographs some fusion takes place within us; however different the education, the traditions behind us, our sensations are the same; and they are violent. You, Sir, call them 'horror' and 'disgust'. We also call them horror and disgust. And the same words rise to our lips. War, you say, is an abomination; a barbarity; war must be stopped at whatever cost. And we echo your words. (1977: 21)

For Woolf, the feeling aroused by the photographic images *is* shared by men and women. As indicated by Stein, however, having the same category of emotion as another person does not necessarily mean sharing the same inner experience, especially when that person has a different experiential structure; in Woolf's example, that of gender. Meghan Marie Hammond accordingly notes that Woolf immediately follows her statement of feeling the same things as her interlocutor with 'an elaboration of the differences between them', thereby indicating that 'empathy can do little to close the gap of psychological distance between men and women' (2014: 161). Although Woolf and her interlocutor may look at the same images, and feel the same emotions about them, they nevertheless see them through very different eyes.

In Woolf's imagined scenario, her correspondent has written to her as a means of accessing and addressing a much larger group of women; Woolf is therefore positioned by her interlocutor as representative of a 'we' that is inclusive of all women. Her essay probes not only whether she can imagine a community of 'we' that encompasses men and women, but also whether she feels able to speak for, or on behalf of, a broader female collective. Certainly, when war is the topic, it seems that there is an unbridgeable divide between men and women: no matter how much care she takes to express her viewpoint clearly, 'there would still remain some difficulties so fundamental that it may well prove impossible for you to understand or for us to explain' (1977: 7). Central to these difficulties, for Woolf, is that women do not understand the urge to fight in the first place. How, then, can they find even the most basic common vocabulary to discuss the subject of war with men? More than this, Woolf is at pains to establish that the 'we' on whose behalf she speaks does not represent all women. It is, rather, a category that is carefully and precisely circumscribed by the boundaries of class, education, and economics: she speaks only for the daughters of educated men who have enough to live upon. If Woolf represents a 'we', which affords her the voice of political solidarity, it is therefore a small collective of those women who have rooms of their own; she claims to speak only for those whose views and feelings she feels confident in representing, and in doing so she indicates that, if it is to remain meaningful, the empathetic circle cannot be too wide. For Hammond, there is a political manoeuvre in Woolf's self-positioning that is indissociable from pacifism. Pacifism thus depends on a refusal to invade the other's borders, or to subsume their interior as one's own. Woolf rhetorically and strategically demonstrates that 'there is something distinctly non-pacifist about speaking as one of many . . . To speak as "we" rather than "I" always carries the threat of invasion, annexation, or appropriation' (Hammond 2014: 160). Woolf's carefully circumscribed 'we' thus seeks a form of solidarity that does not tip into the violence of appropriation; in so doing, she inscribes other-directed empathy as both a feminist and a pacifist project, and one that takes on particular urgency and vitality in a Europe poised precariously between two World Wars.

The photographs that formed the basis of Woolf's discussion of affect in *Three Guineas* were of Fascist atrocities and were sent to British supporters by the Republican government. They documented the violence and brutality inflicted against both bodies and homes:

> Here then on the table before us are photographs. The Spanish government sends them with patient pertinacity about twice a week. They are not pleasant photographs to look upon. They are photographs of dead bodies for the most part. This morning's collection contains the photograph of what might be a man's body, or a woman's; it is so mutilated that it might, on the other hand, be the body of a pig. But those certainly are dead children, and that undoubtedly is the section of a house. A bomb has torn open the side; there is still a bird cage hanging in what was presumably the sitting-room, but the rest of the house looks like nothing so much as a bunch of spillikins suspended in mid air. (1977: 20–1)[16]

Although Woolf describes these photographs in evocative terms, she does not reproduce them in the text, leaving it to the imagination of the reader to visualise the scenes described. The photographs of atrocity are thus marked as an absence in *Three Guineas*, images that are not shown and that we cannot see. In their place, visible and on display in the essay, were five published newspaper photographs depicting 'A General', 'Heralds', 'A University Procession', 'A Judge', and 'An Archbishop'.[17] Woolf's contrast between the two sets of photographs puts in play a series of correspondences. For cultural studies scholar, Maggie Humm, they establish a visual pattern in and through which 'women are absent in the present public world', while the masculine, military world 'has created an absent, dead world' (2003: 659). In so doing, the photographs link patriarchy and Fascism, as tyrannical systems that inflict invisible violence on women and children in the domestic sphere. Literary critic Lili Hsieh adds to this that Woolf's presentation of the photographs critiques a broader politics of (in)visibility. Woolf re-circulates already published images celebrating masculine, public achievement, but she also reveals their hidden underside, in the privately circulated photographs of atrocity. Woolf thereby represents the picture of patriarchy as 'double-sided', but she also opens up to question how a politics of affect is produced in and through the circulation and/or suppression of images. Hsieh accordingly argues that '[i]t is as if a third gaze *beyond* the pictures was needed' (2006: 38), one that pays close critical attention to why certain images are so prominent in the media, and what political interests they might potentially serve. What other images are being obscured or hidden by them, and with what effects?

Together, Ahmed and Woolf articulate a feminist response to humanitarian discourse that complicates and critiques a liberal politics of sympathy. Both women ask how imagery of others' pain is mobilised within a broader politics of affect. The question of agency has surfaced as one important concern. In looking at the image of another's pain, who or what is seen to be its cause, and how or by whom can it be ameliorated? Does the viewer represent an agent of change, or is she positioned as complicit in the very structures that have caused the suffering in the first place? A second focus has been that of good and bad feelings. Is humanitarian discourse inherently one in which images of pain evoke negative emotions, which then require or demand action in order to feel better? Might there be value for a feminist politics in dwelling with and in negative emotion? Could holding on to feelings of anger, for example, motivate or energise political change? Third, the section has attended to the language of community, asking who is the 'we' constructed by humanitarian discourse, and what commonalities are thereby assumed. Might the boundaries of the 'we' productively be called into question? How do we balance the politics of solidarity against potential misrepresentation or appropriation? Finally, the section has emphasised the politics of (in)visibility, focusing critical attention not only on the images of suffering that we see, but also on those that are not circulated or reproduced. Judith Butler (2004) has powerfully argued that the difference between visibility and invisibility can mark the distinction between those whose lives matter enough to be publicly mourned, and those who are deemed ungrievable and expendable, and who can therefore be killed with impunity. Central to a feminist politics of affect, then, is the question of how and for whom we care – which suffering bodies become the focus of our attention, and which do not – because our relation to the other is implicated in broader trajectories of violence and exploitation.

Positioning the empathetic gaze

Pat Barker's *Life Class* focuses on the role and purpose of art in response to the suffering of war.[18] The first half of the novel is set before the war and follows a group of young artists – Paul Tarrant, Kit Neville and Elinor Brooke – as they train under Henry Tonks, instructor of life drawing at the Slade School of Art. In the second half of the novel, the students' training is set against the experience of war, and the artists must apply what they have learned to representing their own and others' war experience. Together, the students represent the generation that defined the artistic response to the First World War: Paul Tarrant is loosely based on Paul Nash and Stanley Spencer, Kit Neville on Christopher Nevinson and Mark Gertler, and Elinor Brooke on Dora Carrington and Virginia Woolf. Critic Simon Avery has remarked that *Life Class* represents 'a *Bildingsroman* narrative – or more rightly a *Kunstlerroman* of the kind prevalent in early twentieth-century texts, such as D. H. Lawrence's *Sons and Lovers* (1913) and James Joyce's *Portrait of the Artist as a Young Man* (1916)' (2011: 132). Avery's literary comparisons suggest that the narrative trajectory of the novel is towards a maturity of artistic voice; that the war acts as a crucible in and through which the protagonists can find an authentic mode of aesthetic expression. Certainly, there is something of this in *Life Class*: the pre-war years are repeatedly evoked by its leading characters as a period of immaturity and inexperience that they have now left behind. For Barker, however, the aesthetic response to war is more troubled, and less resolved, than such a reading would imply. As in Haddon, the contemporary novel evokes, but ultimately refuses, the consolation afforded by the coming-of-age narrative; Barker offers in its place what Fiona Tolan has described as an 'image . . . of humanity cast adrift after World War I, unanchored by moral codes or liberal certainties' (2010: 377).

Barker's exploration of what it means to represent war artistically is in dialogue with Susan Sontag's *Regarding the Pain of Others*; *Life Class* is a continuation – and even to some degree a reworking – of her previous novel, *Double Vision* (2004), focused on the ethics of contemporary war photography and in explicit conversation with Sontag's work. Elinor Brooke shares certain features with Virginia Woolf, and particularly with her feminist, anti-war stance of the 1930s. Sontag's response to Woolf emphasises the importance of interrogating the 'we' that is designated as the viewing subject: 'No "we" should be taken for granted when the subject is looking at other people's pain' (2003: 3). The effect of war images is dependent on who is viewing them, and from what vantage point: 'Photographs of an atrocity may give rise to opposing responses. A call for peace. A cry for revenge. Or simply the bemused awareness, continually restocked by photographic information, that terrible things happen' (2003: 11). An unthinking affective alliance with suffering – one that is not cognisant of its own framing and positionality – is for Sontag 'too simple', because it elides relations of power and privilege: 'So far as we feel sympathy, we feel that we are not accomplices to what caused the suffering. Our sympathy proclaims our innocence as well as our impotence' (2003: 91).

Elinor's stance on war echoes Woolf's feminist conviction that it is a man's game; in conversation with Paul she refers to war as 'the great bully' that silences women, even as it uses them as justification (Barker 2007: 245). For her, war does not represent 'a proper subject for art' because it 'has been imposed on us from the outside . . . It's unchosen, it's passive' (2007: 176). Her solution is to turn her back on the conflict as far as her own artistic practice is concerned. To some degree, this position is justified in the novel; it is a response that is, like Woolf's, attuned to Elinor's own position as a woman, and the limitations and restrictions that it imposes. If teaching at the Slade, and under Tonks in particular, emphasised the importance of drawing from direct observation, Elinor's position reflects a recognition that women are denied access to war, making it difficult to know what they *are* to draw in wartime. Challenged by Paul as to whether her rejection of the war would hold up if her brother, Toby, was killed in the fighting, she responds: 'I'd go home. I'd paint what made him, not what destroyed him' (2007: 244). Threatened by the 'single bullying voice' of war, 'shouting all the other voices down', Elinor seeks to preserve an untainted aesthetic; one that is rooted in the landscape around her home and that reflects the only vantage point on the conflict that is actually permitted to her as a woman (2007: 116). Her arguments with Paul refuse the 'we' of a community of war artists that does not take into account women's very different perspective on the conflict. Like Sontag, Barker is interested in a mode of empathy that refuses to take for granted the 'we' of the viewing subject.

Barker is also interested in the ways in which the 'we' of female solidarity is cut across by class and economics. In this sense, she echoes Woolf's precise alignment of herself with women of the same socioeconomic category, so that her views represent a very particular class position; for Barker, however, Woolf's upper-middle-class background imposes restrictions on her radicalism. Elinor's feminist politics accordingly exist in tension with the conservatism of her upbringing, complicating any straightforward validation of her stance. Refusing the limitations of movement imposed upon her as a woman, Elinor passes through Belgium, disguised as a nurse, to spend time with Paul in the 'forbidden zone'. Gazing from the train window across an as yet unspoilt rural landscape, she reflects:

> Rain-drenched fields. She tried to imagine this land churned up by wheels and horses' hooves and marching feet, but she couldn't. And why should I? she thought, hardening again, when this was the reality. Grasses, trees, pools full of reflected sky, somewhere in the distance a curlew calling. This is what will be left when all the armies have fought and bled and marched away. (2007: 167)

Elinor's vision of the scene inclines towards the Romantic sublime, placing its faith in a timeless nature that transcends the contingencies of history.[19] We have seen that a permanent and unchanging landscape is also her defence mechanism against her brother, Toby's, death. In its upholding of an authentic 'reality' that is immune to war and violence, Elinor's viewpoint speaks of her underlying conservatism; Barker holds Elinor's rebellious rejection of the codes and conventions of gender in balance and in tension with her conformity to the orthodoxies of her class, indicating that positionality is both complex and contradictory. Barker's representation of Elinor also gives us a contemporary perspective on Woolf that, without discounting her feminist politics, brings into focus more problematic attitudes arising from her class position.[20]

Paul Tarrant in *Life Class* exemplifies another key figure in Sontag's *Regarding the Pain of Others*: Spanish artist Francisco Goya (1746–1820).[21] For Sontag, Goya's series of etchings, *The Disasters of War* (1810–20), embody an ethical commitment to representing the horrors of war. Sontag is particularly drawn to a quotation from Goya's *Disasters* that also forms the epigraph to *Double Vision*: 'One cannot look at this. I saw it. This is the truth' (Barker 2003: no pagination). Paul's pre-war art, dismissed by Kit Neville as 'anaemic', is based on the same pastoral idyll that Elinor invokes; in Paul's case, however, this is an escape from, rather than an expression of, his class background, as he literally turns his back on the industrial scenes of Middlesbrough's ironworks to focus on the surrounding countryside. Kit scathingly dismisses Paul's expression of a timeless, rural vision that both excludes and denies his own working-class background: 'Oh well, you know, this is the *real* England. *Bollocks*. . . . If this was the real England, what did he think Middlesbrough was? A mirage?' (Barker 2007: 85; italics in original). Tonks reinforces Kit's damning judgement of Paul's pre-war art, noting with characteristic directness that the paintings have no 'feeling' and 'nothing to say' (2007: 29).

Paul's contact with the war is transformative for his aesthetic practice. Based on his nursing experience in Belgium, Paul produces powerful canvases that depict the war-damaged body, and that receive Tonks's rare seal of approval. Although it seems that the journey to artistic maturity has been achieved, Barker is, however, notably more equivocal on the matter. From the opening of *Life Class*, Paul's art is shadowed by the concern that observation might tip over into voyeurism. In the pre-war section of the novel, this theme plays out in Paul's relationship with life-drawing model Teresa; lingering outside her house, Paul reflects uneasily that he is not far removed from Teresa's abusive and predatory ex-husband, Jack. Paul's discomfort extends into the second half of the novel, and is focused on anxiety about what it means to be a war artist; the observation and representation of others' pain seems troublingly close to appropriation and exploitation. Paul speaks to Kit of his 'Faustian pact' (Barker 2007: 240), which represents the uneasy compromise between witnessing the other's suffering, and the artistic achievement and recognition that is to be gained in and through its aesthetic depiction. For Kit, too, the Faustian image speaks of the commercial benefits accrued by the successful war artist, which conflict with and undercut more moral considerations. Barker does not let the more negative connotations of war art negate its role as an ethical act of witness, however; the two aspects co-exist, revealing, in the words of Tolan, that art represents both 'a potential good' and 'a messy and. . . ambiguous pursuit' (2010: 391, 386). In dialogue with Sontag, Barker reminds us just how fine the line can be between compassionate witness and voyeurism, especially when the gaze is focused on another's pain. She also draws to our attention the uncomfortable truth that war art frequently commands high prices in the commercial market, and so represents valuable social, cultural and economic capital.[22]

This section has argued that Barker engages closely with Sontag's emphasis on positionality in relation to representations of pain. As a contemporary novelist, she is particularly interested in thinking through the ways in which the class privileges of the Bloomsbury set place certain restrictions on their political radicalism. Barker is also keen to balance war art's ethical dimension against its more troubling aspects, rejecting any assurance that art is, or can be, an essential good. There is, however, a more positive, or less ambivalent, treatment of art in *Life Class*, if we shift our focus to its temporal aspect. Throughout the novel, Barker is interested in the long, painstaking labour of working up studies for a finished artwork. Emphasis is placed on art, not as an act of spontaneous creation, but rather as a difficult struggle towards expression. Drawing is represented as an extended process of absorption with and in the other; in reworking material, the artist can experiment with a range of viewpoints in relation to the subject, and examine the effects of different modes of framing. In this sense, art provides a vehicle for engagement that facilitates both positionality and objectivity. During Elinor's night crossing on the ferry to Belgium, she is struck by a woman breastfeeding an infant, remarking of the mother's absorption in her child: 'her whole body seemed to be a wax candle feeding the child's flame' (2007: 216). Elinor sets to work to sketch the scene, spending over an hour testing out what it means to look at the female form, and the subject of the maternal relation more specifically, through the eyes of another woman. Finishing only when she has 'exhausted the possibilities' (2007: 164), Elinor's mode of engagement represents a different kind of absorption to the mother's: a form of attention that is attuned to the limits and boundaries between self and other. The artistic act of looking is one that takes its time, and that slowly explores the different possibilities in its subject. In and through this process, Elinor is working out how she, as a woman, is positioned in relation to the mother and her child. The boundaries of the 'we' – the community formed between Elinor and the other woman, between the mother and her child, and between Elinor and the mother–child bond – are again at stake, and art provides a means to explore the complex tension and interplay between proximity, distance and difference.

Empathy and the institution

In *Life Class*, Paul produces powerful images of the war-damaged body that look at that body from the perspective of medical intervention: he bases his canvases on his experience as an ambulance driver in Belgium. He produces his work within an institution that is both medical and military, and this chapter section asks what effect the institution has on the artistic act of looking at, and responding to, the pain of another. My approach to the military hospital is aligned with that of historians such as Joanna Bourke (1996) and Ana Carden-Coyne (2007, 2008), who have positioned these institutions as part of a wider war machine that influenced how the casualties of war experienced treatment within them. In *Life Class* and *Toby's Room*, Barker is interested in how the empathetic relation is bound to, and located within, particular institutional structures and practices, which are themselves already marked by the hierarchies of rank, dis/ability, class and gender. In this sense, Barker's treatment of the military hospital in her later fiction can be read as an extension or continuation of her representation of Craiglockhart Hospital in the *Regeneration Trilogy*.

In *Life Class*, Paul's connection with the military is through his experience as an ambulance driver. Volunteering for this service provided one of the only routes for men not enlisted in the army to gain access to the front early in the war; Paul and Kit both put themselves forward as a means of gaining artistic access to the effects of the fighting. On arrival at the front, both men soon find themselves performing nursing and orderly duties in a highly pressurised environment. Literary critic Santanu Das (2005) has drawn attention to nursing memoirs as overlooked acts of witness to the First World War, and highlights as central to these texts the awareness of others' physical pain through the repeated contact with wounds. A frequent task for nurses in the First World War was the dressing of a gangrenous wound with hydrogen peroxide or carbolic acid, a painful procedure that entailed close bodily contact with the patient and the concomitant risk of infection.[23] As the point of contact with the injured body, the hand acts as a particularly important trope in nurses' memoirs. Das elaborates: 'Hands dress wounds, clean instruments, habitually comfort, may even cause fresh pain, are frequently disgusted, and in rare moments of leisure, the hand writes its varied life' (2005: 26). Barker, too, attends to the 'varied life' of Paul's hands, which are similarly employed. When he dresses infected wounds, he wears protective rubber gloves, and in a letter to Elinor he uses this as an image to represent his state of self-protective numbness: 'most of the time I go around in a kind of dream state. Like being inside a rubber glove that covers all of you, not just your hands' (2007: 147). Paul's protective sheath is breached by the arrival at the hospital of novice Richard Lewis, for whom everything is new, and Paul explains that he too 'starts *seeing* it all again' (2007: 147; italics in original). The resulting emotion finds expression for Paul through painting, and his hand, in its rare and precious moments of leisure, reaches compulsively for the brush.

Literary critic Margaret Higonnet has argued that the question of framing is particularly crucial in nursing memoirs: 'how', she questions, 'is one positioned in relation to war's trauma?' (2002: 94). For Barker, the answer depends on the recognition of the other's alterity or difference. Removing a dressing, Paul involuntarily mimics the patient's response to the pain that he inflicts, as if he too experiences it: 'He clenches his teeth, as if he were in pain.' Here, then, Paul's response seems to collapse the other into the self, appropriating the pain as his own. However, this feeling is blocked even as it is invoked: 'the pain was not his and never could be' (2007: 136). Although Paul feels for those whom he treats, he is cognisant of the incommensurability between their experiences: 'These men suffer so much more than he does, more than he can ever imagine. In the face of their suffering, isn't it self indulgent to think about his own feelings?' (2007: 145). Emotion gives way to a reflective dimension, which acknowledges positionality and recognises that the patient's experience of the war is very different from his own. Returning to the boundaries of the 'we', Paul does not claim to know or to understand – to share a bond of community – with the patients whom he treats, positioning himself differently in relation to the trauma of war.

The most important canvas that Paul produces in Belgium depicts a nurse dressing an infected wound. The nurse represents an impersonal and swaddled figure that seems to have lost connection with the patient's pain:

[The] figure by the bed was by no means a self-portrait. Indeed, it was so wrapped up in rubber and white cloth: apron, mask, gloves – ah yes, the all important gloves – that it had no individual features. Its anonymity, alone, made it appear threatening. No ministering angel, this. A white-swaddled mummy, intent on causing pain. The patient was nothing: merely a blob of tortured nerves. (2007: 203)

Although the description of the painting claims an indifference, or lack of feeling, towards the patient, the rendering of the latter as a 'blob of tortured nerves' is indicative of a dense, textural handling of paint that would draw the viewer's eye, insisting on the patient not as 'nothing' but as a suffering and fleshly materiality. Moreover, even as Paul completes the painting, he succumbs to a fever that results from accidentally cutting through his glove while dressing a badly infected wound.[24] For Paul, at least, it seems that there is a breach in his protective psychic shield, so that he does not experience the numbness depicted in the canvas, but retains something of the emotion of witnessing at close proximity the wounds of war. Swathed and gloved, it appears that Paul's surface is nevertheless still capable of penetration.

Paul's canvas depicts the hazards of a medical practice that becomes too identified with, and absorbed into, the machinery of war. At the hospital where he works, novice Lewis stands at one extreme of a spectrum of affective response. Lewis's hand is repeatedly described as being in direct contact with the patient, and he lacks any capacity for the suspension of feeling. This is particularly true of his relation to the suicidal patient Goujet, who is being nursed back to health after attempting to take his own life, only to be executed by firing squad. Lewis develops an obsession with the patient, sitting for hours by his bedside and 'clasping his wrist' (2007: 158). Lewis is hindered by this excess of feeling from carrying out his nursing duties effectively. At the opposite extreme is Sister Byrd, who is the closest approximation in the novel to Paul's depiction. From her first introduction, she is representative of an emotional detachment that risks losing touch with feeling altogether. Paul notes on his arrival at the hospital the rows of soldiers' feet on the ward, skin thickened by marching: 'yellow, strong, calloused, scarred where blisters have formed and burst repeatedly'. His attention shifts to Sister Byrd, whose surfaces are similarly hardened by war; Paul notes that she is 'tough, tougher even than she looks' (2007: 129). Although this enables her to perform her duties efficiently, Paul worries that there is something 'machine-like' about her (2007: 145). Sister Byrd appears as an increasingly robotic figure, indistinguishable from the military machine that she serves. Although a capacity for objectification is needed in order to get the job done, it seems to become hazardous for Barker when it is placed at the service of a militarised medicine that is over-identified with the industrialised warfare within which it operates. Paul's painting probes the troubling question of his own and his colleagues' relation to the patients in their care; the swathed, masked and gloved bodily surface may be insulated from the other's pain, but it also signals its own complicity with, and absorption into, the wider war machine.

Another portrait forms the central focus of *Toby's Room*: Tonks's pastel study of Kit, after he has been invalided home with severe facial injuries and admitted to Gillies' care. Confronted in the First World War with unprecedented numbers of facial injuries, Gillies pioneered new techniques in reconstructive surgery, first at the Cambridge Military Hospital in Aldershot and subsequently at Queen Mary's Hospital in Sidcup.[25] Tonks was one of a number of artists attached to Gillies' surgical team, who produced surgical drawings and documented the process of recovery. However, his artistic practice notably differed from that of the other artists attached to Gillies, in his insistence on drawing his subjects from life; the other artists worked from photographs of the injured men. Curator Emma Chambers has emphasised that Tonks's portraits occupy an uncertain ground between surgical record and portraiture. Nevertheless, she notes that his artistic practice of drawing from life necessitated 'an interaction between Tonks and the patients, whether at their bedsides or in his office', and that the sustained and concentrated attention of the artist would have had 'similarities to a conventional portrait sitting' (2009: 597). For Chambers, then, the formality of the procedure, and the detachment of the artist's gaze, would have been beneficial for the sitters, for whom the experience of being looked at would often have been intensely painful:

> the artist engages in a process of close looking and non-judgmental attention with the consent of the sitter, and this consensual interaction of looks counteracts the disfigured sitter's usual experience of inappropriate forms of looking, and informs the meaning of the portrait. (2009: 597)

Chambers' description is reassuring in its account of the therapeutic effect of the portrait sitting for the patient; the positive aspect of the process is, however, emphatically dependent upon the patient's consent ('with the consent of the sitter', 'consensual').

In *Toby's Room*, Tonks's work is initially viewed through Elinor's eyes as she shadows him on the ward. She closely echoes Chambers' account of Tonks's working practice, emphasising his personal connection with the patients, and she observes that the patients view him as a 'trusted' and 'fatherly' presence. In contrast, Elinor perceives her own presence on the ward to be 'dangerous' to the injured men, posing a sexual threat to them (2012: 166).[26] Barker is thus attentive to the ways in which gender dynamics inform and shape the relationship between artist and sitter, tipping Elinor's act of looking towards the voyeuristic gaze. More than this, however, Barker also imagines Tonks's working practice from the patient's perspective, through the eyes of Kit, and his account refuses the consolations offered by Chambers' description because the sittings are decidedly not 'consensual'. Indeed, Kit's first 'sitting' takes place on the ward when he is in a barely conscious post-operative haze, and so can hardly be said to have taken place with his informed consent.

Kit's second sitting takes place in Tonks's office and the emphasis is, from the outset, on the *dis*comfort of the experience. Neville feels 'cruelly exposed' to Tonks's 'pitiless stare', which is described as a 'continual needle prick' (2012: 195, 198). The benevolent paternalism that Elinor identified in Tonks on the ward shades into a more authoritarian character. Tonks famously displayed his portraits of Gillies' patients on the wall of his office at the hospital, and they proved a popular attraction for visitors; encountering the wall of portraits, Kit's primary concern is with who sees them. Tonks reveals that the sitters are not shown their own portraits, although he offers to make an exception for Kit on the grounds that he is an artist. Kit refuses Tonks's offer, but the exchange takes us back to the question of how images of pain circulate, and who has (or is denied) access to them.[27] Tonks's authority is further underlined when Kit asks whether he can refuse the sitting. Tonks's response brings into focus the military and institutional context of their encounter, and is a far cry from Chambers' reassuring description of mutual consent: 'You're in the army. Mr Neville. What do you think?' (2012: 195). Although Tonks has not enlisted, Kit as a patient is bound by military as well as medical orders to submit not only to Tonks's pastels but also to (Major) Gillies' surgical knife. For Barker, then, emphasis is placed on a military-medical institution that denies Kit any agency or control.

Barker's 'Author's Note' to *Toby's Room* describes Chambers' account of Tonks's pastels as 'a thought-provoking examination of the aesthetic and ethical questions raised by the portraits' (2012:

265); as with Sontag in *Life Class*, Barker consciously enters into dialogue with a prominent critical thinker, so that her novel is itself an act of reframing an existing debate on empathy. Barker's strategic intervention introduces into the frame the structures and dynamics of institutional authority, emphasising that they cannot be dissociated from the empathetic relation. The emphasis of mainstream medical humanities on the individual protagonists within the scene of medical treatment has often diverted attention away from its institutional setting. In Barker, the scene announces its historical and institutional setting; she thereby rejects the presumed homogeneity of a mainstream 'medicine' and probes the specific pressures in and on a medical system that is struggling to respond to the demands placed upon it in the early years of the First World War. Barker's fiction examines the complex tensions between opposition and implication that mark the relation between the institution and those who operate within it; in this space of entanglement, she opens up the dense, knotted and ambiguous relationship between the medical, the gaze, the body, affect and power. In its shifting of viewpoint between Paul, Elinor and Kit, Barker also emphasises that the clinical scene looks very different according to the vantage point one occupies, and how that is inflected by gendered, classed and sexed hierarchies. Finally, Barker also asks how art is positioned in relation to the medical scene. Angela Woods and I have recently argued that in the mainstream medical humanities, art acts as a kind of third party to the scene: art is looking at medicine looking at the patient (Whitehead and Woods 2016: 2). While this aesthetic could be seen to describe Paul's canvas, albeit complicated by the implication of the artist's gaze within the scene that it observes, Barker's dialogue with Chambers effectively reframes Tonks's artistic gaze so that it does not stand simply as a humanist act of compassionate witness, nor as a look that stands outside Gillies' surgical practices. Rather, Barker emphasises art's implication in, and complicity with, the authority, the anonymity, and the indifference of its institutional framework.

Conclusion

This chapter has argued that the construction of empathy in the mainstream medical humanities has close affinities with the ideas emerging out of human-rights scholarship, both in its understanding of empathy as a mode of perspective taking and in its belief in the social value and utility of reading fiction. I have engaged critically with these liberal-humanist approaches, arguing for an account of empathy that is both other-directed in its orientation and cognisant of its own implication in structures and hierarchies of power and privilege. I have also called for an approach to literature, and to art more broadly, that does not pressure it into fulfilling civic and social agendas, but that attends instead to its own distinctive qualities and attributes. I have pointed particularly to the novel's capacity to foster a slow and exploratory unfolding of the relation to the other that does not claim knowledge or understanding, but rather that dwells in ambiguity, difficulty and uncertainty. The chapter has brought into dialogue a range of cultural texts that, in different ways and from a variety of perspectives, respond to the political aftermath of 11 September 2001. In so doing, they are concerned with how, confronted by a negative identity politics, we might work towards an ethical position from which to engage productively with the urgent political question of engaging with and across difference. Woolf surfaces as an intellectual touchstone in many of these texts. She acts as an important interlocutor for thinking through not only the response to images of pain, but also how these images circulate and become visible to us in the first place. I position Barker as deeply engaged in and with this ongoing cultural conversation about empathy; her fiction intervenes strategically into these debates, explicitly responding to key critical voices and reflecting on the complex, troubled, and yet necessary, relation between art, war, violence and ethics. There are no answers, and few consolations, in Barker's work. Rather, she challenges us, like her protagonists, to think, act and respond to the crises of our times without falling back on the reassuring platitudes of humanist rhetoric, but engaging instead with a more entangled, messy and contingent politics and ethics.

Notes

1. For more on the emergence and development of human-rights scholarship as an interdisciplinary field, see Elizabeth Swanson Goldberg and Alexandra Schultheis Moore (2012). This chapter focuses on Susan Sontag (2003), but other key works include Judith Butler (2004), Darius Rejali (2007), Kay Schaffer and Sidonie Smith (2004), and Joseph R. Slaughter (2007). More recently, human-rights scholarship has focused attention on the urgent political questions of migration and displacement, to which the question of empathy is also central.

2. The works by Sontag and Barker are themselves important contributions to the cultural debates on war, ethics and representation that followed the attacks of 11 September 2001. Barker's *Double Vision* (2004), focusing on the experiences of war photographer Ben Frobisher in Afghanistan and loosely based on the experiences of Don McCullin, initiated her dialogue with Sontag's *Regarding the Pain of Others*, which continues to resonate throughout *Life Class* and *Toby's Room*.

3. Barker's exploration of the military hospital as setting has its roots in her celebrated representation of Craiglockhart Military Hospital in the *Regeneration Trilogy* (1996). There, too, the military hospital influenced the relation of W. H. R. Rivers to the soldiers in his care, as well as acting as the setting for artistic production in the work of war poets Wilfred Owen and Siegfried Sassoon.

4. For an insightful discussion of how contemporary fiction has responded to and critiqued the care institution in the context of the so-called 'Alzheimer's epidemic', see Lucy Burke (2016).

5. For an extended discussion of art, violence and beauty in Pat Barker's *Toby's Room* (2012) and Louisa Young's *My Dear, I Wanted to Tell You* (2011), see Anne Whitehead (2015).

6. Hunt privileges the genre of the epistolary novel because its lack of a single authorial point of view, and highlighting of characters' perspectives as expressed in their letters, produces 'a heightened sense of identification, as if the character were real, not fictional' (2007: 42).

7. In the context of critical thinking, Nussbaum gives particular weight to Socratic argument, arguing that, like the novel, it requires 'the ability to understand other positions from within' (2010: 72).

8. As Nussbaum indicates, her linking of empathy, reading, education and respect for difference chimes closely with the beliefs of American President Barack Obama (Nussbaum 2010: 136). His 2007 speech on empathy and literacy argued that the largest social deficit in America was an 'empathy deficit' and prescribed reading as the solution: 'it's books more than anything else that are going to give our young people the ability to see other people. And that then gives them the capacity to act responsibly with respect to other people' (Obama 2007).

9. Claims for narrative empathy leading to pro-social action rely heavily on the empathy–altruism hypothesis, formulated in the early 1980s by C. Daniel Batson and influential across a range of academic disciplines. According to the hypothesis, we act for the good of others not (only) when the perceived benefits of doing so outweigh the cost, but (also) when we are motivated by empathy to do so (see Batson 1991, 1998). Batson's theories have not been uncontroversial. Keen notes that in applying them to narrative empathy, an additional step is taken in 'substituting experiences of narrative empathy for shared feelings with real others' (2007: vii). For the most recent critique of empathy as the basis for well-informed social action and decision making, see Bloom (2017).

10. While agreeing with Keen's distinction between feeling for fictional characters and sympathy for real others, I find the language of expenditure and waste somewhat uneasy in this context, with its implication that we have a certain allocation of empathy that we would be advised to invest wisely and well.

11. See Neil Hertz (2004) and Carolyn Williams (2004) for readings of Eliot that Berlant includes in her edited volume on compassion, and that run counter to Nussbaum's liberalism.

12. In particular, Berlant reads Sethe's flight from slavery across the Ohio river as a reworking of 'poor Eliza's' journey across the same river, while carrying her son. Morrison's emphasis is on Sethe's inability to escape, and for Berlant her embodied knowledge of slavery resists being passed on through empathy and identification.

13. The figure of Henry Tonks dominates the life-class studio in the novel, and he was renowned for both his portraiture and his life-drawing skills. I will return to the question of empathy and time in my reading of Aminatta Forna's *The Memory of Love* in Chapter 4.

14. Rudolf Makkreel (1996) has helpfully returned to the German etymology of empathy to explain that, for Stein, *Einfühlung* should not be confused with *Einsfühlung*: *Ein* in *Einfühlung* means 'into' not 'one', and thus empathy is a process of 'feeling into' not 'feeling one with'.

15. For a thoughtful discussion of waiting in the context of British healthcare, that addresses its ambivalent relation to the question of care, see Sophie Day (2016).

16. For a discussion of this quotation in relation to beauty and aesthetics in Barker, see Anne Whitehead (2015).

17. The published images were removed without comment from the American edition of *Three Guineas*. This has led Lili Hsieh to speculate that Sontag's misplaced critique of Woolf in *Regarding the Pain of Others* as holding a transparent and communal view of sympathetic feeling may result from her lack of knowledge that these images formed part of the original text. See Hsieh 2006: 33–6.

18. Historical critiques of the contemporary representation of the First World War have focused on the over-representation of the 'myth' that it only comprised mud, slaughter, tragedy and futility, which occludes the pride and patriotism that many felt at the time; see Daniel Todman (2007). Although Barker's fictions of the First World War centre exclusively on the Western Front, they do nevertheless engage critically with many of the prevailing 'myths' about the conflict, giving voice in fiction to viewpoints that are often absent from the historical record, and looking from different perspectives at leading figures in the contemporary remembrance of the conflict, such as Siegfried Sassoon and Wilfred Owen.

19. For a discussion of the negotiation of art's essential or transcendent qualities between Elinor, Paul and Kit in their discussion of a medieval church painting of the Last Judgement, see Tolan 2010: 385–6.

20. Barker's treatment of Woolf is comparable to her earlier treatment of the war poets in *Regeneration*. It becomes more explicit in *Toby's Room*, when Elinor visits Charleston and encounters Woolf. Reporting Woolf's views over dinner that 'women are outside the political process and therefore the war's got nothing to do with them', Elinor indicates a shift in her attitude as she marks out her own difference from this position, recognising that the women of Deptford, at least, have proved 'amazingly and repulsively belligerent', throwing bricks through the windows of German shopkeepers and handing out white feathers (2012: 71). The working-class dockyard area of London throws Bloomsbury into sharp relief, and troubles the 'we' of a feminist collective.

21. In *Double Vision*, artist Kate Frobisher provides a template for Goya and acts, like Paul, to witness artistically the suffering of others.

22. This, of course, applies not least to the writing of Barker herself, who won the Booker Prize and garnered attention as a major British novelist only when she turned to the subject of the First World War in the *Regeneration Trilogy*. In many ways, war has produced some of Barker's best work, and so the Faustian pact of Paul and Kit is also very much her own.

23. Historian Christine Hallett has noted that the various forms of pain relief available to nurses in the First World War each came with their attendant hazards: morphine repressed circulation, while anaesthesia could cause respiratory problems and vomiting. Given these dangers, it was often seen as preferable for the patient to endure the pain (2009: 106).

24. Hallett notes: 'One of the most common complaints suffered by nurses was "septic finger", a condition in which a small cut or abrasion on the finger became infected with a virulent microorganism . . . from a heavily infected wound' (2009: 210).

25. Gillies' facial injury unit was opened at Queen Mary's Hospital in 1917, after the Somme campaign had rendered the facilities in Aldershot inadequate for the numbers of men requiring treatment.

26. This scene is comparable to Sarah Lumb's inadvertent encounter with amputees on a hospital ward in *The Regeneration Trilogy*, itself a reworking of Wilfred Owen's poem 'Disabled' from the woman's viewpoint.

27. Although Tonks permitted hospital visitors a view of the private gallery of portraits, he was firmly of the view that they should not be exhibited to the general public, and they were published in Tonks's lifetime only as medical illustrations to Gillies' definitive study of facial surgery techniques.

Chapter 3

Empathy and Interdisciplinarity

Introduction

In Chapters 1 and 2 I have argued that contemporary interest in empathy is fuelled both by recent scientific developments relating to neuroscience and genetics, and also by an ethical turn in the humanities, which has focused on literature as a vehicle for imaginative connection with others, promoting action on their behalf. The concepts of empathy emerging from the sciences and the humanities do share some common ground, but their differences are such that I have asked whether a single term is adequate to describe the range of ideas that the term encompasses. This chapter does not seek to elide or evade the evident discontinuities between the scientific and the humanistic accounts of empathy. Rather, I ask how, in the context of the burgeoning field of the medical humanities, we might most productively and creatively think across and between disciplinary domains or boundaries. In mainstream medical humanities, the arts and humanities have been routinely subordinated to biomedical science, acting in the role of an assistant that can help to soften and to humanise its practices. Work in the critical medical humanities has accordingly asked whether a different kind of relationship between the sciences and the humanities might be construed, and if so, what it might look like. This question involves, on the one hand, an enquiry into what we mean by interdisciplinarity; how best we might think and work in a conceptual space that is constructed between medicine and the arts. It also engages us, on the other hand, with how empathy might potentially be reconfigured in and through such a space. Rather than humanism acting as the counterpoint to biomedicine, we might then begin to ask different questions of both science and the humanities. Thus, as Angela Woods and I have recently indicated, we could think instead about 'what the biomedical sciences might have to tell us about empath[etic feeling], or how the arts and humanities might speak of affective distance, or even a lack of care' (Whitehead and Woods 2016: 5).[1]

In his recent fiction, Ian McEwan has engaged not only with the question of empathy, but more particularly with how science and literature understand and negotiate the term. For McEwan the novel is, *par excellence*, the artistic mode that enters into and explores another consciousness. McEwan has for many years been an avid reader of popular science, engaging enthusiastically with developments in neurobiology and genetics. His later novels can productively be read as creative explorations in constructing a space between literature and biomedical science, or as formal experiments in how contemporary fiction can most adequately represent consciousness in the neurobiological era. None of his novels are more explicitly engaged with the literature–medicine intersection than *Saturday* (2005), with neurosurgeon Henry Perowne as its protagonist. Perowne places all his faith in science and tolerates reading fiction only as a concession to his daughter-poet, Daisy, who seeks to provide him with the kind of literary education of which Martha Nussbaum would surely approve. McEwan knowingly mobilises the literature–science debate in the context of a protracted history of disciplinary posturing and wrangling, extending back through the mid-twentieth-century 'two cultures' debate between C. P. Snow and F. R. Leavis, to the nineteenth-century spat between T. H. Huxley and Matthew Arnold. This chapter draws on *Saturday* as a focus for positioning the question of interdisciplinarity within a longer historical frame, arguing that the 'two cultures' debate has exerted a particularly strong influence in the British cultural context. The chapter also assesses McEwan's position in relation to the 'third culture' movement, which has emerged as one new mode of literature–science interdisciplinarity. My turn to McEwan is not intended to signal that I view his work as a positive treatment of either empathy or interdisciplinarity; on the contrary, I argue that his fiction displays both a lingering humanism and a troubling conservatism. Rather, read against the grain, McEwan's writing can open up and illuminate what we have invested historically in the academic disciplines, which then inflects how and on what (or whose) terms interdisciplinarity then becomes imagined. *Saturday* also stands as an example of the serious, if not unproblematic, engagement with popular science – and the neuroscientific revolution in particular – on the part of contemporary British novelists, marking out the literature–science question as an important theme of twenty-first-century British fiction, with McEwan in the vanguard.[2]

As with the texts in the previous chapter, *Saturday* debates the question of empathy in the political aftermath of 11 September 2001. The novel's depiction of a day in the life of Henry Perowne is set on 16 February 2003: the date of the mass protest in London against the invasion of Iraq.[3] The march of the political demonstrators to Hyde Park forms the backdrop to the events of the novel, and is never far from Perowne's thoughts as he moves through the city.[4] In a *Guardian* article published on 15 September 2001, McEwan explicitly linked empathy, reading and the 9/11 attacks in a formulation that underpins the writing of *Saturday*. Reflecting on the new technologies that now characterise sites of catastrophe, McEwan notes that, in their last moments, those caught in the attacks used their mobile phones to leave last messages for their loved ones. Again and again, these final calls repeated the same words: I love you. For McEwan, these parting words 'compel us to imagine ourselves into that moment'; now we know what we, too, would say from the burning tower or the hijacked plane. Drawing on empathy as perspective taking, McEwan goes on to observe: 'This is the nature of empathy, to think oneself into the minds of others'. If empathy is what binds us together, 'the core of our humanity', then for McEwan the hijackers could only act as they did by suppressing their empathetic facility: 'The hijackers used fanatical certainty, misplaced religious faith, and dehumanising hatred to purge themselves of the human instinct for empathy. Among their crimes was a failure of the imagination' (2001: no pagination). Here, then, empathy counters religious fundamentalism. One effect of McEwan's association, as critic Dominic Head has noted, is to 'valoriz[e] the secular love that McEwan evokes earlier in the article'; the love that urgently speaks its name before the mobile phone connection is cut off (2007: 180). McEwan's logic also operates according to an empathy deficit, anticipating Simon Baron-Cohen's (2011) thesis that evil equates to a lack of empathy, which enables cruelty to happen. In this context, fiction takes on a decidedly moral dimension, enabling us to practice, and even to enhance, our ability to imagine ourselves into other lives. McEwan's emphasis on empathy also notably resonates with Barack Obama's approach to the 11 September attacks; while acknowledging the importance of social and geopolitical factors, including poverty, hopelessness and despair, Obama's main emphasis was on the origination of the perpetrators' actions in a 'fundamental absence of empathy' (Remnick

2010: 337). Although Obama's vision of empathy – like McEwan's – promotes a universal humanism, Carolyn Pedwell has observed that it can also be read politically 'as linked . . . to . . . promoting American cultural and moral exceptionalism' (2014: 57). Perowne's belief that, if regimes do not embrace democratic governance independently, then military intervention is justified, is striking in this context.

McEwan's liberal humanism connects our curiosity about the lives of others with the inquiry that underpins scientific endeavour. For him, the same imagination thus motivates both novel writing and scientific discovery. Nowhere is the connection between the two disciplinary domains more evident or more fertile than in the neurological, and *Saturday* has often been discussed as an example of the syndrome novel that I considered in Chapter 1. As with *The Curious Incident*, there are in relation to *Saturday* significant questions about the extent to which the biological and the neurological subsume, or even replace, the political; I am therefore interested, at the close of the chapter, to assess whether the novel can be read against the grain of its own inherent conservatism. Can the syndrome novel offer a potential model for interdisciplinary thinking, or is it ultimately something of a dead end? I also turn at the close of the chapter to the vexed question of what kind of empathetic relation we, as readers, are invited to enter into with Perowne. Aligning ourselves with McEwan's own position on empathy, we would approach the novel as a vehicle for entering imaginatively into the consciousness of Perowne, suggesting a strong degree of identification with him. This entails aligning ourselves not only with Perowne's political views, but also with his notably first-world vision of empathy, which applies the 'enclosed' and 'foreshorten[ed]' perspective of the operating theatre to a broader social attitude: 'The trick, as always, is to be selective in your mercies. For all the discerning talk, it's the close at hand, the visible, that exerts the compelling force. And what you don't see . . .' (2005: 11, 127). In Chapter 1, I cautioned against interpretative approaches that focus on entering into the interiority or subjectivity of the protagonist, drawing on Edith Stein's account of empathy to highlight an encounter with alterity; an alternative perspective on the world that might potentially reshape our own view, but that can also simply provide a different vantage point from our own. To what extent does *Saturday*, and particularly the novel's ending, allow scope for a critical distance from Perowne? Does McEwan offer any viable alternatives to Perowne's perspective? Does the novel sustain the political enquiry opened up by the date chosen as its setting, or is the political ultimately subsumed into the very liberal humanism, and its problematic casting of geopolitical crisis as the drama of individual affect, that Perowne embodies? In addressing these questions, this chapter continues our ongoing investigation into how a range of British novelists variously utilise the notion of empathy, in combination with the trope of medicine, to position themselves in relation to the complex legacies of humanism, liberalism and morality that continue to haunt, disturb and play out, in and through contemporary fiction.

The two cultures

The theme of the 'two cultures' of science and literature is explicitly presented in *Saturday* through Perowne's exchanges with his daughter, Daisy, and his reflections on their relationship. A 'diligent' reader of the literary curriculum that Daisy plans out for him, Perowne nevertheless knows that in his daughter's eyes he represents a 'coarse, unredeemable materialist', who 'lacks an imagination' (2005: 134). At a historical moment when reality is 'strange enough', Perowne is impatient with fictions that 'make things up' and hankers after explanation rather than escape (2005: 66). Perowne calls into question whether, and how, literature matters or can make a difference, either socially or culturally; although he notably does so within the context of a work of fiction, and by invoking – through Daisy's presumed judgement of him – a deficit of the imagination, that, as I have already noted, assumes a particular moral valence for McEwan in the context of 9/11. Perowne's primary opponent in the novel is Daisy, who, under the influence of her father-in-law, the respected poet John Grammaticus, is now making her own way as a published poet. The science–literature divide maps on to the political affiliations in the novel, as Perowne is largely persuaded that the war would be a good thing, while Daisy acts as its most vocal critic. As critic David Alderson has noted, McEwan's alignments of character and perspective put into play an all-too-familiar series of oppositions: 'objective/subjective, science/culture, masculine/feminine' (2011: 225).

The binaries that Alderson identifies in the novel are also mapped onto the template of the family unit: across the Perowne family, there is a notable – if somewhat exceptional – balance of aptitudes, with Perowne as neurosurgeon, his wife Rosalind as lawyer, daughter Daisy as poet, and son Theo as musician. Empathy might initially be thought to be associated only with the culture side of the family, entailing that Perowne will receive a more effective lesson in the imagination that he lacks, and that he will learn the consequences of such a deficiency. In many ways, through the Baxter plot, this is indeed the case: Perowne's initial humiliation of Baxter, which harnesses the former's medical knowledge of the symptomatology of Huntington's disease, but entirely fails to imagine the encounter from Baxter's point of view, leads directly to the attack on Perowne's family, and the resultant demonstration of poetry's efficacy in the world. Yet, McEwan is more of a proponent of science than this reading allows, and through Perowne's musings on his profession, the novel asks important questions concerning the materialist foundation for empathy, and what science might contribute to our understanding of how we engage with and relate to others.[5] In a work of fiction that is explicitly committed to a vision of order, the family stands in for a broader balance of attributes that would characterise the ideal society; in such a community, the binaries named above would – like the Perowne family – complement and work in harmony with one another.

McEwan's mobilisation of the literature–science question draws on the longer history of the 'two cultures' debate; *Saturday* draws on Arnold as an intellectual touchstone, and, as with the numerous references throughout the novel to Virginia Woolf's *Mrs. Dalloway* (1925), it is somewhat ambiguous as to whether the intention is one of revision or of claiming authority. The phrase 'two cultures' was coined by British physical chemist and novelist C. P. Snow, in the title of his 1959 Rede Lecture at Cambridge University, 'The Two Cultures and the Scientific Revolution' (Snow 1998). The extension of an article published in the *New Statesman* three years earlier, the lecture was quickly published and became the subject of vigorous debate. Snow was particularly concerned that, with the British education system requiring students to specialise at an early stage, 'a gulf of mutual incomprehension' had emerged between 'scientists' and 'literary intellectuals', which meant that they held 'a curious distorted image of each other' (1998: 4). While conceding that no single individual could hold all knowledge – '[i]n the conditions of our age . . . Renaissance man is not possible' (1998: 61) – Snow nevertheless believed that both academic domains were suffering as a result of the divide opening up between them.

Snow's description of the man of science could be read as a blueprint for Perowne: he is 'very intelligent' and his culture is 'exacting and admirable', although he does not count traditional artistic culture as 'relevant' to his interests, 'with the exception . . . of music' (1998: 13–14).[6] Snow concludes of scientists that, because of their lack of engagement with literary culture: 'their imaginative understanding is less than it could be. They are self-impoverished' (1998: 14). On the literary side, in a description that could encompass Daisy and Grammaticus, Snow discerns an equivalent impoverishment, which results from a blindness to the culture of the physical and natural sciences: '[a]s though the scientific edifice of the physical world was not, in its intellectual depth, complexity and articulation, the most beautiful and wonderful collective work of the mind of man' (1998: 14). This evocation of the beauty and the wonder of the natural sciences can be glimpsed in *Saturday*, in the refrain from Charles Darwin's *On the Origin of Species* (1859) that echoes in Perowne's thoughts throughout his day: '*There is grandeur in this view of life*' (2005: 55; italics in original). The enthusiasm of Snow's description also betrays something of his sympathies; although he calls for greater communication between the sciences and the humanities in education, he clearly regards science to be the dominant force for the contemporary age, and at times he barely conceals his animosity towards the literary intellectuals, whom he memorably refers to as 'natural Luddites' (1998: 22).[7]

Snow's allegiances were not lost on influential literary critic F. R. Leavis, who launched his first counter-attack in his Richmond lecture, 'Two Cultures? The Significance of Lord Snow', delivered at Cambridge University in 1962. The majority of the lecture comprises a scathing attack on Snow, or, more specifically, on the question of his authority. Invited to speak on the literature–science question because of his status as both published novelist and respected scientist, Snow comes under attack from Leavis, first as a novelist – 'Snow is, of course, a – no, I can't say that; he isn't; Snow thinks of himself as a novelist' (1972c: 44–5) – and then as a scientist: 'Snow rides on an advancing tide of cliché' (1972c: 51). Under Leavis's withering gaze, Snow materialises in the lecture as a 'portent' of the triumph of style over substance, of celebrity status over critical acumen. If the main thrust of Leavis's offensive is therefore the question of cultural authority, of whose voice is heard, and in what mode or tone it speaks, he turns to the subject of education at the end of the lecture, explicitly presenting an alternative vision of the university to that of Snow:

> I am concerned to make it really a university, something (that is) more than a collocation of specialist departments – to make it a centre of human consciousness, perception, knowledge, judgement, and responsibility . . . I would [see] the centre of [the] university in a vital English school. (1972c: 63)

Leavis's manifesto for the university was further expounded in his second response to Snow, 'Luddites? Or, There is Only One Culture' (1972a), in which Leavis made clear that, while he supported an interdisciplinary liberal arts education, with English at its core, interdisciplinarity did not, for him, extend as far as the sciences. Indeed, as critic Joe Moran has pointed out, Leavis's understanding of interdisciplinarity could more properly be described as disciplinary in nature:

> If disciplines are defined fundamentally by what they exclude from their remit, then Leavis's project was thoroughly disciplinary, since it involved limiting its area of concern to a small canon of recognized texts and studying other forms of culture only insofar as they failed to live up to its standards. (2010: 29)

Equally, if Leavis regarded the culture created in and through the university to act as 'the sustaining creative nucle[us] of a larger community' (1972a: 98), it remained unclear exactly how this transfer of knowledge was to be effected, especially when, as Moran observes, the university and the English school 'remained such closed institutions' (2010: 30).

In many ways, the 'two culture' debate can be seen to exemplify Snow's point about the 'curious distorted view' that literature and science hold of each other, across the disciplinary divide. Science is, from the perspective of Leavis, representative of a crassly technocratic and utilitarian society, while the arts are, in Snow's eyes, dangerously out of touch with the demands of the contemporary age. The debate can also be seen to exemplify the difficulty of promoting a vision of interdisciplinarity that does not have its own disciplinary base or affiliation; we are, after all, trained within particular areas of expertise and these will inevitably colour our sense of what matters, and of how and why it is important. More than this, the dynamic of class runs as a peculiarly British faultline through the 'two cultures' question, and Leavis's defence of culture against the imposter Snow reads uncomfortably as an attack on Snow's own background, as well as a desire to preserve the university as an elite bastion of high culture. Further, Moran rightly notes that for Leavis, as for Snow, the debate seems to take place independently of the material, political and economic base of the university itself: '[it] overlooks the nature of universities, and of *all* the disciplines within them, as institutions organized by the hierarchical distribution of privileges, and inextricably connected to the broader power networks of government, society and culture' (2010: 32; italics in original). While this may be more pronounced today than in the mid-twentieth century, the point remains that interdisciplinarity does not and cannot operate in a vacuum, but is necessarily negotiated in a highly contested environment, which is characterised by intense competition for resource, as well as by a need to be responsive to government agendas and priorities.[8] Returning to McEwan's modelling of the ideal, balanced society around the unit of the nuclear family, it is clear that the university acts as a more difficult and resistant template for such a vision; indeed, the attempts of Snow and Leavis to impose such an idealised community upon the university act to illuminate what must be left out of the picture for such a vision to be possible – if ultimately unrealisable – at all.

Leavis's vision of literature as a vehicle for cultural renewal invoked the nineteenth-century figure of Arnold; for Leavis, T. S. Eliot and I. A. Richards, Arnold was, as Stefan Collini has noted, 'the chief of those recruited to preside over and give legitimacy to a new professional specialism' (1988: 113). In the 1920s and 1930s, Arnold thus became irrevocably associated with a vision of 'high culture' that could stem the rising tide of mass or popular cultural forms. Representing a prescriptive notion of culture, as well as promoting its capacity to heal social conflict, Arnold stands today as 'a negative touchstone' (Collini 1988: 117). In this context, it seems hardly surprising that, in his influential review of *Saturday*, novelist John Banville dismissed the work as 'a neoliberal polemic gone badly wrong' (2005: no pagination), while critic Elaine Hadley described McEwan's treatment of 'Dover Beach' in *Saturday* as 'doggedly Victorian' (2005: 94). Arnold was a particularly apposite figure for Leavis to invoke, not only because of his cultural weight and authority, but more particularly because, in delivering the Rede lecture for 1882 – the same Cambridge University lecture series, in the same Senate House, as Snow would speak in over half a century later – Arnold chose to address the topic of 'Literature and Science'. Furthermore, he did so in response to a lecture by distinguished naturalist and comparative anatomist T. H. Huxley, delivered in Birmingham two years earlier, that defended a scientific education as, in the words of Collini, 'offer[ing] a rigorous mental training, as well as making an indispensable contribution to national well-being' (1998: xiv). In criticising the traditional classical education as outdated and irrelevant, Huxley observed that its proponents drew on Arnold for inspiration; in his Rede lecture, Arnold accordingly took up the gauntlet, and in so doing, acted as an important precedent for Leavis's own response to Snow.

Introducing his lecture, Arnold posed the question of the relative value of literature and science in explicit terms, which can be seen to echo through the later exchange between Snow and Leavis: 'The question is raised whether, to meet the demands of our modern life, the predominance [in education] ought not now to pass from letters to science' (1964: 210). Arnold then proceeds to collapse the marked division between literature and science, arguing that the category of 'literature' encompasses not only the traditional classics but also the great works that have emerged out of the physical and natural sciences: 'Literature is a huge word; it may mean everything written with letters or printed in a book. Euclid's *Elements* and Newton's *Principia* are thus literature' (1964: 214; italics in original). Broadening his scope to the present day, Arnold also includes within the scope of the literary 'what in modern times has been thought and said by the great observers and knowers of nature'; not least among them, the towering figure of Darwin (1964: 215). If the major scientific thinkers can be counted as literature, then literature equally is not for Arnold a mere 'superficial humanism, mainly decorative', but rather holds the rigour and the discipline that are usually associated with the scientific: 'all learning is scientific which is systematically laid out and followed up to its original sources, and . . . a genuine humanism is scientific' (1964: 213). Nevertheless, in spite of his apparently flexible and compromising approach, Arnold's conclusion makes it unequivocal where his allegiances truly lie. The scientific education can provide an accumulation of facts, but for Arnold it struggles to extend beyond this level: 'still it will be *knowledge* only which [the scientists] give us' (1964: 222; italics in original). It is only the literary education that can relate its knowledge to 'the need in man for conduct, and the need in man for beauty', and in so doing create not a specialist but an educated man (1964: 232). As with the subsequent 'two cultures' debate, the question of science and literature cannot avoid partisanship, and Arnold's concluding comparison does not avoid the snobbery and elitism that Leavis would later display. With an eye on what was to come, Collini aptly summarises Arnold's lecture in the following terms: 'Not for the last time in British history, questions about the proper place of the sciences and the humanities . . . appeared to be inextricably entangled with elusive but highly-charged matters of institutional status and social class' (1998: xvi).

The politics underpinning Arnold's lecture come into clearer focus by placing it within the context of his other writings. Arnold explicitly refers in his lecture to his earlier claim in *Culture and Anarchy* (1869) that in our culture we ought '*to know the best which has been thought and said in the world*' (1964: 211; italics in original). As Collini notes, Arnold's attention to the verbal immediately prioritises literary and philosophical culture over the visual or musical, and so 'faithfully represents Arnold's own cultural tastes' (1988: 85). Further, the phrase signals Arnold's belief in culture as a human ideal – a vision of beauty, morality and intellect, towards which we should aim and aspire. Such a model of culture is set, in the first instance, against the philistinism of middle-class mediocrity (a precedent for Snow as the man of celebrity and cliché), which is characterised, in Collini's eloquent terms, by 'its puritan moralism, its provincialism, its smugness and complacency, its lack of interest in ideas or feeling for style, its pinched and cramped ideas of human excellence' (1988: 78). Culture also stems the tide of anarchy that Arnold associates with the working classes, who no longer conform to 'the strong feudal habits of subordination and deference' but display a dangerous 'worship of freedom in and for itself' (1971: 61, 62). In a particularly impassioned passage, Arnold evokes the vision of a gathering threat to the social order:

> More and more, because of this our blind faith in machinery, because of our want of light to enable us to look beyond machinery to the end for which machinery is valuable, this and that man, and this and that body of men, all over the country, are beginning to assert and put in practice an Englishman's right to do what he likes; his right to march where he likes, meet where he likes, enter where he likes, hoot as he likes, threaten as he likes, smash as he likes. All this, I say, tends to anarchy. (1971: 62)

The immediate political background to this passage was the Hyde Park demonstrations of 1866 and 1867. In 1866, the Reform League organised a march to Hyde Park, which attracted large numbers of demonstrators; the government chained the park gates and protesters breached the railings to occupy the Park. The meeting was held without undue disturbance, although there was minor unrest over the following days. In 1867, a further march to Hyde Park was unopposed by government, and on 6 May, up to 200,000 demonstrators converged to hear talks and speeches.[9] Given the largely peaceful nature of the demonstrations, Arnold's rhetoric of escalating violence is telling of his own concerns. For our purposes, it is also worth noting that Arnold's solution to political inequality lies in culture, which acts as a unifying and healing force that can harmonise the disparate interests of the various social classes and political parties. Its long view of history can subsume and overcome the narrow, divisive and temporally immediate concerns of the barbarians at the gates.

Saturday is set on the date of a more contemporary protest march to Hyde Park and the descriptions of the rally, viewed through Perowne's eyes, subtly shift in the opening section of the novel. Initially, the spectacle of the marchers seems to Perowne to hold 'an air of innocence and English dottiness', and its surge and force are experienced as a 'seduction and excitement . . . an intimation of revolutionary joy', that could potentially, but does not, sweep the sceptical Perowne into its flow (2005: 62). By the time of his first encounter with Baxter, however, Perowne's associations have shifted and the march feels more akin to the violence and threat of Arnold's description, characterised by 'the funereal beat of marching drums', '[t]he unrelenting throb of drums', and 'the tribal drums' (2005: 84, 85, 87). The closure of the street on which the confrontation takes place means that it is deserted, and Perowne is isolated as Baxter attacks. With his 'simian air' (2005: 88), the materialisation of Baxter in the back street evokes what Alderson has summarised as 'the moral and physical degenerate of the sort which for long has haunted the racially inflected imperial imaginary' (2011: 232) – an imaginary that also shadows Arnold's fearful vision of the violent mob – and simultaneously stands as a figure for the new barbarian at the gates, the 'other' not of class riots but of global terrorism; the hijackers who were so central to McEwan's initial response to the 9/11 attacks. In shifting the narrative to a scene of individual confrontation, with the political both literally and metaphorically consigned to background noise, McEwan performs the very gesture of liberal humanism that Lauren Berlant has so eloquently exposed; replacing political action and critique with a highly personal, subjective drama, the theatre of which distracts from broader structural issues.

The contest between Baxter and Perowne is played out in the second confrontation scene, with the rest of the Perowne family assembled. Forcing Daisy to undress, and with the threat of rape hanging in the air, Baxter is mesmerised by Daisy's rendition of Arnold's 'Dover Beach', disarmed by the beauty of the poem. Here, then, we witness in action Arnold's vision of culture as both healing and unifying, a force that can overcome the threat of anarchy. With his sidekick Nigel disappearing in disgust, Baxter is now isolated, and is vanquished as Perowne and Theo combine forces to push him down the stairs. Arnold's poem reinforces the simple moral message of the family drama, that love is what we – like those caught in the terror attacks, leaving last messages on their mobile phones – can set against the hijackers. In an uncertain and anxious time, when 'ignorant armies clash by night', and the 'sea of faith' has ebbed away, leaving in its wake 'the vast edges drear and the naked shingles of the world', only love remains as the solace and comfort that we can offer to one another: 'Ah, love, let us be true to one another!' (2005: 221–2). The scene of Baxter's intrusion enacts at once his own humanisation – his conversion from thug to aesthete, through his susceptibility to the beauty of the poem – and Perowne's recognition that poetry can make a difference in the world. In so doing, however, it turns its back on the political, leading Hadley to conclude that liberalism 'is . . . too often about itself, about the drama of its own confrontation with the world' (2005: 100). The drama of individual subjectivity is, furthermore, one that offers only a temporary solution; as Alderson aptly observes, 'reality . . . can only be redeemed momentarily by the art which aspires to humanise, not politicise' (2011: 234). The need for reiteration is immediately evident in *Saturday*, as the male rescue of the threatened female family members must be reinforced by Perowne's life-saving operation on Baxter. If the ties of empathy – between Perowne and his family – are what bind 'us' together, then *Saturday* reveals that this comes at a cost; the price, it seems, is that of political engagement, agency and critique.

As Perowne's day closes, he stands at the bedroom window, looking out over the Bloomsbury square. Behind him, Rosalind sleeps uneasily, and Perowne reflects on the vulnerability and defencelessness of London in the face of a more extensive terrorist threat than Baxter has posed:

A hundred years ago, a middle-aged doctor standing at this window in his silk dressing gown, less than two hours before a winter's dawn, might have pondered the new century's future. February 1903. You might envy this Edwardian gent all he didn't yet know. If he had young boys, he could lose them within a dozen years, at the Somme. And what was their body count, Hitler, Stalin, Mao? Fifty million, a hundred? If you described the hell that lay ahead, if you warned him, the good doctor – an affable product of decades of prosperity and peace – would not believe you. Beware the utopianists, zealous men certain of the path to the ideal social order. Here they are again, totalitarians in a different form, still scattered and weak, but growing, and angry, and thirsty for another mass killing. A hundred years to resolve. But this may be an indulgence, an idle, overblown fantasy, a night-thought about a passing disturbance that time and good sense will settle and rearrange. (2005: 276–7)

Here, the long historical view does not discount the violence of the twentieth century but, in the grand scheme of things, it is contextualised, calmed, and future disasters are soothed into 'passing disturbance'. Perowne's vision is reminiscent of Elinor's view through the train window on her way to the forbidden zone; an aesthetic of consolation, that focuses on what will remain after the forces of violence have all been spent. As we saw in Chapter 2, Barker critiques Elinor's perspective by placing it in dialogue with the views of other characters, and thereby exposing the class ideology that underpins it. In *Saturday*, no alternative viewpoint is offered to Perowne's thoughts, and the novel ends with his loving embrace of Rosalind and his slow slide into unconsciousness: 'there's only this' (2005: 279). Arguably, though, the framing of Perowne's vision by the bedroom window – as Elinor's by the train window – points to an awareness that 'this', the warm and secure embrace of his family, is *not* all that there is; that the marchers, too, have their place on this particular Saturday in February, and that Perowne's view of the world is, ultimately, limited, partial and open to critique.[10]

A third culture?

In his 'Introduction' to *The Two Cultures*, Collini identifies as a particularly 'encouraging sign' for interdisciplinary thinking a new wave of scientific writing that combines 'creative scientific work at the highest level with communication with a wider audience' (1998: lviii), highlighting in particular the achievements of evolutionary biologists Stephen Jay Gould and Richard Dawkins, and theoretical physicist Steven Hawking. A few years later, John Brockman, the influential literary agent of numerous popular scientists, including Dawkins and cognitive psychologist Daniel Dennett, published a collection of essays entitled *The Next Fifty Years: Science in the First Half of the Twenty-First Century* (2002). Here, Brockman advanced a vision of scientists not only asking the big questions, but also communicating their ideas directly to a broader public, rather than looking to the arts and humanities to disseminate their work in forms accessible to a wider audience. Here, then, the arts and humanities are positioned, in the first instance, as subservient to the sciences – a vehicle for communicating the big ideas, but lacking a constitutive role in their shaping or formation. Even this secondary position has now been subsumed, however, as scientists themselves assume the mantle of the public intellectual, thereby rendering the arts and humanities redundant. Horton observes of Brockman's tone in the collection: '[t]he clear confidence . . . of this expression . . . suggests a new level of popular scientific autonomy, going beyond the self-defensiveness of the earlier debates' (2014: 684). If Snow envisaged a 'third culture', in which the literary intellectuals would be in communication with the scientists, for Brockman the failure of the humanities to engage with science in a sustained way entails that they are simply taken out of the equation. McEwan has visibly aligned himself with the 'third culture' debates, and this section accordingly asks whether his stance can, in the words of Collini, be read as an 'encouraging sign', or whether the 'third culture' simply represents the most recent incarnation of scientific imperialism masquerading as interdisciplinarity.

The most promising vein of literary criticism for the 'third culture' movement has been the neo-Darwinian, evolutionary criticism advanced by American biologist E. O. Wilson. Adopting the term 'consilience', Wilson is particularly interested in the reconfiguration of disciplinary boundaries within and between the sciences, with new areas of academic enquiry emerging, such as biochemistry, physical chemistry, or chemical ecology. In this context, 'consilience' represents a call for greater collaboration between the sciences, the social sciences, and the humanities, better to understand the effects of biological evolution. Wilson draws on the rhetoric of interdisciplinarity, but as we have seen with other projects that seek to think across science and literature, partisanship is again at work, with biology now acting as the nodal point of disciplinary convergence. Moran accordingly observes of 'consilience' that 'this kind of project could be seen as a scientific version of Leavis's vision for English: the call for interdisciplinarity is presented as a project of intellectual synthesis, but is actually based on the vested interests of one discipline' (Moran 2010: 164). Further, Wilson's vision of literature effectively subsumes it into the biological, rather than according it autonomous epistemological status: given that we all have biological brains, culture, as the product of the brain, is not only biologically determined, but is also itself a manifestation of biological evolution. In the words of Wilson, '[t]he narratives and artifacts that prove most innately satisfying spread and become culture. The societies with the most potent Darwinian innovations export them to other societies' (2005: ix). Here, then, literary narratives are not only based in biology but operate according to their own principle of natural selection. With evolution as the explanation that can harmonise the disciplines into a common intellectual project, 'consilience' is particularly attractive to Wilson because it offers certainty in deeply uncertain times; literary criticism is characterised for him solely by 'confusion', and Darwinian criticism therefore offers 'an unbeatable strategy to replace it' (2005: vii).

For McEwan, at least, it would seem that Wilson's arguments hold a persuasive force. A 2001 *Guardian* article originally published to mark the republication of Darwin's *The Expression of the Emotions in Man and Animals* (1872), was republished in a volume that explicitly sought to advance the field of evolutionary criticism, *The Literary Animal: Evolution and the Nature of Narrative* (Gottschall and Wilson 2005).[11] McEwan's contribution draws on evolutionary psychology to argue that, as a species, we have an innate neurological capacity to empathise: 'We have, in the terms of cognitive psychology, a theory of mind, a more-or-less automatic understanding of what it means to be someone else' (McEwan 2005a: 5). It is this facility for empathy that fiction both responds to and satisfies. For Head, McEwan's combination of evolutionary criticism and empathy has 'a benign, even utopian impulse' (2007: 202), in that it minimises the superficial differences between us in order to focus on the deeper commonalities that bind us together. McEwan thus avers:

> [W]e are descended from a common stock of anatomically modern humans who migrated out of East Africa perhaps as recently as two hundred thousand years ago and spread around the world. Local differences in climate have produced variations in the species that are in many cases literally skin deep. We have fetishized these differences to rationalize conquest and subjugation. (2005a: 10)

Head also distinguishes McEwan's aims from the remit of the volume more broadly, arguing that he accords more significance to cultural specificity than the evolutionary framework might typically accommodate (2007: 202). Yet, the predominant impetus of McEwan's essay is undoubtedly towards a human universal, and he uses the evolutionary framework to emphasise the long temporal perspective that we have already encountered in Perowne's reflections at the close of *Saturday*. The 'biological view' is important to McEwan because it is based on stasis and equilibrium; if evolutionary change happens, it does so over an 'immeasurable tract of irretrievable time' and in response to 'a powerful adaptive pressure' (2005a: 14, 11). He sets this 'dull continuum of infinitesimal change' against the 'literary' fascination with the 'explosive, decisive moment', the dramatic 'rupture with the past' (2005a: 14). While McEwan has a valid point in cautioning against a fixation on the catastrophe or the traumatic break, which can obscure more quotidian and insidious modes of harm and violence, I argue that his own emphasis nevertheless reflects a troubling conservatism that also characterises the broader evolutionary turn in popular science.[12]

In common with a range of popular science texts about empathy, McEwan notably mobilises the biological in his essay – and also in *Saturday* – to explain both individual behaviour and the workings of society more broadly. According to this logic, we are hard-wired by our biology to be empathetic, to utilise our innate sociality for the benefit of the species, and by harnessing this embedded capacity at an individual level we can effect broader social change. Frans de Waal has thus argued that 'biology constitutes our greatest hope', holding the potential to usher in a 'new epoch that stresses co-operation and social responsibility' over 'greed' (2009: ix). Significantly, however, it can only do so if we do not succumb to 'the whims of politics, culture and religion'; in terms notably similar to McEwan (and Perowne), de Waal takes the long historical view, which again acts to frame politics as a momentary, passing disturbance: '[i]deologies come and go, but human nature is here to stay' (2009: 45). Although de Waal rhetorically separates biology from politics, Pedwell notes that his work mobilises a version of empathy that correlates closely with 'neoliberal capitalism's demand for an enterprising and emotionally adaptable citizenry' (2014: 153). Further, in spite of positive claims for social transformation, evolutionary biology is politically invested in maintaining existing hierarchies. Pedwell observes of claims that homeostasis represents the optimum functioning of the individual body, and, by analogy, also of the social body, that they 'frequently work in the interests of maintaining the Euro-American neoliberal status quo and the social and political . . . exclusions that underscore it' (2014: 153). In the remainder of this section, I argue that McEwan's emphasis on the family unit as the model not only for balance and equilibrium, but also for co-operation and social responsibility, acts problematically both to ally empathy with political stasis and exclusion, and also to bridge the gap between individual and social in a mode that effectively bypasses political action.

In the previous section, I discussed Baxter as the materialisation of the new 'other' of the Western imaginary, merging Arnold's class anxiety with the contemporary spectre of the global terrorist. His defeat by the Perowne family represents an affirmation of middle-class values, as well as of civilisation's power to overcome and expel externally threatening forces. In the light of McEwan's interest in evolutionary biology, Baxter's Huntington's disease also assumes particular symbolic weight in the novel, defining difference not in cultural or political terms, but rather on the biological grounds of genetic inheritance. Throughout *Saturday*, Perowne repeatedly reflects on the ways in which genetics now play a determining role in our lives; from his scientific perspective, it is 'which sperm finds which egg, how the cards in two packs are chosen, then how they are shuffled, halved and spliced at the moment of recombination' that decides 'the sort of person' that we are, while other factors 'have little or no influence' (2005b: 25). McEwan's choice of Huntington's disease to define Baxter makes the argument for 'biological determinism' particularly compelling, as there is a 'fifty-fifty chance' of inheritance of the condition from a parent, and it stands in the popular imaginary as an effective shorthand for a genetic disease that is currently incurable (2005b: 93). On the one hand, if biology, rather than social and political inequality, determines who will have a life on the margins of society, the prospect of medical advance holds out significant hope for change; not least for Baxter, for whom Perowne's false promises of a cure lure him upstairs, enabling Perowne and Theo to overpower him. On the other hand, such a vision of the social order discounts the need for political critique and transformation. In Perowne's decision to operate on Baxter, *Saturday* enacts what Head has aptly described as a 'new mode[l] of agency and responsibility' (2007: 196), adapted for the biological age. As he watches Baxter tumble down the stairs, Perowne discerns in his eyes:

> a sorrowful accusation of betrayal. He, Henry Perowne, possesses so much – the work, money, status, the home, above all, the family . . . ; and he has done nothing, given nothing, to Baxter who has so little that is not wrecked by his defective gene, and who is soon to have even less. (2005b: 227)

The implication is not that Perowne can, or indeed should, change the status quo by giving up any of these things, or by enabling the Baxters of the world to have access to them. The most that can be offered is that Perowne should 'do what he can to make [Baxter] comfortable'

(2005b: 278). Although Perowne has some agency in creating the second confrontation with Baxter – using his professional knowledge against him to avoid a beating, and humiliating him in front of his friends – the logic of the narrative is that he is not responsible for the roll of the genetic dice that, in the end, marks out the difference between the two men. Implicated, but not the guilty party, Perowne's operation on Baxter is an act of atonement for the privileges that he enjoys, and that Baxter lacks. Critic Jane F. Thrailkill has noted that Perowne's is a metaphorical, as well as a literal, act of reparation, and that in structuring the narrative around this impulse, *Saturday* 'tends towards homeostasis, the prompt restoration of equilibrium following moments of instability or impairment' (2011: 179). In line with evolutionary biology more broadly, McEwan's novel reinforces the existing political and social hierarchies, and their exclusions.

I have argued in the previous section that the family drama of the confrontation with Baxter distracts from, and even replaces, the political. It might, however, be more productive to see the family in *Saturday* as an alternative vehicle for exploring the global questions of the post-9/11 age. Taking this approach, we can read McEwan's fetishisation of the balanced family as a move that, in Alderson's terms, 'symbolically reconciles our gendered outlooks on the world (objectivity and subjectivity) and our dispositions towards it (aggression and nurture)' (2011: 224). By acting as a unit, the Perowne family co-operate to defeat Baxter, enacting a social responsibility that puts the good of the whole above considerations of individual safety, and exemplifies neoliberalism's 'emotionally attuned citizenry' (Pedwell 2014: 153). The ideal balance of the family symbolises the broader society that both underpins and sustains it, so that the restoration of order within the Perowne family unit simultaneously naturalises the existing social and political order. Here, then, empathy is mobilised by McEwan as the force that harmonises and cements the Perowne family, harnessing the different aptitudes and dispositions within it for the service of the greater good. Alderson observes, however, that the family is not a neutral template, but is itself highly ideological, and 'has symbolically served to police all kinds of distinctions, extending outwards from public and private to those which define the communal or national, and even the human' (2011: 221). The expulsion of Baxter by and from the family unit accordingly introduces a more troubling version of empathy, in the form of a travelling affect that fails to move very far. With affective ties in *Saturday* invested primarily within the family unit, empathy notably does not extend beyond the nuclear family, and the conquest of Baxter ultimately serves to confirm his position as outsider: communally, socially and biologically. It is appropriate that Perowne's act of atonement can be also be read as a gesture of 'at-one-ment'; the operation brings Perowne a sense of calm and resolution, of being at one with himself, precisely through its confirmation of the Perownes' moral elevation above the revenge enacted by Baxter. Equally telling is the first action of the family once Baxter has been expelled from the house. All of the family members work in harmony to prepare the family meal: 'While Perowne reheats his stock and takes from the fridge the clams, mussels, prawns and monkfish, the children lay the table, Rosalind slices a loaf of bread and makes a dressing for the salad, and Grammaticus puts down his icepack to open another bottle of wine' (2005b: 231). Again, an innate and instinctive empathy between the family members co-ordinates their activity into a seamless whole that reinforces the bonds between them, demonstrating their effortless 'at-one-ment' with each other, but this is a mode of affect that is neither outward-directed nor other-oriented, and that acts rather as a conservative, exclusionary force.

An unbounded view

I have argued that reading *Saturday* through the lens of McEwan's own positioning of the novel, in alliance with the 'third culture' movement and with evolutionary criticism, focuses attention on Baxter's Huntington's disease, and a mode of genetic determinism that upholds the status quo and locates the possibility of change not in social or political movements, but in scientific and biomedical advance. There is, however, an alternative framing of medicine in the novel, in Perowne's mother, Lily's, Alzheimer's disease. Perowne's visit to Lily in the nursing home acts as a significant feature of his day, first in his efforts to fit it into his busy schedule and, later, in the unexpected surfacing in his thoughts of the conversation with his mother. Lily's neurodegenerative disorder means that, as for Baxter, the threads that bind her identity together are gradually loosening; unlike Baxter, however, Lily does not display violent behaviour, but rather a new and different form of insight. Although this might seem suggestive of a problematically romanticised approach to Alzheimer's, this section asks whether Lily's notably lyrical and avant-garde stream of association offers an alternative aesthetic for thinking through the interdisciplinary relation between medicine and literature in the novel. I suggest that McEwan's portrayal of Perowne's response to, and reflections on, his mother, not only offers a vision of empathy that is open, mobile and other-oriented, but that it can also provide a timely critical intervention into debates in the medical humanities concerning the role and function of narrative as a vehicle for communicating and understanding the illness experience.

If Perowne's relation to genetic medicine is one of authority – asserting a knowledge of Huntington's disease that is superior to that of Baxter, and using that display of knowledge to defeat Baxter twice over – his attitude towards his own specialist area of neuroscience is noticeably different. Here, Perowne expresses feelings of wonder, both at the marvels that science has already revealed about the human brain, and at the mysteries that remain to be solved:

> For all the recent advances, it's still not known how this well-protected one kilogram or so of cells actually encodes information, how it holds experiences, memories, dreams and intentions. He doesn't doubt that in years to come, the coding mechanism will be well known, though it might not be in his lifetime. Just like the digital codes of replicating life held within DNA, the brain's fundamental secret will be laid open one day. But even when it has, the wonder will remain; that mere wet stuff can make this bright inward cinema of thought, of sight and sound and touch bound into a vivid illusion of an instantaneous present, with a self, another brightly wrought illusion, hovering like a ghost at its centre. Could it ever be explained how matter becomes conscious? He can't begin to imagine a satisfactory account, but he knows it will come, the secret will be revealed – over decades, as long as the scientists and the institutions remain in place, the explanations will refine themselves into an irrefutable truth about consciousness. (2005b: 254–5)

On the one hand, this passage could be read as confirmation of biomedicine's primacy, in its ultimate capacity to explain consciousness, and in its priority for institutional funding and support; Head observes that, in comparison, 'other mental activities – writing a poem or novel, say – might be deemed secondary, mere consequences of the consciousness that they cannot comprehend or preserve' (2007: 192). On the other hand, there are glimpses here of what Horton has designated a more 'feminine' vision of science, aligned with potential rather than with 'a patriarchal use of science as a source of control and progress' (2014: 690). Such an approach, based in the recognition of knowledge's limitations, opens up the possibility for a more collaborative interdisciplinary dynamic between the sciences and the humanities, neither of which can claim an authoritative position in relation to consciousness. Critic Thom Dancer has accordingly argued that Theo's declaration of a commitment to thinking small, to intellectual modesty, offers a viable alternative to Perowne's grand view in the novel, and one that is, moreover, demonstrated throughout the day to be the most effective (2012: 218–19).[13] In what follows, I argue that, through Lily, McEwan offers us further glimpses into a mode of consciousness that resists Perowne's scientific authority, and that suggests the basis for a different mode of interdisciplinarity to the 'third culture' model.

Perowne's visit to Lily takes place between the two encounters with Baxter, and offers an alternative insight into the neurodegenerative condition. Lily no longer recognises her son, but relies on cues from his behaviour and tone of voice to guide her affective responses. Perowne's interactions with Lily do not attempt to instate the reality of the present situation, but focus instead on offering her comfort through a soothing demeanour. His thoughts return to the woman she was during his childhood, a proud housekeeper and a champion swimmer. Critic Laura Salisbury has observed that McEwan's evocation of empathy in Perowne's engagement with Lily is again tied to the liberal subject; if Alzheimer's strips Lily of her own narrative of identity, this is shored up in and through Perowne's memory work. Although this act of conservation consoles Perowne, it evades the challenge of engaging with a consciousness rendered radically other by neurological damage. Salisbury thus notes of McEwan's fiction:

> the preservation of the capacity . . . to imagine ourselves into the minds of others remains constrictively tied to a more liberal notion of making contact with those whose images of who or what they once were are retained in the subject's *own* narratives of self-legibility. (2010: 904; italics in original)

An alternative approach to brain damage is offered by French philosopher Catherine Malabou, who argues that Alzheimer's disease gives rise to a new form of suffering that does not conform to the psycho-analytical model of continuity of personality: 'A person with Alzheimer's Disease . . . is not – or not only – someone who has "changed" or been "modified", but rather *a subject who has become someone else*' (2012: 15; italics in original). Malabou's description of Oliver Sacks's writing resonates with Perowne's visit to Lily; Sacks's patients, like Lily, '*never cease to feel emotions*', and this allows an emotional dynamic in which the doctor can, like Perowne with his mother, 'be *affectionate* with [his] patien[t] and *affected* by [her]' (2012: 187, 188; italics in original). Yet, for Malabou, this narrative mode misses the radical potential offered by neurological damage, which resides in our common vulnerability to becoming radically other to ourselves:

> At every instant we are all susceptible to becoming prototypes of ourselves without any essential relation to the past of our identities. Alzheimer's disease is a particularly important example of such loss. A form of life appears that bids farewell to all the subject's old modes of being. (2012: 213)

Recognition of this emergent form of life, or of the new wounded, necessitates a mode of empathy that does not cling to the illusion of a continuous individual, but that is other-directed, and capable of registering the unprecedented new identity.

If we look beyond Perowne's visit to the nursing home, and to its later resurfacing in his consciousness as he is carried away by the music at Theo's concert, a mode of empathy emerges that is arguably more attuned to Malabou's description. Engulfed by the music, and lifted emotionally by it, Perowne recalls the words spoken by Lily during his visit: 'He knows what his mother meant. He can go for miles, he feels lifted up, right high across the counter. He doesn't want the song to end' (2005b: 172). His thoughts take us back to Lily's parting words to her son, that speak, allusively and poetically, of what critic Peter Boxall has termed 'an unbinding that leads to a kind of release, a swelling pleasure' (2013: 158). Lily's full observation reads as follows:

> Out here it only looks like a garden, Aunty, but it's the countryside really and you can go for miles. When you walk here you feel lifted up, right high across the counter. I can manage all them plates without a brush, but God will take care of you and see what you're going to get because it's a swimming race. You'll squeeze through somehow. (2005b: 167)

For Boxall, this more lyrical poetic mode offers a very different aesthetic to that of Arnold, an investment in a momentary liberation and a form of 'utopian energ[y]' (2013: 157). It is also a mode of the poetic that is tied to an experimental avant-gardism, suspending logical constraints to make unexpected, indeed uncontained, imaginative connections. Boxall's reading of this 'unbound poetics' (2013: 158) is political: in the post-9/11 context, it offers an alternative to the defensive and self-protective expulsion of Baxter, in order to conserve the familial, and more broadly national, body. It speaks, rather, of an opening-up of subjectivity, which is based in an awareness of our common vulnerability to injury, and to the potential for radical otherness that resides within ourselves. *Saturday* thus reaches towards the kind of political vision offered by Judith Butler in *Precarious Life*; a call that we resist the urge to toughen the boundaries of the political body against harm and attack, and develop instead modes of governance that both maintain openness and recognise contingency: 'the dislocation from First World privilege, however temporary, offers a chance to imagine a world in which . . . violence might be minimized, in which an inevitable interdependency becomes acknowledged as the basis for global political community' (2004: xii). If the body politic is closely mapped on to the individual body throughout *Saturday* – a body that is repeatedly identified as being bound to its biological determinants – then here, briefly, is a different mood, that asks what it might look like to relinquish the containing frame, and to look at the unbounded view.

In the context of the medical humanities, Lily's 'unbound poetics' can lead in a different direction, speaking to debates on how the illness experience might be communicated and conveyed. In an influential article, Angela Woods has argued for a more critical approach to narrative, in a field which has seen a prolific deployment of the term. As I have outlined in the Introduction, narrative has been positioned in relation to the patient as central to the prioritisation of illness as subjective experience; it is, Woods notes, 'frequently promoted as the primary vehicle through which the ill person can express her changing sense of self and identity, explore new social roles and gain membership of new communities' (2011: 73). With the rise of narrative medicine, narrative has also been placed at the heart of clinical training: 'more recently, and more radically, "narrative competence" has come to be seen as the essential skill' for the medical or health practitioner (2011: 73). In the face of narrative's ubiquity, Woods calls for a more critically informed approach, centred first on questioning the equation between narrative and wellbeing; second, on the importance of non-narrative modes of representing the illness experience; and third, on narrative's embeddedness in Western, liberal, upper- and middle-class subjective norms (2011: 75–6). My reading of *Saturday* has already addressed narrative's problematic alliance with liberal and middle-class ideologies. Of particular interest for my purposes here is Woods's challenge to the primacy accorded to narrative for communicating illness experience; she indicates, as a key point of departure for a critical medical humanities, the recognition that 'language is not the only medium for communicating matters of medicine, health and illness' (2011: 76). In place of narrative, she turns instead to the aesthetic modes of metaphor, phenomenology and photography.[14]

Taking an explicitly medical humanities approach to *Saturday*, critic Catherine Belling has picked up on the lyrical, as opposed to the narrative, mode of literary discourse in the novel. Associating the narrative mode of literature with the forward momentum of plot – the steady trajectory of Perowne's progression through the day – Belling defines the lyric mode as an 'absorption in the present' that disrupts and 'evade[s] plot' (2012: 3). Belling identifies a number of lyrical episodes throughout *Saturday*: Perowne's listening to the jazz music at Theo's concert; during sex with his wife; playing squash; and during the operation on Baxter. For Belling, however, the importance of these moments is that they are distinguished not only from Baxter's neuropathology, but also from Lily's dementia. She thus avers:

> There is a fundamental difference . . . between Lily's and Baxter's confinement in the present and Perowne's escape to it: neither Lily nor Baxter is capable (as far as McEwan allows us to know) of recognising that position or reflecting on it. The lyric mode requires one not only to step out of the current of narrated time, but then, from such a position, to examine what it means. (2012: 4)

Belling's intervention into the medical humanities is particularly concerned with narrative medicine; reading Perowne's absorption in the present moment as a state of 'mindfulness' (2012: 3) that is no longer available to Baxter or Lily, because they are stranded permanently within the present tense, she argues that *Saturday* offers its readers instruction in the lyrical position, in stepping – momentarily and reflectively – outside narrative time. The implied reader is thus equated with Perowne's position as doctor, and *Saturday* is interpreted, in a familiar hermeneutic gesture, as a form of training manual – not in empathy this time, but in mindfulness.

In reading the lyrical dimension of *Saturday*, my focus is not on clinical training but on the communication of the illness experience. Laura Salisbury has recently taken up Woods's challenge to narrative as the privileged vehicle for representing illness, and while acknowledging its importance, she has cautioned against a move beyond or outside language, noting that it might . . . be important not to mistake narrative for language. For language, even as it might orientate itself towards the proposition-ality that subtends the very possibility of making a narrative, also consists of other modes of more explicitly embodied expressivity, of meaning-making. (2016: 456)

Drawing on the formal similarities between aphasia – another mode of neurological disturbance that renders the subject fundamentally other to herself – and modernist writing, Salisbury is attentive to the potential of 'disordered language' (2016: 450) for conveying the subjective experience of illness. Such experimental, avant-gardist literary modes not only contest the priority accorded in the medical humanities to realist, linear narrative structures, but also draw on the poetic as a mode of orientation that can 'prompt connections between linguistic elements that are not always straightforwardly propositional but can then also become available to conscious reflection' (2016: 456). Lily's parting words to Perowne exemplify what Salisbury refers to as a 'confusion of tongues' (2016: 458). Lily's mode of expressivity draws attention to language's materiality and its allusive quality provides Perowne with a vehicle for reflecting on his own, less conscious experience. Lily's unbound language offers a communication of neurological illness that captures its radical otherness, its different modal space, at the same time as refusing to place it entirely outside language and representation. As such, it represents a potential resource for exploring illness in a mode that does not assume its transparency and comprehensibility. In recalling his mother's words, Perowne thus does not seek to gain access to Lily's consciousness, which Alzheimer's has already rendered radically other. He accepts her different orientation to the world, drawing upon what he cannot understand or explain to open up an alternative, less restricted, mode of engagement and attention.

In the context of interdisciplinarity, debates about the role and function of narrative in relation to illness reflect unease about the ways in which mainstream medical humanities have reified narrative representation and defined it in limited and circumscribed ways; namely, as realist, linear and working towards closure. Under the guise of interdisciplinarity, medicine has colonised a selective version of literature, which is stripped of its historical, social, geographical and theoretical contexts. Woods's critique seeks to initiate a more critically informed debate around narrative, including why it has taken on such importance in the field. Yet, as Salisbury has indicated, it is important not to throw out the baby with the bathwater;

in moving to non-narrative modes of representation, Woods passes over those more experimental linguistic modes that tend towards the non-linear, the anti-realist, the open-ended. In moving forward, then, we need to expand our understanding of the possibilities of narrative, and to engage with the multiplicity of its forms. Gender theorist Lisa Diedrich has aptly asked of the medical humanities: 'Where are the stories of failure? Where are the stories not of consolation or of a compensatory imaginary that screens the real, but of dissolution and perhaps even a desire for dissolution?' (2007: 54). One response, emerging out of my reading of *Saturday,* is that such stories are there to be read, but that to do so is to read against the grain. In closing, I also suggest that it is illuminating to consider where, and how, the story of Perowne's desire for 'dissolution' is articulated. Critic Claire McKechnie has observed of Woods's turn to the non-narrative that, even in aesthetic modes which have no apparent narrative, the recipient will make meaning by using narrative: 'in order to be interpreted (indeed interpretable) the types of non-narrative representation and communication [Woods] discusses in fact require a narrative response' (2014: 2). This approach leads us back to the unfolding of Perowne's day, and the distinction between his positioning while he is with Lily – which is, in Diedrich's terms, one of 'consolation', and of a 'compensatory imaginary' – and his later harnessing of his mother's mental dissolution to make meaning of the music by which he is so carried away. Perowne's return to Lily's words makes provisional meaning of the non-narrative aesthetic mode of music; it does so in a creative, loose and open-ended manner, which is suggestive for developing a more expansive and flexible mode of narrative interdisciplinarity in the medical humanities.

Conclusion

The question of empathy is central to a reading of *Saturday* at a number of levels. Critical responses to the novel have typically centred on how much scope there is – in a free indirect narrative discourse, centred throughout on Perowne's perspective – for a questioning of, or critical distance from, his views. Thus, Alderson's critique of *Saturday* rests on feeling corralled into sympathy with Perowne's politics: the 'subtle ironisations' of his perspective are outweighed by the extent to which the novel 'impresses on its presumed liberal audience – probably anti-war, cultured and sceptical of the claims of genetics to explain human behaviour – the value and integrity of

Henry's rather different values' (2011: 225). To achieve this feat, Alderson points to McEwan's 'painstaking realism', which blurs the line between fact and fiction not only in setting the novel on a particular historical day, but also in McEwan's shadowing of a neurosurgeon, and in the use of his own home as the model for Perowne's (2011: 226). For critic Laura Marcus, on the other hand, a more sympathetic response to the novel is underpinned by a greater sense of its interpretative play; while Perowne carefully tracks and monitors his own thought processes throughout the narrative, he does not have access either to the political events that have intervened between the date of the novel's setting and the date of its publication, or to his own intertextual relations to *Mrs. Dalloway*, and – in the context of this chapter's focus – Matthew Arnold. For Marcus, the gap opened up between the reader's consciousness and that of Perowne – and, by extension, between Perowne's consciousness and that of McEwan – is indicative of a critical distance on McEwan's part from his own stated position on narrative empathy as an ethics of fiction. Distinguishing the work of the novel from McEwan's authorial persona in interviews and articles, Marcus thus avers: '[t]he novelist's imaginative entry into other minds can never obviate the fact that these minds are, ultimately, his or her own creation' (2009: 94). The question of whether we can, or should, read with or against the grain of McEwan's views on empathy thus itself becomes bound up with the question of whether we can, or should, read ourselves empathetically into Perowne's consciousness.

In line with the broader impetus of the monograph, this chapter seeks to reposition debates on empathy away from the individual consciousness – whether that of Perowne, McEwan, or the reader – and towards a more politicised account of empathy's effects; what it is that the work of empathy *does*. Although empathy is widely linked with visions of social transformation, I have argued that its alliance in *Saturday* with the discourses of popular science has produced a conservative narrative of hard-wired emotions that both reinforces and naturalises existing divisions and hierarchies. Genetic determinism is combined with Arnoldian liberalism to indicate that, in a biological age, ethical action does not reside in effecting change but in doing what one can to ameliorate the suffering of those who are, inescapably, at the bottom of the evolutionary-social scale.[15] The work of empathy is that of depoliticisation: the affective drama of individual confrontation subsumes broader structural questions, and a change in the emotional atmosphere replaces the urgent – and ongoing – political questions mobilised by the date on which the narrative is set. The family acts as a mediating force between individual and social: the family crisis of the Baxter invasion distracts us from the bigger picture, while the innate flow of feeling and understanding across and between the Perownes performs a normalising, and normative, function in the novel. We might usefully think back here to the discussion of Haddon's *The Curious Incident* in Chapter 1, in which the novel's harnessing of popular science debates on autism again acted to limit and contain its potential for social and political critique, so that the vision of a post-Thatcher landscape of social alienation was muted into background scenery. In Haddon, however, the ideological associations of the family unit are mobilised in a contrary direction to that taken by McEwan: where *Saturday* reifies the nuclear family as a model of social balance and harmony, Haddon's family unit is fractured and dispersed, and is significantly neither conserved nor repaired at the novel's close. Haddon does not provide a consoling narrative of familial understanding, but rather draws on the *dis*connection between Christopher and his mother, combined with the love between them, to reach towards a more radical notion of empathy as an openness to, and an accommodation of, difference and alterity.

My reading of *Saturday* does not, however, relinquish the transformative potential of empathy. I argued in Chapter 1 that an important aspect of the syndrome novel lies in its phenomenological exploration of the protagonist's interactions as an intentional agent with other intentional agents in the shared world that the novel constructs. For neo-phenomenologists, the pre-reflective is a central component of intersubjectivity, which is embedded in an embodied mind that is necessarily entangled within, and a unique centre of orientation upon, the world. In numerous passages of *Saturday*, but perhaps most notably in the extended sequence at the beginning of the novel that describes Perowne's gradual awakening and in the squash match that forms its narrative centrepiece, McEwan is orientated towards a distinctly phenomenological mode of description that conveys the marvellous complexity of our routine movements and interactions; the ways in which the embodied human consciousness engages with, shapes, and is shaped by, its everyday encounters.[16] Thrailkill has thus commented upon the novel's 'stitching motion', that sutures Perowne's mind to the world that he inhabits and moves continually inward and outward between the two, mimicking the work of perception (2011: 185). While this could be read as another instance of *Saturday*'s reparative impulse, it also has the effect of estrangement; of opening up to our attention the wonder and the mystery of who we are. Pressed further, this impulse works in the representation of Lily's Alzheimer's to ask how Perowne as intentional agent interacts with someone whose intentionality has been irreparably damaged by neurological disease. How, the novel asks, do we engage with those for whom the thread that stitches mind, body and world together has been frayed, if not cut through? I have indicated that Perowne's interpretation of Lily's disordered speech offers a glimpse into a radical form of empathy; one that is more open and mobile than elsewhere in the narrative, and that recognises otherness without seeking mastery or exclusion. Like Haddon's linguistic and visual experimentalism in relation to Christopher's autism, the lyrical and avant-garde poetics of Lily's conversation reaches towards a mode of expression that does not sentimentalise – Haddon evokes Christopher's fear and confusion in his journey across London, while McEwan conveys the sense of a self that has lost its bearings and for whom the centre no longer holds – but that equally refuses to place neurological difference outside language and representation.[17] In doing so, it renders the work of empathy – for Christopher's mother and for Perowne – as the recognition of a very different mode of orientation to the world.

This chapter has also focused on empathy and interdisciplinarity. *Saturday* has spoken to the limitations of our contemporary modes of imagining interdisciplinary conversation. The 'two cultures' debates have not only exposed the difficulties of moving beyond disciplinary partisanship, but have also been mired in a politics of class that continues to reverberate through McEwan's novel. The 'third culture' movement, with which McEwan aligns himself, represents a more disciplinary than truly collaborative impulse, reifying the biological and assessing other disciplines only as they interact with, and contribute to, its advancement. In closing, I turn to an alternative model of interdisciplinarity that is currently being articulated in the medical humanities. For Patricia Waugh, just as the biomedical sciences are being transformed from the conceptual models of molecular biology and genetics, which conceived of life as a predetermined script, into the post-genomic understanding of 'the network, as a complex process of entanglement' (2016: 154), so too is interdisciplinarity shifting and being re-imagined. Gravitating towards the model of the network, new modes of interdisciplinarity are challenging the idea of 'pre-packaged individual disciplines retaining and contributing their particular strengths in constrained and appropriate spaces and simply reframing epistemic objects already securely positioned in other specific disciplines' (2016: 155). More messy and more contingent than previous models have envisaged, such an interdisciplinary praxis is based in a belief that, as Des Fitzgerald and Felicity Callard outline, the 'concerns, objects, methods and preoccupations' of the medical sciences are not 'neatly separable or dissociable' from those of the humanities; they are, in fact, always already entangled (2016: 35). As such, the space of interdisciplinarity is neither one of overcoming difference, nor of integration; it is, rather, a vibrant and lively domain of 'animacies, vitalities and pathologies, which flow across different practices and preoccupations' (2016: 45).[18]

What, then, is the work that empathy might do in this new form of interdisciplinary working? The answer, I propose, is both conceptual and critical: empathy can itself be reconceived as a relational network, in which each element is affected by those other elements to which it is constitutively connected. Feminist theorist Elizabeth A. Wilson has begun to articulate what such a vision of empathy might look like: harnessing 'the entanglement of biochemistry, affectivity, and the physiology of the internal organs', she seeks to develop 'more vibrant' approaches to the human body, conceived precisely as a relational network connecting psyche and soma, psychology and biology, nature and culture (2004: 14).[19] Pedwell has built on Wilson to argue that the neural and biological flows and circuits, which shape and influence our affects and emotions, can themselves be shaped by 'repeated historical encounters and experiences of privileging and exclusion' (2014: 172). Empathy, then, emerges as at once biological, cultural and historical; it can also speak, through the circuitry that it follows, of embedded and embodied relations of power. Importantly, this feminist (re)thinking of an alliance with neurology does not entail that neural coding and circuits are fixed and predetermined, and so – as with popular science – naturalise existing social and political inequalities. Rather, it articulates the complex ways in which history and biology can interconnect to produce material affects, at the same time as retaining a commitment to the possibility of re-routing established circuits and flows. Here, then, empathy is, in Pedwell's terms, 'both "biological" *and* amenable to modification' (2014: 177; italics in original). If such a politics can be glimpsed in McEwan, it is in the momentary exaltation of Perowne at Theo's jazz concert; a different kind of flow or circuitry fleetingly enters the horizon of possibility, even if it is quickly closed down. In the remaining two chapters, I accordingly propose to hold open the critical potential of empathy as network, asking how it might intervene into, and potentially transform, the structural and political hierarchies and exclusions in our globalised, capitalist and neoliberalist times.

Notes

1. The question of what fiction can tell us about emotional distance and a lack of care will be the focus of Chapter 5, which examines the relation between empathy and capitalism through a reading of Kazuo Ishiguro's *Never Let Me Go*.

2. In addition to McEwan, contemporary novelists as various as A. S. Byatt, David Lodge, Zadie Smith and Graham Swift have all engaged in different ways with popular science in their writings. For critic Emily Horton, this trend in contemporary fiction 'reflect[s] a new cultural outlook, creatively reimagining the modern and postmodern ideas of truth and progress, while at the same time learning from these' (2014: 684). My own account of the intersection of literature with medicine in contemporary fiction focuses on empathy as the primary vehicle for reimagining questions of ethics, governance, distance and difference.

3. This date marked a co-ordinated campaign of demonstrations in opposition to the imminent invasion of Iraq in over 600 cities across the world, with Rome hosting the largest anti-war rally. The London demonstration is probably the largest protest march to date in British history.

4. Secretary of State for Culture, Media and Sport, Tessa Jowell, vetoed the use of Hyde Park for the rally on the grounds of safety. This decision was overturned by 5 February 2003. As I will argue, the Hyde Park venue has particular resonance with the figure of Matthew Arnold.

5. The description of Perowne's first encounter with his wife, in which he fell in love at once and inextricably both with her and with neurosurgery, seems particularly resonant in this context in its unexpected entanglement of science and affect or emotion.

6. Perowne is aligned with music not only through his musician son, Theo, but also by his habit of listening to music, and particularly J. S. Bach's *Goldberg Variations* (1741) while he is in the operating theatre.

7. Patricia Waugh notes of Snow's subsequent career:

   > Five years later, Harold Wilson acceded to office as Prime Minister of Great Britain with a commitment to a new scientifically planned culture. Snow was now given a prominent place in a government ostentatiously committed to an ethos of no-nonsense social rationalisation. (1997: 145)

   In spite of having no previous ministerial experience, Snow held a position in the newly formed Ministry of Technology. Snow's use of the term 'Luddite' to dismiss the literary intellectuals was picked up in the title of F. R. Leavis's 1966 response, 'Luddites? Or, There Is Only One Culture' (Leavis 1972a).

8. Moran discusses in this context a backlash against interdisciplinarity that is emerging in some quarters, based not only on whether the work

that it produces can, without a clear rationale, tend towards a 'vague, bland eclecticism', but more particularly on concerns that it 'can easily be appropriated in pursuit of the market-oriented university's aims', so that 'merging departments into interdisciplinary programmes can be a form of downsizing and cost-cutting' (2010: 170, 166).

9. Home Secretary Spencer Walpole (1839–1907) subsequently resigned over the issue of free speech in Hyde Park, and the Reform League campaign resulted in the 1867 Reform Act which gave representatives of the working class the vote for the first time.

10. At various key points in *Saturday*, Perowne's vision is either framed by windows or focused and restricted by medical technology and equipment. The cover image of the novel directs us to Perowne's typical vantage point, which is not only behind a window but also at an elevation above the scene observed.

11. The volume included a Foreword by E. O. Wilson, and McEwan was the only novelist included within the collection, thereby giving his contribution particular prominence, especially as the collection was published in the same year as *Saturday*.

12. Postcolonial and gender criticism of trauma theory has pointed out that the punctual model of trauma fails to recognise, and can potentially efface, structural and institutional modes of violence; see, for example, Stef Craps (2013) and Ann Cvetkovich (2003). Horton has also considered McEwan's fiction alongside that of Martin Amis and Philip Pullman as an example of New Atheist writing, and asked whether his celebration of popular science can be read 'as a . . . justification for condemning faith' (2014: 708).

13. Dancer's reading offers a version of the novel that seems closer to Barker's narrative technique of juxtaposing different narrative perspectives as a mode of critique. However, this approach is limited in *Saturday*, both because Perowne is always the narrative focaliser, and because the contrasting viewpoint is – like that of Daisy discussed earlier – from another member of the Perowne family.

14. Woods points to phenomenology as 'a way of grasping the transformations – subtle and profound – to embodiment and "unworldedness" in illness' (2011: 76). Her wording resonates with Matthew Ratcliffe's phenomenologically informed account of radical empathy.

15. For a counter-position that defends evolutionary criticism and its potential, see Jonathan Kramnick (2012).

16. For a suggestive article on the potential of wonder for the medical humanities that might further illuminate these passages, see Martyn Evans (2016).

17. It is striking in this context that even as Haddon evokes mathematics and McEwan music as a means to convey neurological difference, both combine this with a more experimental linguistic mode.

18. As with the 'two cultures' mode of interdisciplinarity, it should be noted that this model will of necessity be operating within, and challenged by, the material and political structures of the university, and higher education policies and initiatives more broadly, which tend towards an intensely competitive and highly defensive research environment.
19. Wilson has usefully extended this project in her subsequent publication, *Gut Feminism* (2015).

Chapter 4

Empathy and the Geopolitical

Introduction

In Chapter 3, I examined the ways in which, during the geopolitical upheaval of 9/11 and its aftermath, fiction could be mobilised to shore up the familiar world order, harnessing a liberal version of empathy to reinforce the status quo. It is only in reading Ian McEwan's *Saturday* against the grain that the potential for a different, more open aesthetic can emerge. This chapter turns to a novel that stages the relation between medicine and empathy in the context of the mobility and cosmopolitanism of people and cultures under contemporary global capitalism: Aminatta Forna's *The Memory of Love* (2010) portrays the journey of British psychologist Adrian Lockheart to Sierra Leone, in the aftermath of the civil war (1991–2002). Forna focuses less on whether we can or should understand others empathetically, than on how our affective interactions are necessarily embedded in, and inflected by, structural and material relations of power. In the Introduction, I noted that, when mainstream medical humanities has engaged with globalisation, it has tended to reproduce a binary conceptual model of the 'West' and 'the rest'. This chapter aims to articulate the more complex entanglements that characterise contemporary globalised movements, which can more productively – and more critically – be addressed through the vocabulary of transnational networks and encounters. Twenty-first-century identities and subject positions are typically mobile, hybrid and migratory, although not in the mode of postmodern play; rather, in the wake of 9/11 and the subsequent economic crises, fiction's challenge is to reflect (on) a new scepticism about the promise of global community. Forna's writing both emerges out of and exemplifies a new wave of fiction that examines and holds up to view the fractures and tensions in the idea of globalisation, not least its uneven distribution of material, cultural, and – of particular interest for my purposes – medical resource.[1] Empathy emerges in this context as an affect that typically follows the paths already traced out by the circuits of economic and political privilege. At the same time, however, it is not entirely exhausted in and through such trajectories, but can potentially be re-routed by the affective openings that are created by transnational migration and mobility (Pedwell 2014).

Peter Boxall has identified as particularly distinctive of twenty-first-century world fiction the emergence of authors whose 'hyphenated identities' speak of 'postnational . . . subject positions' (2013: 168). Forna typifies this trend, with a Scottish mother and a Sierra-Leonean father; born in Scotland, and currently living in Britain, Forna grew up travelling between Britain and Sierra Leone, as well as spending time in Iran, Thailand and Zambia. Boxall observes that, for writers with hybrid identities, fiction often 'derives its energy from the failure of its various historical components fully to cohere' (2013: 174). Critic Zoe Norridge has tellingly remarked of Forna's writing that it 'seems to reflect a split experienced by Forna herself: the negotiation of British privilege in tension with a desire to remain committed to Sierra Leone' (2013: 176); it is not, then, simply that different cultures and identities fail to unite, but more particularly that this failure is grounded in the unequal relation between them. Often categorised as an African writer, Forna has resisted any straightforward classification of her work that would close down its complex hybridity; in interview, she has thus questioned: 'What makes you an African writer? I'm half Scottish' (Akbar 2010: no pagination). Her first book was *The Devil That Danced on the Water* (2002), an acclaimed memoir of her doctor-politician father, Mohamed Sorie Forna, which examined his execution for treason in 1975, under the dictatorship of Siaka Stevens. This was followed by two novels set in Sierra Leone: *Ancestor Stones* (2006) and *The Memory of Love* (2010). *The Hired Man* (2013) is set in Croatia and deals with the betrayals and complicities that play out in communities in the aftermath of civil war. Forna's writing thus uncovers and analyses the complex global forces that bring different peoples and histories into contact.

More than this, Forna is particularly interested in civil war as a lens to think critically about the connections and tensions in the global imaginary. Moving her third novel to the setting of Croatia enabled Forna to open up questions for the reader about the similarities and differences between two more-or-less contemporaneous conflicts: the Croatian war (1991–5) and the civil war in Sierra Leone

(1991–2002). Resonating across the two wars are the atmosphere of fear and suspicion that Forna so powerfully diagnosed in the memoir of her father, and the silences that linger in their aftermaths. Distinguishing them from one another is the ethnic killing that characterised the war in Croatia, making it more comparable in many ways to the Rwandan civil war (1990–4), and the weapons used: if the rebel army in Sierra Leone used machetes to sever hands and limbs, Croatia was a snipers' war. Forna thus observes: 'We were a nation of farmers and they were a nation of hunters. When people go to war they pick up the first thing to hand, be it a machete or a rifle' (2015: no pagination). Importantly for our purposes, the nature of post-war investment and rebuilding also differed across the two nations: Croatia's European links were strengthened by its creation as a holiday and tourist destination, while the hotels built in Sierra Leone catered for United Nations aid workers and Non-Governmental Organisation taskforces.[2] Forna acts to complicate Euro-American perceptions of African conflicts, exposing some of the assumptions that are often in place; by addressing the commonalities of civil war, she works against an 'othering' of the African experience. Significantly, Forna does so by pointing to the 'West' as an ideological concept that fails to recognise the internal heterogeneity of Europe, and that needs to register the parallels, as well as the differences, between Europe and Africa. She maps out an alternative cartography to 'the West' and 'the rest', which is based on a complex and uneven relationality.

In reading Forna's civil-war fictions, Norridge has harnessed the concept of empathy to humanitarian, peace-building agendas. Attending to Forna's detailed characterisation, Norridge argues that this technique 'leads to an empathetic identification – a *feeling with* – the character' (2014: 103). In *The Memory of Love*, such feeling is attached to the character of Elias Cole, a dying man who is being treated by Adrian in the Freetown hospital to which he has been posted, and who is eventually revealed to have been morally complicit with the repressive regime in Sierra Leone. Forna's deployment of this technique is heightened and intensified in *The Hired Man*, a novel in which the protagonist shades from complicity to perpetration: he has been involved in killing enemy soldiers and he approves the 'cleansing' of Serbs from his nearest town. For Norridge, the gradual unfolding of character gives rise to complex feelings in the reader, which undercut expectations of moral clarity, and that are 'essential for rehumanising peace-building processes' (2014: 103). In one sense, Norridge's reading takes us back to my discussion of slow reading in Chapter 2; a mode of narration that deliberately makes us take our time, and that suspends quick or easy moral judgements. However, if my discussion of such a hermeneutics focused on its resistance to social utility, Norridge's argument reinforces the idea of fiction as training manual: we are instructed in how to respond appropriately to offences committed during civil conflict.

My reading of *The Memory of Love* turns to an alternative model of empathy that takes into account the necessary imbrication of the knowledge gained through empathy in location and embodiment; we cannot separate feeling from structural and material relations of power. In order to elaborate on what I mean by this, I turn first to feminist theoretical physicist Karen Barad, who has produced an influential analysis for thinking about how observation cannot be independent, but is necessarily composed of a specific, materialised relationship. Speaking of the scientific experiment, Barad calls in to question the idea that the world is populated by individual things or entities with their own independent properties.[3] Rather, she notes:

> there is something fundamental about the nature of measurement interactions such that, given a particular measuring apparatus, certain properties *become determinate*, while others are specifically excluded. Which properties become determinate is not governed by the desires or will of the experimenter but rather by the specificity of the experimental apparatus. . . . Significantly, different qualities become determinate using different apparatuses, and it is not possible to have a situation in which all qualities will have definite values at once – some are always excluded. (2007: 19–20; italics in original)

It follows from this that we need to attend more closely to the experimental apparatus; the complex material and discursive conditions that interact to determine who or what comes to matter, and who or what becomes excluded. Barad evocatively describes the apparatus as:

> a complex network of human and nonhuman agents, including historically specific sets of material conditions that exceed the traditional notion of the individual. Or perhaps it is less that there is an assemblage of agents than there is an entangled state of agencies. (2007: 23)

Extrapolating out from Barad's model, Carolyn Pedwell has noted that: 'the discursive-material "apparatus" . . . through which emotion is produced *matters* to the specific ways in which it is materialised and felt' (2014: 121; italics in original). The question of empathy thus becomes an examination of the structural, discursive and material conditions that underpin emotional relationships, and that play a critical role in how we affect, and are affected by, one another. Barad's description of an 'entangled state of agencies' also acts as a reminder that feeling does not only flow between one person and another, but engages a range of agencies that might, in Pedwell's terms, be 'human or non-human, animate or inanimate, material or conceptual' (2014: 128).

Another important implication of Barad's thinking is that subjects are not fixed in advance of the experiment; knowledge-making practices, including empathy, are 'material enactments that contribute to, and are a part of, the phenomena we describe' (2007: 32). Subjects, then, emerge through their interactions; they do not exist as individual elements but are materialised only in their entanglement with each other. To explain the implications of this approach for understanding emotion, I turn now to Sara Ahmed. Working against the notion that emotions are entities that we 'have', Ahmed argues that it is precisely through our emotions, how we interact with and respond to others and to objects, that we are given any definition at all: 'emotions create the very effect of the surfaces and boundaries that allow us to distinguish an inside and an outside in the first place' (2004: 10). Such responses are typically shaped by the repetition of norms, which act to materialise bodies and worlds along the lines of existing power relations; we thus act and react by repeating previous parallel encounters. If we are shaped and moulded in and through our relationality, it also follows, however, that contact with new objects, ideas and others can reshape the surfaces of individual and collective bodies. While bearing in mind Lauren Berlant's caution that changes in feeling do not equate to a changed world, Ahmed nevertheless articulates a commitment to the relation between emotion and the potential for change. Such transformative possibility is predicated not in the pre-existing subject, who already knows what she wants or expects, but in the unexpected and unforeseen encounter, that can move us forward in different ways, and open up surprising new directions. Returning to Barad, a shift in the entangled network of agencies can change what becomes determinate, and what is excluded; it can produce an affective shift that is at the same time also material, structural, and political.

Emotion is not, for Ahmed, 'inside' the subject or the social; the circulation of affect allows different objects or bodies to take shape for us (2004: 10). Central to her work, then, is not only a focus on surfaces and boundaries – both personal and cultural – but also on the effects of emotion rendered precisely as a mode of movement or mobility. Ahmed thus avers:

> Emotions after all are moving, even if they do not simply move between us . . . Of course, emotions are not only about movement, they are also about attachments or what connects us to this or that. The relationship between movement and attachment is instructive. (2004: 11)

Here, then, movement reinforces the situational and material embeddedness of our affective relations, connecting bodies to other bodies; while attachment is conceived of as movement that has become stuck, emotionally invested in a particular body or idea. We can thus productively attend to how feelings circulate, and where they stick, within and across cultures. What particular attractions and/or tensions cause the sticking points? How do the literal movements of travel or migration map on to the circuits of affect? In reading Forna, I am interested to bring her narrative interest in the physical mobility produced by the globalised economy into dialogue with the idea of empathy as affective movement, to address how feeling might both replicate the structural and historical legacies of colonialism and civil war, and produce the possibilities for new and different kinds of attachments.

In bringing together the physical migrations of contemporary geopolitics and the affective circulation of empathy, I will structure this chapter around the conceptual vocabulary of movement. The first section examines the geographical mobility produced by medical migration; that is, the relocation of skilled healthcare professionals to work in a country that is different from their place of origin and/ or where they trained. I analyse current debates about the relation of medical migration to inequalities in world health, and I ask how Forna's representation of medical migration in *The Memory of Love* speaks to such discussions. In tracing the circuits by and through which medical resource – including, but not limited to, trained professionals – is distributed, this section identifies a material-discursive apparatus of entangled agencies, which underpins how the characters affect, and are affected by, one another in the course of the novel. The detailed attention that Forna pays to the uneven global economics of medical resource ensures that the question of empathy is grounded in an awareness of the structural and material effects of power. The second section moves on to the question of emotion, or of being moved. Here, I use Adrian as a focus to ask how affect circulates in the novel;

to whom or what does it attach, and what are the tensions or sticking points? How do these map on to the circulation of medical resource analysed in the first chapter section? My analysis draws on literary critic Joseph R. Slaughter's reading of humanitarian narratives as a form of enchantment, to analyse the significance of Adrian's empathetic misrecognition in his treatments of Elias Cole and Agnes – the latter, his most elusive and enigmatic patient in Sierra Leone. The final section turns to the question of moving on, or moving forward, asking what possibility of transformation or change is offered by the novel. Pedwell's reading of *The Memory of Love* has placed the affective relationship between Adrian and Sierra-Leonean doctor Kai Manderley as central to this question. Drawing out the significance of the novel's double time frame, set both in the post-civil-war Freetown of today and in the decolonisation period of 1969, I also turn to the charismatic figure of Julius Kamara – who is closely modelled on Forna's own father – to think about the legacy of his political activism, and whether the unfulfilled promise of the past can help to shape the politics of the future. I draw upon Ahmed's analysis of how feeling can materialise as a sense of being impressed upon by others, to articulate how attachment can work to reshape our bodies, and to create new impressions and affiliations.

Medical migrations

Sociologist Hannah Bradby (2016) has recently observed that, in twenty-first-century Britain, we are accustomed to the idea that healthcare professionals trained elsewhere are employed by the National Health Service, and that this has historically been the case since its foundation in 1948. Drawing on imperial routes of education and migration, whereby trained doctors and nurses were dispatched to colonial territories to establish medical schools and curricula in the language of the colonial power, Britain was able to access a reserve work force to compensate for labour shortages. In the wake of the catastrophic impact of the human immunodeficiency virus epidemic in sub-Saharan Africa, however, concerns were raised by the World Health Organization (WHO) that such economic migration was leaving the healthcare workers' countries of origin vulnerable to poor health outcomes and low life expectancy. A causal link was made between the migration of skilled professionals and declining health statistics in sub-Saharan Africa, and this narrative gained considerable purchase in the media. Its attraction can be explained in part, Bradby notes, because it acts as 'a powerful symbol of gross global inequity . . . of sub-Saharan Africa's suffering at the rich world's expense' (2016: 495). In spite of its narrative appeal, however, Bradby observes several problems with the argument: it relies on a generalisation about sub-Saharan Africa that fails to register variation across the healthcare systems of different countries; it assumes that the motivation for migration is solely economic, and ignores other aspirations; and it medicalises an issue that is political and socioeconomic in origin (2016: 495, 497).

In addressing the declining health outcomes in Africa, the focus on the 'brain drain' caused by medical migration resulted in initiatives that sought to redirect the flow of labour. Parvati Raghuram has noted of the policies that resulted:

> [T]he Code of Practice on recruitment of international medical workers adopted by the UK in 2004 . . . encourages recruitment agencies to sign up to a voluntary code of practice that restricts direct recruitment from states with critical shortages in medical workers. However, mechanisms such as ethical recruitment guidelines (Department of Health, 2001) are a blunt instrument because they appear to threaten individuals' human rights to freedom of movement . . . especially if they are not supplemented by much stronger commitments to generate benefits for countries of origin. The introduction of such regulation may simply provide a veneer of responsibility with little effects. (2009: 28)[4]

More than this, Bradby observes that the 'plumbing' model of global healthcare renders the work force a human-resource commodity that can be redirected at will, and with the assumption that 'altering the location does not affect the quality of service provided'; it is, in other words, premised on a neoliberal faith in 'perfect human capital transferability' (2016: 498).

For Bradby, narratives of a global health labour crisis overlook, and even potentially erase, the relation of both medical migration and declining health outcomes to specific socioeconomic conditions, which have an identifiable political origin. In the global debt crisis of the late 1970s, African countries – including Sierra Leone – entered into structural adjustment agreements with the World Bank and the International Monetary Fund (IMF) that required them to prioritise export currency at the expense of investment in the health and education sectors. The effects of this economic programme were felt in the 1980s and 1990s as the public health sector shrank, leading to 'the emigration of health professionals from rural to urban settings, from public service to private sector jobs, and abroad to better-paid opportunities' (Bradby 2016: 497). This was combined with, and exacerbated by, underinvestment in equipment, training and buildings. The loss of resource across the health and education sectors impacted on health statistics, especially among the most vulnerable populations. It is not, then, that medical migration is causing declining health; rather, both can be seen politically as 'outcomes of the same "brute neoliberalism"' (2016: 497). This distinction matters not only in terms of healthcare policy, but also in relation to responsibility or accountability; the medical migration explanation places the moral burden of health in African nations on healthcare professionals who have left their countries of origin, rather than on the underlying socioeconomic factors.

Although Forna does not engage explicitly in this debate, the mode of detailed realism that she engages in *The Memory of Love* documents the effects of a sustained and systematic underinvestment in the healthcare services of Sierra Leone. The Freetown hospital at which Adrian and Kai both work thus becomes much more than a setting for their interactions; it exposes a lack of even the most basic equipment and material resource. Forna's 'Acknowledgements' reveal that her research for the novel involved observations at the Kissy Mental Hospital, Freetown, and on the orthopaedic surgery ward of the Emergency Medical Hospital, Goderich. While this practice links back to McEwan's shadowing of a neurosurgeon in preparation for writing *Saturday*, there seems to be a more political edge to Forna's background research; it gives weight and authority to representations of deprived medical resource that might seem exaggerated and unbelievable to a Euro-American readership. In this section, I focus on Forna's representation of a range of Sierra-Leonean healthcare workers: Kai as orthopaedic surgeon; Doctor Attila as director of a mental-health hospital on the outskirts of Freetown; and Doctor Bangura, a researcher into Lassa fever, who had a significant impact on Kai when he met him during his medical training. Forna leaves us in no doubt about the international significance of the work that each of these men perform; she also portrays a resourcefulness and agency in the face of a chronic lack of medical supplies. For all of these men, eminent in their respective fields, the question of medical migration has emerged, and Forna stages their response in a mode that reveals both that the effects of underinvestment provide a strong motivation for moving away, and that the decision is often motivated by a complex and contradictory combination of factors.

Kai's work as an orthopaedic surgeon in Freetown is framed by his letters to his childhood friend Tejani, who has migrated to work in America and encourages Kai to join him there. The question of medical migration lingers for Kai throughout the narrative, returning to his thoughts as he gradually comes to a decision. *The Memory of Love* is framed by two powerful scenes of death in childbirth: the first a stillborn baby witnessed by Adrian from his window, the second the death of his own lover Mamakay in giving birth to their daughter. These act as a reminder that, even in peacetime, mortality rates are high in Sierra Leone and medical treatment does not have the same chance of success as in Britain; indeed, Adrian berates himself for remaining in Freetown for the birth: 'if he had taken [Mamakay] away from here, back to England – she would be alive, too' (2010: 422). Kai worked as a surgeon at the Freetown hospital throughout the civil war, and dealt with the worst of its atrocities. Confronted by large numbers of amputees, the first priority was to save lives where he could, operating a triage system to select those with the most chance of making it through surgery. After this, the task was to carry out surgical interventions that would restore basic function. The operations that Kai performs make possible actions that are simple, but essential for an independent life: 'a man once again able to hold his own penis when he pissed, a mother place her nipple into her child's mouth' (2010: 121). They are also inventive, turning to techniques not practised since the First World War to fashion a hand out of the muscles and bones of the wrist. Such innovation extends not only to surgical technique, but also to an improvisation with materials: 'making do with whatever instruments were available, even kitchen utensils' (2010: 92). Forna makes clear that material shortages are not simply a consequence of the civil war; they extend into the post-war period, and result from a chronic lack of funding and investment. Somewhat paradoxically, then, Kai himself represents a highly desirable and exportable commodity in the labour marketplace. His extensive experience with amputations has placed him ahead of young orthopaedic specialists anywhere else in the world, and he would have no difficulty in joining Tejani in America, should he choose to follow him there. In the end, Kai decides to remain in Sierra Leone in a gesture of commitment to the future of the country that is at once affective, political and social; economic consideration is not, in other words, the only motivation in weighing up the question of migration. Further, Tejani writes to tell Kai that he will shortly be returning home from America; for Forna, leaving Sierra Leone is not a one-way ticket, and medical migration can bring back into the country valuable skills, knowledge and expertise that could not otherwise be gained.

The Freetown hospital at which Kai works is paired with Attila's psychiatric hospital on the outskirts of the city. In both cases, Forna contrasts the conditions of work and treatment against the expectations of her Western readers, filtered through Adrian's responses. Due to a lack of resource, the hospital is reliant on sedating patients with behavioural problems and chaining drug addicts who are in withdrawal. Touring the ward, Adrian expresses shock at these treatment methods, only to be given a lesson in economics: it would cost 2 million dollars to cover the infrastructure, staff and training required if the restraining methods were to be removed. Attila has a formidable international reputation through his published work. Trained abroad, he returned to Sierra Leone in the 1980s, when 'the country was being run into the ground' (2010: 85) and many overseas workers were leaving and being replaced by Africans. Taking on the directorship of the hospital at an early age, he quickly gained respect and authority, and during the civil war used the asylum to provide a refuge for peace-workers and members of the population vulnerable to the rebels. Attila's psychiatric work afforded him advance warning of the effects of the socioeconomic policies in Sierra Leone that presaged the civil war to come: 'Hundreds, thousands of young men, high on drugs and very, very angry. No jobs. No families. No futures. Nothing to lose' (2010: 86). Here, then, Forna indicates that the violence of the civil war was preventable, precisely because it was rooted in social, economic and political conditions. Although Attila sounded a warning to the government of Sierra Leone, the international media and the WHO, he went unheeded.

In a conversation with Adrian, Attila underlines the politics of the global circulation of capital. Aid and resource is directed at those medical conditions that are of interest to the West, such as Adrian's specialism of Post-Traumatic Stress Disorder (PTSD), rather than at the social problems that underlie the conflict. Investment also follows those who import 'expertise' from the global north to the south, rather than those who have worked on the ground throughout the conflict and its aftermath. Driving Adrian to a shanty town, Attila tells him of a medical research team who visited Freetown for six weeks to survey the population, concluding that ninety per cent were suffering from PTSD, and recommending that 150,000 dollars be invested in further research. Through Attila's eyes, the institutions of world health represent a vast enterprise of self-generating income and activity that fails even to register, let alone to address, the actual conditions in which the majority of the population in Sierra Leone struggle to survive from day to day: 'You call it a disorder, my friend. We call it *life*' (2010: 319; italics in original). The most concrete and visible effects of the investment of capital in Freetown are the hotels that accommodate the incoming aid workers and medical personnel, further insulating them from the lives of their subjects: 'Western rates. Television. Minibar' (2010: 319). Across both physical and mental health, then, declining health outcomes in Sierra Leone are linked by Forna to the effects of a neoliberal economy that not only marks the present, but that also preceded, and arguably contributed to, the civil war.

Forna's representation of Doctor Bangura demonstrates that medical research, too, is chronically underfunded in Sierra Leone. Her 'Acknowledgements' reveal that Bangura is the only character in the novel who has been taken from life, based on 'the late Dr. Aniru Conteh, a specialist in [L]assa fever who in 2004 died of the disease he had spent his life combating' (2010: 447). Although world leading in his specialism, Bangura is researching into a disease that affects only rural populations in West Africa, and so is not of interest to the West; he has consequently failed to attract international funding for his work, and there is no internal resource to support him. Kai becomes fascinated with Bangura when he is a medical student, and travelling upcountry he finds him at work using the resources that he has to hand: 'handling samples of contaminated matter, wearing a snorkel and mask, and a pair of household rubber gloves' (2010: 94). Finding himself in the same area some years later, Kai enquires after the doctor, only to be told that he has died: 'Not the war, a pinprick to his finger. He was infected by the disease he's been researching' (2010: 303). Bangura has died in agony, because he had no capital or resources; he worked with a single assistant beneath a 'lone, insect-spotted forty watt bulb' (2010: 94). We might instructively compare Bangura's infection through the torn glove with Pat Barker's deployment of the same image in *Life Class*, discussed in Chapter 2. Where Barker used the image to signify that Paul Tarrant's frontline nursing experience had not (yet) rendered him invulnerable to feeling, Forna centres on the household rubber glove that has been made to substitute for more adequate protection. Here, the glove symbolises the uneven economies of global medical institutions, which are revealed to lie at the source of Bangura's infection and subsequent death.

A sombre postscript to Forna's representation of Bangura emerges in the Ebola outbreak that affected a number of countries across West Africa, including Sierra Leone, in 2014. Writing in the *Guardian*, Forna addressed the crisis by engaging with different aspects of mobility. Discussing a conversation with her mother about whether she should visit her in Freetown, Forna remarks that the decision is probably an academic one, because British Airways have cancelled all flights to Sierra Leone until the end of the month, in spite of criticism by the WHO that there was no reason to do so, and that it meant that health workers could not get into the country. At the same time as movement into Sierra Leone is arrested, so too are there attempts to prevent movement out of the country. Forna notes: 'In the U.S., Donald Trump tweeted that American Ebola victims should not be brought home' (2014: no pagination). Having traced the (proposed) obstructions to physical movement, Forna goes on to address the movement of global capital, in terms of investment in medical research and resource. Looking back to *The Memory of Love*, Forna observes:

> Some years ago I met the Sierra Leonean expert in haemorrhagic fevers, Dr. Aniru Conteh, who headed the country's Lassa fever research unit. He had struggled on with his work for years despite a lack of proper equipment – reportedly at one point using a snorkel and mask while handling samples. He died after being accidentally contaminated by a patient.
>
> His successor, Dr. Sheik Umar Khan, spearheaded initial efforts to combat the Ebola outbreak. He too died in the line of duty, as did most members of his unit: researchers, nurses, and even a driver. (2014: no pagination)

Forna's point is about media coverage; poor understanding of the nature of Ebola is leading to an overreaction in the West that compounds the crisis, while the efforts of Sierra-Leonean medical teams to save lives go unremarked. Lacking sufficient resource, these efforts too often result in infection and death, although these fatalities are not the ones that make the news headlines.

Discussion of the Ebola crisis in *The Lancet* drew attention to an unprecedented decision by the IMF to make funds available in order to help alleviate the situation. Alexander Kentikelenis et al. thus observe: 'the [IMF] has announced US$430 million of funding to fight Ebola in Sierra Leone, Guinea and Liberia. By making these funds available, the IMF aims to become part of the solution to the crisis' (2014: 69). Looking back to the structural adjustment agreements, however, the authors of the article question whether it was not rather the case that 'the IMF had contributed to the circumstances that enabled the crisis to arise in the first place' (2014: 69). In particular, they note, the required reduction in government spending absorbed funds that could be directed to major health challenges; the reduction of public sector employment eroded the number of trained healthcare professionals who could respond to the crisis; and the decentralisation of healthcare systems made co-ordinated, central responses to disease outbreaks difficult. Together, these factors produced a cumulative effect, 'contributing to the lack of preparedness of health systems to cope with infectious disease outbreaks and other emergencies' (2014: 70).[5] The article reinforces Bradby's argument that socioeconomic factors are an underlying cause of poor health outcomes in sub-Saharan Africa. In the context of Forna's writing, the Ebola crisis affirms the need to redirect attention in the West from the narrative of short-term crisis and catastrophe to the longer-term effects of systematic underinvestment in healthcare infrastructure and resource. In spanning the historical period from 1969 through to the 2000s, Forna conveys in *The Memory of Love* the slow, insidious and gradual collapse of the country's infrastructure, foregrounding the importance of a steady erosion of material, social and economic resource.

This section has highlighted Forna's careful documentation in *The Memory of Love* of the political and socioeconomic factors that gradually, and hardly noticeably, combine to weaken a nation, and that underpin the highly visible humanitarian emergencies of civil war and disease outbreak. Across three Sierra-Leonean doctors, working in very different fields of specialism, Forna provides a complex and varied picture of medical migration, and builds a powerful sense of how medicine carries on in spite of physical and material hardship. This is a portrait of resilience and creativity, but also of unnecessary fatality. The material-discursive apparatus of the novel comprises a network of agencies – institutional, human and conceptual – that produce PTSD as what matters in Sierra Leone, and that exclude the socioeconomic reality of the shanty town; a network within which Adrian is, as Attila indicates, inextricably entangled. In what follows, I focus on Adrian's interactions with Elias Cole, Agnes and Kai, to assess whether, and in what ways, they make a difference. In so doing, my attention is not on empathy as the relation between two individual entities, but rather on how affect moves, and where it sticks, within and across a complex network of human and non-human agencies; as such, my analysis builds on and extends my argument in Chapter 2 that empathy cannot be extricated from its material, structural and institutional settings. Norridge has aptly remarked of *The Memory of Love*: 'healing work is not an idealised gesture, removed from economic, political and social concerns, but is instead imbedded in a network of power relations' (2013: 177). Given the existing power dynamics that Adrian's feelings for others both enact and reinforce, what, I ask, if anything, does his presence in Sierra Leone actually achieve?

Humanitarianism as (dis)enchantment

Addressing the complex relationship between literary writing and human rights, critics Rachel Potter and Lyndsey Stonebridge have recently diagnosed empathy as something of a problem in the field. An unquestioned assumption that rights writing should produce empathy, and that empathy is in turn inherently good in terms of generating justice in human-rights relations, puts in place a model of escalation, whereby: '[m]ore and better writing both by and about more people produces more and better outcomes for those people' (2014: 4). Instead of seeing empathy as the solution to human-rights infringements, Potter and Stonebridge ask whether there might be other ways of connecting literature with the question of rights. Echoing Berlant's argument in Chapter 2 that fiction all too often depicts our refusal to connect with others, or to respond to their pain and suffering, Potter and Stonebridge likewise indicate that literature is particularly good at representing: 'ambivalence, contradiction and paradox; at pinpointing, often in uncomfortable ways, what it is that is so difficult about imagining others' (2014: 7). Taking a step back from the ethical response to the wound or injury opens up a more troubled, and more critical terrain, that is less about 'participating', through affect, in human-rights work, and more about probing the politics and ideology of human rights as a mode of action or intervention.

Taking up the idea of ambivalence, if not indifference, Joseph R. Slaughter has also challenged the centrality of empathy to human-rights literature. Typically, he argues, the notion of indifference enters human-rights discourse as a sign of the difference between those who suffer and require aid, and those who have the resource to help; the difference could, in this case, be 'moral, geographical, cultural, political, economic, religious, national, ethnic, sexual, gendered, racial, etc.' (2014: 50). The greater the perceived distance between the two parties, the more need there is for fiction to bridge the gap both imaginatively and affectively. Yet, for Slaughter, this is to misread the place of indifference in human-rights narratives, precisely through the liberal imagining of a singular, individualised relationship between 'victim' and 'saviour'. Rather, he suggests, most human-rights stories do not direct our imaginative identification towards the suffering other at all; typically, they 'invite us to empathise with the knight-errant, to share his enchanting vision of a disenchanted world' (2014: 51). Interposed between the reader and the suffering other, the humanitarian aid worker asks us to identify with her own motivations and impulses; we are directed, in other words, to 'identify with *people like us*' (2014: 52; italics in original). Further, such an act of identification directs us towards a moral vision that is aligned not with investment in a singular other, but with affective indifference: the primary commitment for the humanitarian worker is to 'a disinterested humanitarian ideal that everyone deserves assistance in times of need, regardless of subjective differences and circumstances' (2014: 58). The practical directives of humanitarian action, encoded in law, thus emphasise indifference to the social difference of the other: as long as there is demonstrable need, it is not necessary to know the precise socioeconomic and political circumstances within which an action takes place. For Slaughter, a commitment to individualism, to a singular imaginative identification, is incompatible with this disinterested humanitarian ideal, and our persistence in measuring humanitarian action in this way entails that '[f]ailure seems all but inevitable' (2014: 58); there is always going to be more suffering, more wounded, and more injured to rescue. Here, then, a tension can be discerned between the liberal ideal of helping the suffering individual and the humanitarian ideal of disinterested action.

For Slaughter, if the narrative form of contemporary human-rights literature resembles the chivalric quest genre, then it does so in an ironic mode.[6] Irony derives, at least in part, from the mismatch between the liberal sympathetic imagination and a humanitarian disinterest or indifference. Thus, the narrative decision to become a humanitarian actor is characteristically not one of moral gravity and resolution, but of a surprising ambivalence, even indecision. If need is everywhere, decision becomes inconsequential: when one injustice is as worthy of attention as another, it does not matter which way one turns, and individual choice becomes replaced by the whim of transnational agencies. The narrative trajectory of the contemporary aid worker is likewise reactive, and lacking in agency; an 'endless meandering, episodic story-form' (2014: 52). The liberal ideal is placed under pressure in these narratives, which often expose a crisis in the aid worker's sense of confidence and moral purpose; a lesson in disenchantment. The heroic narrative of righting wrongs becomes a less glamorous story in which: 'the "wench" may not be a damsel, may not be in distress, and may not, in the end, be rescued by a knight (who also is no knight)' (2014: 57). Typified by self-questioning, the contemporary humanitarian story is one in which the hero often makes matters worse, due to a misplaced imaginative identification: 'in the name of a disinterested dedication to justice, [the humanitarian actor] is too interested in the individuals he "saves". In other words, [he] misidentifies with the imagined injuries of others' (2014: 61). Imaginative empathy misses its mark, and the resulting dilemmas and misunderstandings offer a relation between rights and writing that is based not in liberal feeling, but in a more critical engagement with, and staging of, what contemporary humanitarian action means and does.

The Memory of Love can be seen to conform closely with Slaughter's analysis, although he does not mention the novel in his essay. Adrian is the main narrative focaliser, forming a point of identification that is 'like us', and that both filters and displaces attention in relation to the Sierra-Leonean characters. The ironic chivalric quest narrative is explicitly signalled through Kai's jaded condemnation of two female American aid workers; a judgement that also implicates Adrian, indicating that he is no simple or transparent vehicle for empathy:

> It was errantry that brought them here, flooding in through the gaping wound left by the war, lascivious in their eagerness. Kai had seen it in the feverish eyes of the women, the sweat on their upper lips, the smell of their breath as they pressed close to him. They came to sell their newspaper stories, to save black babies, to spread the word, to make money, to fuck black bodies. Modern-day knights, each after his own trophy, their very own Holy Grail. (2010: 218–19)

For Kai, as for Attila, those who come out to Sierra Leone in the aftermath of the civil war not only arrive on the scene too late, but are also infected by the fever of their own wants and desires, rather than acting from more selfless principles. Coming to the country for eighteen months or so, and then returning home, it is unclear what lasting legacy they leave behind. In Kai's eyes, Adrian is merely the most recent incarnation of these knights errant. As the narrative unfolds, we learn that Adrian, like those before him, does indeed return to Britain after a brief episode in Sierra Leone. To what extent, then, does Kai's assessment encapsulate Adrian's motivations and achievements? What interpretative weight should we accord to his words, in the broader context of the novel?

Adrian's decision to become an aid worker displays much of the passivity and ambivalence described by Slaughter. Confronted by a failing marriage and a feeling that 'the momentum of his career had dissipated' (2010: 66), Adrian accidentally chances upon an advertisement in a professional journal for a six-week posting in Sierra Leone, and applies on impulse. Initially unsuccessful, he is offered and accepts the job at the last minute, when the successful applicant is taken ill. Following the six-week placement, during which he enjoys a sense of camaraderie with the other volunteers, Adrian accepts a further posting, which takes him to the Freetown hospital. Adrian thus has a vague sense of career development, combined with a desire to remove himself from his present circumstances, but much of his 'decision' seems surprisingly non-momentous, lacking in agency or resolution. Adrian departs from Slaughter's model, however, in his particular commitment to Sierra Leone; although his wife, Lisa, cannot distinguish one civil-war emergency from another, confusing Sierra Leone with Sri Lanka, Adrian knows the difference between the two, because Sierra Leone is 'the country where his mother had nearly been born' (2010: 67). His quest, then, is less a chivalric journey to aid others in distress, than a self-quest for and about his own origins. In the light of Slaughter, this directs our attention to the knight errant rather than to the suffering other. It also enables Forna to map Adrian's journey onto a longer history of colonial migration. Adrian retraces his grandfather's journey as District Commissioner in Sierra Leone, and although his humanitarian venture at first seems far removed from his ancestor's colonial past, neocolonial elements soon come into view. Adrian's ready access to a Land Cruiser connects him to a network of socio-economic privilege that is not available to his Sierra-Leonean counterpart, Attila. The vehicle's 'cool and insulating effect' (2010: 164) reinforces Adrian's separation from the circumstances of those whom he claims to treat and understand, as well as his similarity to the team of medical researchers that Attila described, similarly cocooned in their luxury hotels. Yet, in spite of the self-interest at work in Adrian's decision, there is also a lingering whiff of liberal sentiment(alism). Tired of the fifty-minute appointment slot, and of acting as a service provider to his 'clients', Adrian seeks a more fulfilling, and a more traditional, relationship with those whom he treats. In Sierra Leone, he will treat 'patients' once more, who will queue patiently for his assistance (2010: 64). Unsurprisingly, Adrian is rapidly disillusioned of this enchanted view of humanitarian work on arrival in Freetown, as his initial referrals soon dry up, leading to the realisation that not only is he 'not helping', but that he may be getting in the way of those who can (2010: 64).

The Memory of Love begins with Adrian's treatment session of Elias Cole, who lies in a private room in the Freetown hospital. He speaks to Adrian in an extended first-person narration, which runs alongside and counterpoints the post-war narrative. Adrian's treatment of Elias, who has self-referred and speaks readily about the past, is contrasted with that of his other patients, who speak in a disengaged tone – if at all – of their lives and experiences. Elias's extended flashback opens up a longer history of Sierra Leone, which shifts to the late 1960s and captures the political idealism of the early period of independence; the optimism of a generation of Western-educated African intellectuals who had returned to help build a new Africa, and were keen to be at the forefront of social and cultural change. Central to this group is Julius, who is associated particularly with the moon landing, which symbolises his vision of new global possibility. Elias seeks to erase this unfulfilled history, which might have been realised had it not been for men like himself. His is a narrative of gradual complicity with repressive institutions; his role in Julius's arrest and subsequent death in custody is not one of direct responsibility, but of indirect implication. First, he complies with a request by the Dean of the university to complete a report that he knows will implicate Julius, and then he enters into an arrangement with the police chief to hand over his notebooks. Here, he has recorded that Julius is asthmatic, which leads in turn to the withholding of his medication and his death in the prison cell. Through Elias, Forna examines men – like those whom she interviewed in researching her father's death – who not only survived but thrived under repressive regimes. Elias eventually becomes a university Dean himself, and exemplifies those whose crime is one of inaction or omission.

The dying Elias decides to tell his story to one who is 'new here' (2010: 1). In the course of treatment, Adrian visits him regularly, watches his physical deterioration, and listens to his narrative unfold. Adrian understands his role to be that of a deathbed confessor, allowing Elias to gain a final peace; he describes himself to his lover, and Elias's daughter, Mamakay, as a 'priest, imam, counsellor or layman' (2010: 321). This is, however, a narrative of misplaced identification; Adrian has, in Slaughter's terms, become too interested in the man he seeks to 'save'. He is corrected by Mamakay, who makes clear that

Adrian's relationship with her father is not about Elias confronting his guilt, but concealing it all the more effectively:

> 'He's using it to write his own version of history, don't you see? And it's happening all over the country. People are blotting out what happened, fiddling with the truth, creating their own version of events to fill in the blanks. A version of the truth which puts them in a good light, that wipes out whatever they did or failed to do, and makes certain that none of them will be blamed. My father has you to help him.' (2010: 351)

Adrian records Elias's narrative in his medical notes, acting as a kind of scribe. Through Mamakay's eyes, his uncritical transcription of her father's version of events entails that he, too, is bound into a network of duplicity and deceit; his clinical notes form another layer of the history that is being collectively (re)written, and medical discourse is thereby rendered complicit with those who already occupy a position of advantage. Writing here is decidedly not a mode of righting; it speaks, rather, of the difficulties and the dangers of imaginative identification. In place of Norridge's emphasis on the reader 'feeling with' Elias, my reading focuses on Adrian, and indicates that his empathy for Elias misses the mark precisely because it is founded, not in a universal humanism, but in a material-discursive network of power relations. Adrian's receptiveness to Elias arises out of a class affinity between the two men: Elias is educated, professional and verbally articulate, and therefore identifiable for Adrian in ways that his other patients are not. Looking back to Ahmed, we can see Elias as a 'sticking point' in the flow of affect; he proves 'sticky' for Adrian, acting as a site of emotional investment, because of his familiarity, and this alliance of privilege becomes, in turn, a 'sticking point', or a site of contestation, between Adrian and Mamakay. Forna demonstrates that, in transnational encounters, class can act as a marker of difference that is as powerful as, if less visible than, race or gender. She is also attentive to the limitations of narrative as a vehicle for transformation; it too often works in the service of the powerful, and it occludes the value and importance of silence as a communicative medium.

Adrian's treatment of Elias can productively be compared to his encounters with Agnes. If Elias tells his story (too) easily, Agnes fails to voice what has happened to her, and she takes to its furthest extreme the elusiveness of Adrian's outpatients, as she continually slips out of view. In reading Adrian's treatment of Agnes, it is useful to recall Slaughter's observation that the modern-day knight often finds that he is not rescuing a damsel; that the damsel may not want to be saved; and that the knight may turn out not to be the rescuing hero after all. Agnes regularly disappears from her home, returning without any memory of where she has been, and Adrian diagnoses in her a case of fugue, which has been associated in Europe exclusively with male patients. As a unique case history, Agnes thus shifts – as Kai rightly identifies – from the damsel in distress of Adrian's chivalric tale, to its 'Holy Grail' (2010: 219). Adrian is correct in his diagnosis – Agnes is suffering from fugue states – but he proves unable to access the experience that lies behind the symptom; the life that it expresses. Agnes remains unable to speak of her past, and her story is related to Kai by the women of her community, each of whom relates the part that she knows. Kai learns that Agnes's daughter has unknowingly married the man who killed and beheaded Agnes's husband; she must now therefore live in the same house as her son-in-law without revealing his crime. Agnes's household acts as a powerful symbol for a nation recovering from civil war, in which former enemies have to live side by side, and Kai's response reveals his deep understanding of her predicament: 'the unbearable aftermath, the knowledge, and nothing to be done but endure it' (2010: 325). Kai reflects on Adrian's misunderstanding of Agnes's symptoms, interpreting her fugue states not as a means of escape but as an attempt to find something. As someone who has not been through civil war, Adrian cannot understand the precariousness of Agnes's situation; coming across her unexpectedly, he follows her home to offer his aid, but his knightly gesture goes badly wrong, putting Agnes's life at risk from her son-in-law. Notably, Agnes does not welcome Adrian's attempts at rescue, exemplifying Clare Hemmings's description of the unwilling object of compassion. If the flow of empathy invariably travels from those who occupy a position of privilege to those less fortunate, it may alter the privileged subject by 'expand[ing] her horizons', but it does little to change the life of its target (2011: 202). At the novel's close, Kai writes to Adrian to tell him the story behind Agnes's fugue states; he is given the 'Holy Grail' that will take his career forward.[7] Agnes herself, however, remains fixed in place, living out her intolerable life. It seems that the best she can do, in the circumstances, is to disappear repeatedly from view.

Adrian's treatments of Elias and Agnes reveal the limitations of empathetic understanding, which struggles to be other-directed, adhering to that which feels familiar, and failing to bridge a divide of experience that is marked by class and gender, as well as by war. Forna emphasises that empathetic feeling does not provide access to 'truth'; Elias's narrative turns out to be a dangerous fiction, while Agnes's story relies on Kai as intermediary. Yet, Adrian's treatment methods are not entirely without result during his time in Sierra Leone. The psychiatric patients involved in the group therapy that he practises at Attila's hospital show signs of progress. Most prominently, his treatment session with Kai at the close of the novel enables him to confront his own wartime experience; Kai is able afterwards to drive across the peninsula bridge that he has avoided throughout the narrative.[8] Adrian's treatment session uncovers Kai's memories of abduction by rebel forces; his refusal at gunpoint to rape his nurse, Balia; and the rape that he himself then undergoes. Taken by the rebels to the peninsula bridge, he and Balia are then shot, and Kai survives by jumping from the bridge into the water, using the nurse's body as a shield. Norridge is troubled by the treatment scene, indicating a transnational power dynamic whereby Kai's traumas 'are brought to light by the visiting foreigner-healer Adrian', with the implication that there is 'a need for outside assistance and the heightened therapeutic insights of the foreigner' (2013: 176). While I share Norridge's interest in the power relations at work in and through the medical, I argue that Forna frames Kai's treatment with narrative details that ameliorate an imbalance between the two men. Thus, the treatment session is requested by Kai, placing him in a position of agency. Kai's request is based not in a narrative desire to locate the 'truth' of what happened to him, which would support Norridge's criticism of Adrian's 'heightened . . . insight', but in the pragmatic desire to be able to perform operations without his hands shaking. The scene also mirrors an earlier episode during which Kai nurses Adrian through an attack of malarial fever; Adrian's treatment of Kai is thus positioned as a reciprocal act, which returns a kindness already received. Nevertheless, Kai's responsiveness to Adrian's treatment methods is indicative of his middle-class education and profession. Like Elias, Kai marks a site of attachment for Adrian because of a sense of social familiarity. The effectiveness of the treatment for Kai, in contrast to Agnes, thus acts as a reminder of Angela Woods's point, discussed in Chapter 3, that narrative, and the therapies that it underpins, is historically and geographically located in Western, middle-class norms.[9] If the treatment speaks of a power differential, I propose that this is less between Adrian and Kai, than between Kai and those patients who do not conform to the norms that the narrative cure both enshrines and perpetuates, and who are therefore excluded by a system that invests in them as a primary treatment method.

This section has focused on Adrian to ask how his affective journey maps on to existing routes of privilege and power. Even as Adrian retraces the colonial migration of his grandfather, so his feelings expose the cracks and fissures in contemporary transnational encounters. The 'sticking points' for Adrian are marked by Elias and Kai, as points of affective attachment, and by Agnes as a different site of investment; the key that can unlock Adrian's stalled career progression. Empathy thus circulates along established class and gender hierarchies, and reinforces the existing positionality of the characters. Yet, Adrian's feelings do not equate to knowledge or 'truth', and I have read Adrian's misidentifications in the light of Slaughter's analysis, arguing that they indicate the persistence of liberal sentiment in the form of a stubborn enchantment. The novel charts Adrian's gradual disenchantment, as he learns that his feeling for others is not only misplaced, but often actively unwanted or rejected. Forna's thick description of the historical, material and discursive networks that structure social, political and institutional life in Sierra Leone embed Adrian's knightly quest within a profoundly disenchanted world. His naivety is set against the cynicism of Attila and Kai, and the point is not so much to adjudicate between them, as to register the tension; a tension that is mobilised by Forna to reflect critically on the politics and ideology of humanitarian intervention; on the limitations of empathetic understanding; and on the fractures and fault lines that run through the idea of global community in the twenty-first century.

Moving forward

In the introduction to this chapter, I noted that emotions do not only move along familiar circuits, but also have the potential to be re-routed by the new affective possibilities created in and through transnational encounters. In this section, I accordingly address the question of whether, and how, emotions can move things forward in Sierra Leone. To what extent can empathy motivate or effect change? In one sense, as Pedwell has analysed, transformation is registered in and through Adrian himself, as he becomes more attuned to his new life and deepens his affective relationships with those around him, most notably Kai and Mamakay.[10] This interpretation takes us back to the phenomenological aspects of empathy discussed in Chapter 1, shifting attention away from the perception of the other, and towards our orientations to the world that we share. In assessing the potential for change in *The Memory of Love*, I focus on the epilogue to the novel, which is set two years after the events of the main narrative. Adrian has returned to England and is living in his mother's house in Norfolk. Kai has remained in Sierra Leone, and is raising the daughter of Adrian and Mamakay, who provides an ongoing link between the two men, as well as between them and Mamakay.[11] She also sustains a range of other relationships. Kai pays regular visits with her to Ileana, Attila's assistant at the mental hospital, who developed a close friendship with Adrian during his time in Sierra Leone. On her mother's side, the little girl is the granddaughter of Saffia, who was married first to Julius, and then to Elias Cole. The child thus acts as a point of confluence not only between the transnational differences of the present, but also between the political differences of the past, and she brings the past into living relation with the present. The novel ends as Kai drives across the peninsula bridge, with Adrian's daughter in the car beside him. Examining the figure of the bridge itself, I analyse the connections that it mobilises as a vehicle for thinking through the potential for transformation in Sierra Leone. In so doing, I address Norridge's concerns about the power dynamics at the close of the novel, by locating the potential for change in Sierra-Leonean agency, and by focusing on a child who, like Forna herself, has British and Sierra-Leonean parentage. I also turn to the vocabulary of 'impression' to ask how the unfulfilled political hope of a charismatic young idealist might leave its mark in and on the present, and potentially on the future.

Turning first to Adrian as a marker of change, Pedwell has persuasively argued that a key shift in his relationship with Kai takes place when Adrian succumbs to a malarial fever that leaves him severely weakened, and dependent on Kai to nurse him back to health. With any illusion of sovereignty dispelled, and with Kai ministering to Adrian with tenderness and care, a different kind of intimacy begins to take shape between the two men. Pedwell summarises the shift as a movement from an empathetic feeling based in 'knowledge, accuracy and prediction' to 'a more organic process of becoming in synch', that is based in the gesture of '*surrender*' (2014: 142–3; italics in original). Forna thus deploys in the novel a process of 'affective synchronisation' (2014: 144), in which rhythms and temporalities are intertwined and Adrian becomes more open to the bodily and spatial rhythms of his life in Freetown. These changes are initially mapped in relation to Kai, as the two men's working patterns at the hospital create a flow of movement that harmonises over time into a closely choreographed routine:

In the days and weeks that follow, the rhythms of their lives begin to intertwine . . . Certain days Adrian comes home to find Kai in the apartment, settled into the front room, going through papers or writing up notes. The pattern of Kai's breaks from the operating theatre becomes familiar to Adrian, and he will, on occasion, endeavour to stop work at the same time. He finds he looks forward to the other man's companionship in the evenings. So a new friendship is formed. (2010: 51)

The same dynamic is discernible in Adrian's relationship with Mamakay, which not only signals their deepening feelings, but also affords him a new affective, spatial and temporal experience of Freetown: 'Through Mamakay the landscape of the city has altered for Adrian. For the first time since he arrived, the city bears a past, exists in a . . . dimension other than the present' (2010: 255). In both of these instances, empathetic feeling is not so much directed toward another individual but is rather about being affected by time and space themselves, opening up to a slower pace and rhythm. It is also, as Pedwell notes, an emotional attunement that does not discount difference; it 'depends not on interpersonal, social or geo-political conflict being eliminated or neutralised, but rather on it being felt and critically mobilised' (2014: 147). Thus, Kai and Mamakay continue to experience and express tensions in their relationship with Adrian, and to be critical of his presence in Sierra Leone. Forna's attentiveness to the potential for change in the everyday routines of living speaks to a phenomenological approach to empathy; in sharing a social world, Adrian holds in common a realm of objects, places and environments that exist not only in relation to him, but also in relation to the meaning that they have for others. His shifting rhythms and routines indicate his gradual attunement to the meanings of objects and spaces for those around him. This phenomenological orientation towards navigating anew the relational patterns and habits of everyday living is particularly resonant in the post-civil-war context of the novel, in which the challenge lies precisely in neighbours learning to live together again in the shared everyday spaces of the shops, the market, the schools and the bars. It seems significant in this context that, in *The Memory of Love*, the affective sharing of space can be realised only in the transnational relationships between Adrian and Kai, and between Adrian and Mamakay. It proves noticeably more intractable, and less imaginable, for the Sierra-Leonean characters: Agnes and her family; Elias and Mamakay.

If a way forward for the Sierra-Leonean characters is imagined in *The Memory of Love*, it is glimpsed in the final lines of the novel. Describing Kai, his nephew, and Adrian's daughter, as they drive across the peninsula bridge, the closing sentences read as follows:

> They all see the kingfisher flash from a street lamp down to the water right in front of them. The bird rises, a fish glints on the end of its beak. The little girl screams with pleasure. They do not see, for they cannot, as they cross the peninsula bridge, the letters traced by a boy's forefinger into cement on the far side of the bridge wall half a century ago, beneath the initials of the men who once worked the bridge. *J.K.* (2010: 445; italics in original)

The initials inscribed into the concrete are those of Julius; we first hear of the bridge through Elias, who recalls to Adrian that when Julius was fifteen or so, he had watched its construction every day for months. The building of the bridge is thus linked to Julius from the outset, and Elias describes vividly the moment when Julius added his initials to its foundation:

> Once, at the close of the day's work, Julius told me he crept to the edge of the new section [of the bridge], crawling on his belly, and peered over, exhilarated by the long drop down to the water, the possibility of being blown away. The day before the official opening, [the workmen] lowered him, dangerously, over the side on a trapeze and he wrote all the workers' names in the wet concrete, adding his own initials at the end. (2010: 55)

By inscribing his mark, Julius makes the bridge his own, and Adrian repeats this impression when he sees the bridge for the first time: 'Exactly as Elias described, Adrian is certain of it. Julius's bridge' (2010: 89). The story speaks powerfully of Julius's fearlessness, which is eventually to lead to his undoing. It also renders the bridge into a memorial to the generation of idealists who resisted oppression, and who became, like Forna's father, a lost generation. The initials written in concrete cannot be erased and, although unseen, they will outlast the attempts of men like Elias to cover over the past, to rewrite history to suit their own agendas.

In order to unravel further the significance of Julius's initials impressed into the concrete, I turn now to Ahmed's discussion of the word 'impression'. Noting that the impressions that we form are inextricable from the ways in which objects impress upon us, Ahmed observes:

We need to remember the word "press" in an impression. It allows us
to associate the experience of having an emotion with the very affect
of one surface upon another, an affect that leaves its mark or trace.
So not only do I have an impression of others, they also leave me
with an impression; they impress me, and impress upon me. (2004:
6; italics in original)

Read in this light, Julius's bridge poses the question of whether, and
how, past histories remain alive in the present; to what extent they
leave their mark or impression upon it. The future – represented by
the little girl – bears the impression of Julius's energy and vision,
as well as of Elias's complicity; it will take shape precisely in and
through such impressions. Sierra Leone is poised before an uncertain
future, but it can look to more than one historical legacy to move
it forward, and Forna implies a sense of hope that Julius's political
activism will prove the stronger and more lasting impression. The
bridge is also an object that has impressed itself upon Kai with particular force, as the site of his own (attempted) execution. His fall
from the bridge had signified a collapse of the possibility for connection between one life and another; Kai was unable to share what
had happened on the bridge even with his lover, Nenebah, rendering
the relationship impossible: 'For he'd never told Nenebah about the
bridge. Or of what happened with the young nurse, Balia. He'd hidden these things from Nenebah' (2010: 286). Shaped by fear, Kai's
relation to the bridge was one of avoidance; a desire to remove himself as far as possible from this object that stood in for the violence
of his abduction. Adrian's treatment of Kai demonstrates that emotions involve affective forms of reorientation; he is now able to drive
across the bridge, and to form new impressions: the beauty of the
kingfisher, and the little girl's joyous response to it. Kai's crossing of
the bridge is suggestive that it has been restored as a site of passage
and connection; that movement forward is now possible. The paus-
ing of the novel at the midpoint of the bridge signals, however, that
such transformation is necessarily provisional, yet to be realised. It
also acts as a reminder that, even as a better future becomes imaginable for Kai, this is not also the case for Agnes, who is doomed to
remain in the dead end of her repeated peregrinations; that social
and political change is uneven in its effects.

The vocabulary of impression also calls into question whether
'moving on' or 'moving forward' is necessarily a good thing. Discussing the scar, another way in which our past can mark and shape
our bodily surfaces, Ahmed refutes the truism that 'a good scar is

one that is hard to see' (2004: 201). Rather, she argues in favour of its continued visibility:

> A good scar is one that sticks out, a lumpy sign on the skin. It's not that the wound is exposed or that the skin is bleeding. But the scar is a sign of the injury: a good scar allows healing, it even covers over, *but the covering always exposes the injury, reminding us of how it shapes the body.* (2004: 201–2; italics in original)

In this light, the work of emotion is not to work over the past injury, but rather to work on and with it, to see if we can open up different kinds of attachments. If Elias sought to work over the past, to render it barely visible, then Adrian, for all of his misunderstandings, is committed to working on and with the past, be it Kai's experience on the bridge or Agnes's impossible family history. Scars also speak of the importance of time. *The Memory of Love* is attentive to the time it takes to move, or to move on, and this is symbolised in Kai's surgical procedures, which enable a slow reconstruction and rehabilitation, and one that remains marked by a phantom pain at the site of what is missing.[12] Ahmed observes of temporality: 'It takes time to know what we can do with emotion, and how we can feel differently. Often, this time will exceed the span of the individual life' (2004: 202). Here, too, Forna's work is resonant, as she traces the complex ways in which feelings are, consciously and unconsciously, transferred across and between the generations, and can play out their effects in other lives, and on different bodies. Julius's initials thus signify a past which is currently unseen, covered over by the water, but that remains to be discovered by a different generation. As Jurecic has suggested, part of the work of fiction is to slow us down, so that we, like Adrian, might be opened up to a different pace, rhythm and temporality; a mode of affective attunement that is not about interpretative knowledge or mastery, but that is based in an opening-up towards the unfamiliar. This dispossession signals the alterity of the other, and also gestures to different modes of feeling; new spatial, temporal and affective patterns of orientation towards a world that is shared.

Conclusion

Targeted at European and American markets, *The Memory of Love* cues its readers into an immersive and moving reading experience.

'Profoundly affecting', declares the cover blurb by Kiran Desai, while *The Sunday Times* proclaims: 'Powerful and deeply moving' (Forna 2010: no pagination). My reading of the novel has worked against such narrative expectations, arguing that Forna opens up a critical engagement with empathy's role in the humanitarian project, and probes its hazards and limitations in the transnational context. As such, *The Memory of Love* engages in what postcolonial critic Madhu Krishnan has termed 'a self-consciously ironic critique of the image of Africa as a space for Euro-American humanitarian self-realization' (2015: 4). My analysis has drawn on Slaughter's reading of contemporary humanitarian narrative to deepen and extend Krishnan's description of 'ironic critique'. I have also indicated that, for Forna, empathy cannot be separated from the material and economic flow of goods and resource; the affective flow all too often follows, and even reinforces, globalised routes of wealth, power and privilege. Adrian's movement to Sierra Leone thus maps on to and traces out a complex and unequal infrastructure of medical investment and resource; entangled within this network, Adrian discovers that he is, in many ways, part of the problem. Gradually disenchanted, Adrian learns first that he does not know, and then that there are other ways to know; modes of feeling that can take into account both slowness and silence. My reading highlights the phenomenological aspects of the novel, which point us in the direction of how we might (differently) negotiate our shared world.

The question of where, and to whom, empathy is directed in the novel has surfaced at various points in the chapter. My main emphasis, as in previous chapters, has been on moving away from the individualised empathetic relation between reader and character, which tends to depoliticise the question of empathy. It also does not allow for the mobility and unpredictability of reader response. Nevertheless, the question of identification can raise productive points of discussion. My focus on Adrian has examined the ways in which he functions not only as a 'bridge' character, offering the reader a familiar entry point into an unfamiliar world, but also to focus our attention on the politics and ideology of humanitarianism, which leads not to the suffering other but to the affective disenchantment of the aid worker. Norridge has, however, reported that her reading-group discussions of *The Memory of Love* point in a different direction altogether:

> What I have . . . found fascinating, based on my experiences of working with reading groups . . . is that . . . readers . . . tend to report

identifying not with . . . Adrian, but instead overwhelmingly with Nenebah and Kai. Where the British male is perceived to be steeped in a difficult history of racial and cultural prejudice, readers prefer to align their own identities with those of the articulate . . . Sierra Leonean elite. (2012: 24)

For Norridge, this (re-)positioning of reader sympathies is positive; she argues that it is 'crucial in disturbing the potential voyeurism of the images that still circulate about West Africa' (2012: 24). Certainly, this could be seen as one narrative strategy through which Forna produces a 'de-Othering' of Africa in *The Memory of Love*; I remain troubled, however, by a sense that empathising with those Sierra-Leonean characters who have survived the traumas of the civil war avoids the 'difficult' questions of complicity that the novel poses; empathy thus becomes a means of avoiding, rather than engaging in, critical work. It is particularly noticeable, in the light of Norridge's discussion of Elias as a focus for readerly empathy, that he is not listed here, which again evades questions of moral ambiguity and compromise. My reading has drawn on a feminist politics of affect in order to position empathy as an economy of feeling that overlaps with material and capital economies, so that we can productively map the flow of resource; where, and how, it moves or is blocked. The solution is not, however, one of simply redirecting the flow. Rather, if being moved can also move us forward, I have indicated that it is a more gradual, and a more unpredictable process, in which the affective openings mobilised by transnational encounters can enable surprising new orientations, and different intimacies, to take shape.

Notes

1. Other novelists who are writing in this vein include Chimamanda Ngozie Adichie, Kiran Desai, Zakes Mda, Arundhati Roy and Kamila Shamsie.
2. In interview with Maya Jaggi, Forna has observed that, although Sierra Leone is, like Croatia, a beautiful country and had its own Club Med in the 1970s, tourism cannot now take hold there as a boost to economic regeneration because 'Africa scares the West' (Jaggi 2013: no pagination).
3. For an articulation of interdisciplinarity that draws on Barad's model of entangled agencies, see Des Fitzgerald and Felicity Callard (2016).

4. As Raghuram also notes, such policies on migration are even more contested post-9/11, as the political landscape 'is increasingly being territorialised, securitised and penalised' (2009: 29).

5. In the context of post-war reconstruction, Norridge has helpfully made a distinction in *The Memory of Love* between the 'acute pain' of the war and the 'ongoing experience of chronic suffering in the aftermath' (2013: 208). I argue that this distinction could be usefully extended to think through the longer historical time span of the novel: the acute pain of the civil war, and by extension of the Ebola crisis, is underpinned by the chronic pain of decades of socioeconomic erosion.

6. Slaughter's literary model for an ironic treatment of the chivalric quest is Miguel de Cervantes's *Don Quixote* (1605).

7. It is in the spirit of chivalry's ironic mode that Adrian is not able to find his own Holy Grail. Norridge has noted that, in passing on the story to Kai, the women of Agnes's village ensure that it is 'received by the most traumatised healer in the novel' (2013: 186).

8. Although Forna does not specify the treatment method that Adrian uses, the scene is reminiscent of his former experiments with 'eye movement desensitisation and reprocessing', which have produced 'dramatic' results for PTSD in America (2010: 66). He has attended a training course on using the technique and has practised it with his private clients in England.

9. See Chapter 3 for a more extended discussion of the limitations of narrative in the context of the medical humanities. This chapter adds a postcolonial dimension to the debates; just as the category of trauma has been described by critical trauma theorist Stef Craps as a 'Western artefact', constructed from the experiences of dominant groups in the West, so too has the routine exportation of Western-style trauma programmes as the basis for intervention in post-conflict situations across the globe; treatment programmes that are typically based in the narrativisation of the experience. Craps notes that this uni-directional movement of expertise risks 'imperialism' and excludes local or indigenous knowledge and practices (2013: 20, 22).

10. Adrian's relationship with fellow aid worker Ileana, who is based at Attila's hospital, is also important. Romanian in nationality, Ileana opens up the question of how the history of political repression under Nicolae Ceausescu (1965–89) relates to the erosion of political rights in Sierra Leone under Stevens's presidency. Forna is again inviting us to think in complex ways about commonalities of experience, and, by using an example of European dictatorship, works against the 'othering' of Africa.

11. It becomes evident in the course of the novel that, under the family name of Nenebah, Mamakay was Kai's lover during the civil war; a relationship that could not sustain the trauma of what happened to him on the peninsula bridge. That her daughter remains with Kai in

Sierra Leone is in accordance with Mamakay's own wish to remain in the country, rather than moving to Britain with Adrian.

12. The imagery of phantom pain refers not only to the site of the amputated limb but also to the pain of Kai's separation from Nenebah, another scar in the novel that cannot be worked over, as Kai tries to do, but that needs to be worked on and with.

Chapter 5

Empathy and Capitalism

Introduction

In Chapter 4, I examined empathy in the context of the global economy, arguing that flows of feeling tend to trace out, if not to reinforce, the routes of geopolitical influence and power. At the same time, the migratory impetus of globalisation can produce new and unexpected encounters that disrupt and complicate such flows, making possible new affective openings and affinities. In this chapter, I build on the idea that empathy follows the trajectories of capital by examining the commercial exchange networks that have developed around biotechnology capital; that is, the bodily fragments, tissues and organs that can be extracted from an individual body and are available for transfer to another. In the British context, the existence of such networks came painfully to light in 1999, when the scandal broke of the Alder Hey Children's Hospital in Liverpool. Dirk van Velzen, a Dutch pathologist working at the hospital, was found to have retained thousands of organs from children who had been autopsied between 1988 and 1995, without obtaining parental consent. As further details were released, it emerged that over 2,000 organs were stored at Alder Hey, taken from 800 children. In December 1999, a committee was appointed to inquire into the revelations, led by the United Kingdom's Chief Medical Officer, Professor Liam Donaldson. An audit of National Health Service premises showed that, although not practised on the same scale as at Alder Hey, retention of human organs and tissues was widespread, and over 100,000 organs were found to have been retained at medical schools and hospitals throughout Britain. The Donaldson inquiry also found that organs could be traded for profit; at Birmingham and Liverpool hospitals, thymus glands, removed during heart surgery on live children, had been given to a pharmaceutical company for research in return for financial donations. The Donaldson report recommended changes in the law to ensure that patients, parents and families gave informed consent to the removal of organs during post-mortem examination.[1]

Most acutely, the Alder Hey scandal exposed the conflicting notions of value accorded to the human organ. For the families of the children, the removed organs represented part of a loved one. A statement forwarded to Donaldson by the Royal College of Pathologists asserted the value of the human organ to advance knowledge. The scandal also exposed the commercial value of tissues and organs, which could be sold to companies that extract materials from them for profit. As ever more kinds of tissues can be removed from one body and transplanted into another – including not only human organs, but also sperm, ova, foetal tissue, and embryonic stem cells – the question of the value and meaning that we accord to such material becomes increasingly central to contemporary biomedicine. Social scientist Catherine Waldby has observed that, within biomedical research, the prevailing tendency is towards market exchange and value: 'Within the technical frameworks of biomedicine and the commodity frameworks of biotechnology capital, such fragments are . . . legally regarded as alienable – available for transfer from the originator to others by donation or sale' (2002: 240). This commodity model is, however, contested by a belief that human organs cannot be so readily detached from the person. According to this view, Waldby elaborates:

> Human tissues are not impersonal or affectively neutral; rather, they retain some of the value of personhood for many if not most donors and recipients. Hence, circuits of tissue exchange are not only technical and therapeutic, but also relational and social. To give . . . is to be caught up in a social and embodied circuit in which the significance of one's personhood imbues the fragment. (2002: 240)

Biological exchange is not fully distinguishable from social exchange, and the forms of relationship set up through tissue or organ transfer imply the emergence of new conceptions of identity, personhood, intersubjectivity and empathy.

Feminist theory has provided a key locus for the investigation and articulation of the affective and subjective dimensions of tissue and organ transfer. Gabriele Griffin has noted an emphasis in feminist critical engagements with science on '"messy relationships" where the imbrication of different materialities and species denies the notion of a categorical other. Instead it demands an ethical engagement which registers the claims both of those materialities and species, and their relationalities' (2009: 658). Margaret Shildrick has similarly observed that feminist phenomenology opens up the recognition that 'the normative body [is] already vulnerable, unstable and open to its others' (2014: 58). This feminist vocabulary of risk, openness and challenge to the bounded self, must, however, be set against a recognition that organ and tissue transfer is located within predefined procedures and circuits; Waldby thus notes that biomedicine 'set[s] out the terms of the relational networks that any practice of tissue transfer will create' (2002: 251). The logics of biocapital at once make possible and constrain new, intercorporeal modes of relationality. Social theorist Melinda Cooper has aptly pointed out that the period of the most intense development in the life sciences, namely the late 1980s and 1990s, was also the era of the neoliberal revolution in Britain and the United States, which, she observes, 'sought to undermine the existing foundations of economic growth, productivity, and value, while at the same time it forged an ever tighter alliance between state-funded research, the market in new technologies, and financial capital' (2008: 3). Embedded within bioscience are the economic concepts with which its development is so intimately intertwined, and the intensity of the public and media debates around organ retention speak to the simultaneous registration and contestation of this interchange between the biological and economic spheres. The same traffic between bioscience and contemporary capitalism can also be discerned in the linguistic and semantic pressure points that dominated the public discourse around organ retention, leading anthropologist Kaushik Sunder Rajan to observe: '[w]e live in a world of rapid changes, many of which force us to ask afresh what we mean by words that are an integral part of our lexicon; words like "life", "capital", "fact", "exchange", and "value"' (2006: 3). Certainly, a theory of empathy in the age of biocapitalism will need to be alert to, and cognisant of, the vexed nature of such terms, and to negotiate their highly charged and contested meanings.

Kazuo Ishiguro's *Never Let Me Go* was published in 2005 and provides a complex, if not disturbing, literary reflection on the questions of exchange, value, commodification and subjectivity that are at stake in contemporary bioscientific developments. As the novel unfolds, the reader gradually learns that, in an alternative Britain of the 1990s, human clones are being produced with the specific intention of harvesting their organs once they have reached adulthood. The opening pages gesture towards the linguistic pressure points caused by biocapitalism, through the deliberate unsettling of certain words: 'carer', 'donation', 'completion' and 'deferral'. Here, too, the disquieting narration of Kathy H. is introduced, who we eventually learn is a clone who, in her early thirties, is about to enter the process of organ removal that will, after the fourth operation at most, result in her death. Central to the novel's haunting effect is Kathy's quiet acceptance of her fate, and her lack of anger or resistance in the face of what is to come: her slow, deliberate and painful murder. The problem of Kathy's voice, and the reader's relation to it, has preoccupied critics and located the issue of empathy as central to the novel's reception. Sebastian Groes and Barry Lewis title their introduction to a collection of critical essays on Ishiguro, 'The ethics of empathy' (2011a: 1–10) and argue that, in the face of the recent 'proliferation of new technologies' that 'diminish our capacity to . . . feel and feel *for* . . . Ishiguro's ethic of empathy criticizes this condition' (2011: 5; italics in original). For Patricia Waugh, 'one of Ishiguro's major themes is both the necessity for the cultivation of empathy and the necessity for knowing its limits' (2011: 21).

This chapter accordingly takes up the question of Ishiguro's treatment of empathy in the era of biocapitalism. I begin by addressing the question of affect, or its seeming absence, in the novel, by considering the concept of emotional capitalism; a culture in which emotional and economic practices mutually shape and constitute each other. Focusing on Kathy's labour as carer, I turn to Sianne Ngai's influential analysis of ugly feelings to suggest that there might be more emotion in the novel than has often been recognised, but that it does not take the forms, or assume the attitudes, that we might expect. I then move on to the question of cloning, and read Kathy's narrative in the light of gender theorist Susan Merrill Squier's concept of liminal lives, asking what kinds of life stories are produced in and through biotechnological interventions, and identifying Ishiguro's particular interest in their political, as well as social and ethical, implications. Broadening out to address the novel's treatment of the global organ trade, I develop a parallel focus to the argument in Chapter 4, mapping out the ways in which the extracted human body parts produced by the illegal trade in harvested organs follow the same circuits of transnational capital as medical resource and funding. I ask what such modes of flow and exchange imply about our capacity to care for others, and how such care might in turn be influenced by social and political ideologies. The chapter closes by examining Ishiguro's critical treatment of art as a vehicle for empathy, probing the implications for his own novelistic practice. If art is not straightforwardly productive of empathy, it nevertheless seems that for Ishiguro, developing technologies hold the potential to bring into being new modes of relating to others, and the concept of empathy itself accordingly needs to be re-envisioned in the light of the current biomedical revolution.

Emotional capital

In his critical study of twenty-first-century fiction, Peter Boxall positioned Ishiguro's *Never Let Me Go* alongside the recent fiction of J. M. Coetzee, in a chapter titled 'The Limits of the Human' (2013: 84–122). Referring to the recent advances in technology that have radically transformed the ways in which we conceive the limits of our bodies, Boxall remarks:

> We are now living through a historical period in which the meaning of the human is radically uncertain – as uncertain, perhaps, as it has ever been. It has perhaps never been more difficult to determine . . . what constitutes the nature of our human being, or how we might understand the limits of the human. (2013: 84)

If Coetzee is interested to probe the ethical boundaries between human and animal, Ishiguro is particularly concerned in *Never Let Me Go* to inquire into the question of the human in the context of biomedicine.[2] Ishiguro's portrait of Hailsham, and its place within a network of other institutions, can be linked to Nikolas Rose's influential studies of biopolitics, resonating with his concerns about issues of management and of governance:

> As human beings come to experience themselves in new ways as biological creatures, as biological selves, their vital existence becomes a focus of government, the target of novel forms of authority and expertise, a highly cathected field of knowledge, [and] an expanding territory for bioeconomic exploitation. (2007: 4)

In this section, I address Ishiguro's probing of the limits of the human through Kathy's narrative voice, often read as the culmination of his exploration of protagonists who are not able to articulate their own interiority or feelings, and so fall back instead on repetition and cliché. Reading Kathy's apparent affectlessness in the context of broader questions of authority and governance in the novel, I argue that there is, in fact, a frequent articulation of feelings by Kathy, although it is not the expression of anger and resistance to the system that the reader might anticipate or desire. Occupying an altogether quieter register, Kathy's emotions speak of what can ensue when feeling becomes the object of management within the workplace, and also of the kinds of agentless affect that are produced and circulated in and through cultures of bureaucracy and of commodification.

Sociologist Eva Illouz has traced through the twentieth century the increasing importance accorded in the workplace to emotional capitalism, whereby the management of one's own and others' feelings came to be seen as an essential aspect of leadership, as well as of economic transactions more broadly. From the 1920s on, management theories extolled the business benefits of a professional competence that was defined in emotional terms, and that valorised the skills of listening to and empathising with others. Emotional Intelligence (EI) quickly became classified and categorised, and was assessed in order to predict and to maximise performance and productivity across varying levels and types of labour. Involving capabilities in five areas, EI focused on the commercial value of the affective skills of self-awareness, the management of feelings, self-motivation, empathy and relationality. Harnessed to an economic instrumentalism, emotions have, Illouz observes, 'become entities to be evaluated, inspected, discussed, bargained, quantified and commodified' (2007: 109). Under soft capitalism, the workplace has thus acted increasingly as a site in which one has constantly to be aware of, assess and manage emotions, at the same time as repeatedly demonstrating one's own capacities for sensitivity, collaboration and creative innovation. Sociologist Arlie Russell Hochschild's influential analysis of the work of airline attendants, published as *The Managed Heart* in 1983, called widespread attention to the managerial cultivation of emotion as a resource in improving service quality, and also highlighted the hazards of the commercialisation of feeling, in its potential for the estrangement from one's own emotions (Hochschild 2012). These concerns spoke powerfully to other public-sector workers, not least those involved in the medical and caring professions, for whom empathy had come to represent a key workplace skill and resource, as well as one subject to increasing levels of training, evaluation and assessment.[3]

At first glance, it might seem that the incorporation into the workplace of emotions traditionally assigned as feminine, such as empathy, care and attentiveness to others, represented a positive move, according new value and status to them. Feminists have, however, regarded the developments with a justified degree of caution. Cultural theorist Elaine Swan has noted that the development can work to the detriment of women, in whom such skills are seen to be natural or innate, while male workers displaying the same attributes of feeling are seen to demonstrate mobility and flexibility. Emotion work is, in other words, simply not visible as labour for women, in the same way as it is for men, who are therefore more likely than women to receive affirmation for the performance of emotional labour: 'This means that [women] are not recognized in the exchange of resources for rewards, such as promotion' (2008: 99). At the same time, as David Knights and Emma Surman observe, the commercialisation of feelings has done little to disrupt or challenge the gender balance in terms of who is assigned the work of care within the labour market, or the value that is accorded to such labour:

> job segregation continues to exist such that women more often occupy positions as . . . service workers . . . or those outside the formal economy such as domestic carers. It is significant that these positions are comparatively poorly paid or unpaid and secure a low level of respect and status in society. (2008: 3)

For Illouz, emotions such as empathy are social products, and their integration into the workplace affords us critical insight into the new psychologies that have evolved in response to neoliberalism. If the ideal entrepreneurial self is difficult to achieve, the vocabulary of EI can offer a potential resource for its construction, as well as for dealing with the feelings of failure, disappointment, anxiety and frustration that are likely to develop in response to the impossibility of realising the aspirations of neoliberalism. While this is far from a feminist rebalancing of power, and could even be seen to position emotion work as a means of stabilising and reinforcing the status quo, Illouz argues that EI provides a necessary coping mechanism at a time when no better resource seems to be available. For my purposes, these feminist debates provide a useful framework in indicating not only the instrumentalisation of empathy towards productivity and profit, but also in identifying the range of feelings that emerge in response to the inevitable failure of the neoliberal ideal; emotions that are notably not in the major key, but that are quieter and more passive in tone, unlikely to lead either to agency or to action.

In *Ugly Feelings* (2005), Sianne Ngai has identified a similar range of minor emotions as characteristic of late modernity, a period defined by the total marketisation and commercialisation of culture. Turning away from powerful and dynamic emotions such as anger, Ngai points to the importance in literary texts of more minor and non-cathartic negative states of feeling, including envy, irritation, anxiety and disgust. These emotions are brought together by their association with situations in which action is blocked or suspended, and their attention to states of powerlessness also provides a reflection on the increasingly marginalised and restricted position of literature itself in the market society: '[t]hese situations of passivity . . . can . . . be thought of as allegories for an autonomous and bourgeois art's increasingly resigned and pessimistic understanding of its *own* relationship to political action' (2005: 3; italics in original). Precisely because the feelings that Ngai focuses on are characterised by a weak intentionality, they become a powerful vehicle for analysing situations of passivity and a lack of agency, even as they deny the reader any form of cathartic release. Across the range of feelings that Ngai assembles, she identifies a spectrum of powerlessness associated with them. At the most active end, marking the 'outer threshold' of minor affects, is disgust, which represents for Ngai an 'intense and unambivalent negativity [that] prepar[es] us for more instrumental or politically efficacious emotions' (2005: 354). At the weakest end of the scale is irritation, which is negative affect in its 'most politically effete form' (2005: 181). Ngai defines irritation as vexing – indeed, irritating – for the reader in two distinct ways: on the one hand, it continually slips from view, shifting from emotional experience to physical sensation, and on the other hand, it frustrates our impulse either to feel with or to feel instead of the protagonist, which stronger passions can fulfil. The reader is accordingly placed in as blocked and obstructed a position as the protagonist, creating what Ngai terms a politics of 'suspended agency' (2005: 1).

In describing the literary canon associated with ugly feelings, Ngai evocatively writes:

> [I have a] preference for texts that . . . seem oddly impassive: texts that foreground the absence of a strong emotion where we are led to expect one, or turn entirely on the interpretative problems posed by an emotional illegibility. (2005: 10)

This description resonates powerfully with the aesthetic tone of *Never Let Me Go*, which was published in the same year as *Ugly Feelings*. Kathy H. is 'oddly impassive' in relation to the fate that she shares with the other clones, and her narrative discloses in its inarticulacy a distinct 'emotional illegibility'. Rather than reading these characteristics, as other critics have done, as evidence of Kathy's non-human status, I ask how such an affective register relates to Kathy's work as carer, and beyond that, to her training for such labour at the institution of Hailsham. Read in this light, we can see that Kathy's work as carer for Ruth and Tommy represents the ultimate instrumentalisation of feeling in the service of productivity and profit; the emotional labour that she provides before she herself begins to donate maximises the productivity of the cloning system, which is entirely constructed around profit, conceived of in terms of the health and longevity of the non-clone population. Even as feeling is commercialised, abstracted as a profitable entity, it is simultaneously devalued; the caring work that Kathy performs is labour that nobody else would want to undertake, and it is therefore consigned to the lowest class of worker. Kathy's assessment of her own eleven-year career as carer articulates some pride in her ability to manage the feelings of the donors as they move towards the fourth and final operation:

> I've developed a kind of instinct around donors. I know when to hang around and comfort them, when to leave them to themselves; when to listen to everything they have to say, and when to shrug and tell them to snap out of it. (2005: 3)

From Kathy's story we learn that such management of feeling was structurally embedded in the upbringing of the clones at Hailsham. Introduced gradually to the knowledge of their fates, the clones are brought up in an environment that affords no privacy so that their thoughts and feelings are always shared; the subject of continual observation, discussion and intervention. In this sense, Ishiguro also takes to its logical conclusion the idea of emotion being harnessed to the sphere of public labour, rather than expressive selfhood. Critic Lisa Fluet has argued that, as a result, Kathy and the other clones can 'no longer distinguish personal responsibilities from public ones' (2007: 210). It is this indistinction between private and public, or more precisely the absorption of the former into the latter, that leads Kathy to elevate the responsibilities of public service over personal ties and bonds, including, ultimately, the attachment even to her own life.

Yet, Kathy's narration is not without feeling or emotion. One of the first affects that she names, attributing it to carers less successful than she has been, is resentment:

> If you're one of them, I can understand how you might get resentful – about my bedsit, my car, above all, the way I get to pick and choose who I look after. And I'm a Hailsham student, which is enough by itself sometimes to get people's backs up. (2005: 1)

As a cognate emotion to envy, resentment registers on Ngai's scale of minor feelings. As such, it speaks to the powerlessness of the clones' position: lacking any agency to change the system, they direct negative emotion towards each other, constructing a landscape of internal privileges and hierarchies that constitute the focus for antagonism. Again, this circulation of minor feelings is embedded within the Hailsham education; not only were the clones continually aware of the small distinctions between them, but Hailsham was itself, as Kathy notes, a marker of privilege, conferring on those who went through the institution an elevated status in the eyes of the other clones. It is impossible to distinguish individual selfhood from publicly constructed and managed feelings, and Kathy's personhood continually slips out of sight, blurring both with the feelings of the other clones and with the effects of the institution. At the same time, the objects of resentment – the bedsit, the car, the choice of donors – are indicative of the 'suspended agency' of the clones, for whom the effects of commerce and the market are so total that they eclipse any possibility even of registering, let alone expressing, feelings of resentment towards the larger system of exploitation in which they are enmeshed.

The two emotions that figure at either end of Ngai's spectrum of ugly feelings also play a significant role in *Never Let Me Go*: disgust and irritation. As the most active of the minor affects, disgust is appropriately associated with the guardians at Hailsham and represents their involuntary response to the clones that are in their charge. Kathy first becomes aware of the feeling when she and the other clones catch Madame unawares, crowding around her on one of her visits to Hailsham, only to find that she recoils from them as if she has been confronted with a spider. We subsequently learn that this is the instinctive reaction of all the guardians, and is more or less effectively suppressed. Read in the light of Ngai's analysis, this feeling represents the potential for a more politically efficacious response, and when Kathy and Tommy confront Madame, they learn of her frustrated political efforts, if not to change the system itself, at least to make aspects of it more humane. In Miss Lucy, we also witness the momentary tipping of disgust towards anger, but such an outburst, like those of Tommy, is swiftly managed and contained, deemed not only inappropriate but also futile in the Hailsham environment. For the clones themselves, the feeling most often expressed is that of irritation, the affect that is placed by Ngai at the bottom end of the spectrum of agency. Kathy repeatedly articulates irritation towards her closest companions, Tommy and Ruth, and the feeling circulates like a current between them. It is particularly evident at the Cottages, as the clones occupy a hiatus between their life at Hailsham and their assignment as either donors or carers. Kathy is irritated first by Ruth's mimicking of the gestures that she sees on television, and then by her reading of George Eliot's *Daniel Deronda*. Both of these sources of irritation speak of a desire for connection with the human world, but they do so in an ambivalent and indirect way, and the negative feeling becomes a way to manage and close down more elusive and troubling desires by provoking conflict.[4]

In a broader sense, Fluet argues that irritation also calls attention in *Never Let Me Go* to the kinds of affect that characterise, and become a crucial part of, the system of public service, and that arise out of the tension between a willing attachment to the web of others whom one serves – in Kathy's case, the group of clones who serve each other and ultimately the uncloned public – and the repeated act of letting go of an individual interest – Tommy, Ruth, the baby that Kathy can never have, and ultimately her own life. In Fluet's reading, care becomes decidedly 'creepy' in *Never Let Me Go*; divorced from 'the social valorization of authentic, "deep down" feelings about motherhood, care, and love', it assumes instead an 'antisocial, ugly, affective [form]' (2007: 285, 284). Ishiguro thereby articulates the kinds of psychologies that emotional capitalism can create; if his characters are confronted with lives that are utterly constrained by the system, he shows us not the strong, individual feelings of anger and resistance, but rather the ways in which emotions can themselves be socially and bureaucratically constructed; an essential aspect of the ways in which we manage the behaviours of others and of ourselves, these more minor, elusive and ambivalent feelings speak of how we respond affectively to passivity and a lack of agency, and they effectively resist or block the sympathetic imagination.

Life stories

In the previous section, I have focused on Kathy's work as a carer to argue that her narration is not as lacking in affect as has often been assumed, and to suggest that the minor and ugly feelings that she does express can productively be connected to the effects of an emotional capitalism that both manages and exploits her feelings as a form of labour. In this section, I turn to Ishiguro's representation of Kathy as a clone, reading her and the other clones as representative of what Susan Squier has termed liminal lives. These are lives brought into being through the interventions of biomedicine; the development of stem-cell research, genetic engineering and end-of-life technologies has produced a variety of lives that are, in Squier's terms, 'neither discarded bioproduct nor valued human being . . . And though they partake of human qualities, they share with nonhuman life-forms the possibility of being harvested for a use that transcends their own life' (2004: 4). Liminal lives exercise a powerful hold on the cultural imagination and, as we have seen in the Alder Hey scandal, form the site of highly contested medical, legal and social struggles. For Squier, these new forms of being claim our attention because, in the First World at least, they represent 'a transformation we are all undergoing, as we become initiates in a new biomedical personhood mingling existence and non-existence, organic and inorganic matter, life and death' (2004: 5). As the impact of biotechnology grows ever greater, it looks likely that we will increasingly participate in, and benefit from, these circuits of biological exchange, which places particular pressure on our need to develop a social and ethical response to the liminal lives on which they depend. My reading of Ishiguro argues that he is particularly attentive, not only to the social and ethical dimensions of the clones, but also to their political implications. I read the cloning of humans against the history of race relations in Britain, opening up a convergence between racism and biocapitalism that did not happen, but that might have done so, had history taken a different turn. Ishiguro quietly insists that biomedicine does not take place within a vacuum, but is inextricably tied to, and influenced by, contemporary political and ideological currents.

In opening up the distinction between Squier's social emphasis and Ishiguro's more political focus, it is instructive to address the relation of each writer to the genre of science fiction. Squier is particularly concerned to make a case for the hitherto undervalued genre of science fiction as a crucial testing ground and forerunner of subsequent scientific research and practice. On the one hand, it is uniquely placed as a 'zone of exploration'; because of its 'particular epistemological positioning between knowledge and unawareness' it can imagine possibilities that anticipate and prepare the ground for subsequent biomedical developments (2004: 22). On the other hand, it can also play a crucial role in the normalisation of new advances; with reference to transplant technology in particular, Squier observes:

> throughout the twentieth century, science fiction was as crucial in the cultural realm as immunology was in the realm of medicine in bringing about public acceptance of organ transplant technology. Indeed,

we might think of science fiction as functioning as a kind of ideological cyclosporine. (2004: 183)[5]

Ishiguro's deployment of the science-fiction genre in *Never Let Me Go* does not, however, correspond to either of these models, and he articulates in interview a notable disengagement from the term:

> you can call it science fiction if you like, in that I've used a scientific framework or landscape, in which there are scientific possibilities that don't exist right now . . . I've just imagined a world where there are breakthroughs in science that haven't in fact taken place. I worry less about genres and categories. I use whatever I can. (Kleffel 2005: 62–3)

Ishiguro points here to the complicated temporality of *Never Let Me Go*; set in the 1990s, the novel lays out developments in biotechnology that have not taken place, but that could have done so if postwar scientific developments had taken a different course. The yet to be is thus replaced by the might have been, which establishes a very different interpretative model to that laid out by Squier. The unexpected temporality of Ishiguro's novel not only opens up the space for critical reflection, but also emphasises that scientific development does not follow a predetermined path and is as contingent as any other mode of thought. This indicates that the scientific imaginary is open to influence by broader political movements and ideologies, and it also allows for the possibility of intervention.

In reading what is at stake in Ishiguro's temporal positioning of the novel, I turn now to Nikolas Rose's call for a move away from the dominant rhetoric of our moment in history as 'one of maximal turbulence, on the cusp of an epochal change, on a verge between the security of a past now fading and the insecurity of a future we can only dimly discern' (2007: 5).[6] Rose looks instead to a different intellectual project, which he identifies as a 'more modest cartography of our present', and it is this mode of mapping that I suggest he shares with Ishiguro. Rose elaborates:

> To undertake such a cartography of the present, a map showing the range of paths not yet taken that may lead to different potential futures, it is important to recognize that we do not stand at some unprecedented moment in the unfolding of a single history. Rather, we live in the middle of multiple histories. As with our own present, our future will emerge from the intersection of a number of contingent pathways that, as they intertwine, might create something

new. This, I suspect, will be no radical transformation, no shift into a world 'after nature' or a 'posthuman future'. Perhaps it will not even constitute an 'event'. But I think, in all manner of small ways, much of which will soon be routinized and taken for granted, things will not be quite the same again. (2007: 5)

Never Let Me Go is narrated from the late 1990s and it chronicles the thirty-year life span of Kathy, in terms of a path not taken in post-war scientific development. While the major post-war scientific breakthroughs took place in the realm of nuclear physics, Ishiguro imagines an alternative history of what might have happened if rapid developments in biotechnology had dominated instead (Black 2009). This narrative strategy, undertaken at the very moment that the biosciences are causing such intense public debate, opens up a sense that these developments are not inevitable; that our present, like our past, could lead in multiple possible directions. At the same time, Ishiguro's focus on re-imagining a specific period in British history indicates that the direction in which science does develop is susceptible to political influence. Postcolonial critic Shameem Black has indicated that Ishiguro's imagined enterprise of cloning humans in order to harvest their organs reflects a post-war imaginary 'shaped by the eugenic fantasies of Nazi-era incarceration' (2009: 789). Identifying the moment of Kathy's cloning as the late 1960s, Black suggests a further link to Enoch Powell's famous 1968 'River of Blood' speech against the changing racial composition of Britain, situating Ishiguro's imagined Britain of the 1990s as 'what England might have become, had Powell had his way' (2009: 797). Here, then, Ishiguro powerfully dislodges the sense that scientific discourse can be value-free. *Never Let Me Go* also departs from an epochal vision of history to emphasise the small, almost imperceptible shifts that cumulatively mean that things will never be the same. The force of Ishiguro's novel lies in the ways in which, for all concerned, the fate of the clones is entirely normalised and taken for granted. Critic Liani Lochner thus aptly notes of the novel's intention: 'Ishiguro does not demonize scientific creation; rather, the text's critical focus emphasizes the naturalization of instrumentalist ways of seeing the world' (2011: 227).

Squier's analysis of the new kinds of life stories that can be told in relation to liminal lives further illuminates Ishiguro's political and ideological focus in *Never Let Me Go*. Central to the reconfiguration of human life that is produced by biomedicine is, Squier argues, a shift in the conventional understanding of the human life span: 'people are conceived differently, born differently, grow and live differently, and age and die differently' (2004: 61). Although it is clear that, in the case of Kathy and the other clones, the key phases of the human life course have been radically disrupted, Ishiguro is notably silent on the details. The clones' ignorance of the details of their own coming into existence and mode of death – they know that they have been cloned from humans and that their fate will be that of repeated organ extraction, but they are not told the specifics by their guardians at Hailsham – places the narrative emphasis on the stories that circulate between them about the beginning and end of their lives. The system of donation, which entails 'completion' or death at the fourth operation if not before, leaves the reader to infer the brutal and calculating logic at work; that the donations must begin with those organs such as the eyes or kidneys that can be taken from living donors, and end with a major organ such as the heart.[7] Within this thoroughly instrumentalised system, the clones endure a protracted and painful death, as their lives are prolonged for as long as transplantable material can be extracted from them.

Griffin notes that the clones 'undertake both productive and reproductive labour in that . . . whilst their service is exhausted in its performance, their organs survive in others' bodies' (2009: 652). Nevertheless, the attention of the clones themselves is focused not on their material afterlives in the human recipients of their organs, but rather on the potential for further harvesting of their tissues and cells even after the fourth donation. Tommy raises the subject with Kathy as he approaches his fourth donation, leading her to reflect:

> You'll have heard the same talk. How maybe, after the fourth donation, even if you're technically completed, you're still conscious in some sort of way; how then you find there are more donations, plenty of them, on the other side of that line; how there are no recovery centres, no carers, no friends; how there's nothing to do except watch your remaining donations until they switch you off. (2005: 274)

Through this unsubstantiated rumour passed between the clones, Ishiguro captures not only the relentless logic at work behind the donation programme, but also the deep anxieties that emerge when the boundaries that demarcate the passage from life to death are disturbed. The same difficult question echoes through Rebecca Skloot's *The Immortal Life of Henrietta Lacks* (2010), which reworks the genre of life writing in order to recount the life of Henrietta Lacks, a poor black woman from Virginia who died of cervical cancer in 1951, and whose cancerous cells were taken and retained without familial consent. These cells became the first human material to be reproduced *in vitro*, and they have now been grown in extraordinary numbers in laboratories around the world. Resonating with Tommy's concerns is Skloot's sense of Lacks' cellular afterlife as a potentially ceaseless existence, which cannot properly be termed a 'life' because it is entirely lacking in agency and rights. Boxall has described what is at stake for Skloot in terms that also resonate with *Never Let Me Go*: 'Henrietta's immortal life is . . . a stripped biological life which persists blindly without any agency or sovereignty, outside the legal and cultural institutions which consign personhood upon the body; unending life beneath the threshold of the human' (2013: 89). Analogously, the rumour that passes between the clones articulates their status as what Giorgio Agamben (1998) has termed *homo sacer*, a life that is excluded from citizenship and that can accordingly be killed but not sacrificed; their deaths by organ extraction can produce no higher significance, even for the clones themselves, because they have already been designated worthless.

The same understanding of who they are, or, more accurately, what they represent, underpins the clones' theory of 'possibles', the humans from whom they have been copied or reproduced. In one sense, as critic Mark Currie has outlined, the possibles represent 'the reification of an ideal' (2013: 157). Thus, Ruth's dreams of working in a glass-fronted office momentarily seem to be realised, as her possible is identified working in exactly such an office in Norwich. As the clones pursue Ruth's possible through the streets and into a gallery, however, the dream evaporates and a different sense of where they come from emerges. Ruth thus insists that their possibles do not work in modern offices, but rather represent the social underclass: 'Junkies, prostitutes, winos, tramps. Convicts, maybe, just so long as they aren't psychos. That's what we come from' (2005: 164). Kathy, too, has secretly harboured this belief, flipping through the pages of porn magazines to see if any of the faces matches her own. The clones' putative origin in the 'gutter' and the 'rubbish bin' (2005: 164) is suggestive of Zygmunt Bauman's analysis of human waste. Identifying human surplus as an inevitable outcome of modernity, Bauman distinguishes between two varieties of human waste. The first represents the *homo sacer*, whose life is designated as not worth living, and who is exempted from the protection of the law. This form of human rubbish is representative of the clones themselves. The second form of wasted life is not deliberately targeted, but represents the 'unintended and unplanned "collateral casualties" of economic progress' (2004: 39). This is the surplus population that is rendered redundant by new technologies; the kind of underclass that Ruth identifies as representative of the possibles from whom the clones originate. The narrative of possibles thus captures at once the clones' desire for origin and belonging, and their simultaneous conviction that even if they locate an original from whom they are derived, this person too will represent a social outcast or a wasted life.

Kathy's life story – and the stories that the clones tell each other about their own lives and deaths – captures the destabilising of the conventional boundaries of human life that Squier identifies, but also expands beyond this to indicate that the lives of the clones are liminal not only biologically but also politically. Picking up the connection that I have described between the clones and other socially marginalised groups, Black has noted:

> The implicit analogies between deracinated, genetically-engineered students and exploited workers in a multicultural Britain and a globalizing economy ask us to recognize how many people in our own world are not considered fully human. Like the clones, they are consigned to the barely visible world of service to others that, in extreme situations, give rise to Agamben's *homo sacer*. (2009: 803)

Ishiguro and Skloot both add to Squier's analysis of the biologically liminal life a connection with those whose lives are on the social and political margins. For Skloot, it is no accident that the He-La cell can be traced to the racially marginalised Lacks, while for Ishiguro, it is those who are excluded from economic production who seem most likely to be co-opted for the production of the bare life of the clones. Ishiguro's exposure of the link between socioeconomic vulnerability and the new forms of life engineered through biotechnology, rendering the latter into an exploitative form of commerce or trade, is most fully articulated, however, not in relation to cloning but with reference to organ donation. I accordingly turn in the following section to address Ishiguro's treatment of the illegal global trade in human organs, which has developed in response to the shortage of organs needed to satisfy the demand for transplant operations in the industrialised world.

Ishiguro and biopolitics

The recent development of the drug cyclosporine has revolutionised transplant medicine, drastically reducing the risk of organ rejection. The rapid expansion of transplant operations and procedures throughout the First World has, however, placed pressure on the number of available human organs. The field of regenerative medicine, which aims to reconstruct living organs and tissues *in vitro*, has been widely hailed as the future solution to the various problems associated with organ transplantation, but, in spite of significant breakthroughs, we remain some distance away from the successful engineering of complex organ structures.[8] The transplantation of cadaver organs has now been supplemented with the transplantation of organs from living donors. Many such organs are gifted by healthy relatives and family members, but they can also be procured through an illegal global trade in extracted organs. Anthropologist Nancy Scheper-Hughes has tracked and exposed this illicit commerce in which vulnerable populations are recruited into selling body parts, mostly kidneys. In a movement of medical resource that closely parallels the global circuits outlined in Chapter 4, Scheper-Hughes observes that the traffic in human organs 'follows the established routes of capital from south to north, from poorer to more affluent bodies, from black and brown bodies to white ones, and from females to males, or from poor males to more affluent males' (2004: 36–7). The transplant trade thus exploits and exacerbates existing hierarchies between global north and south, core and periphery. Those whose bodies are most likely to be co-opted for the production of the forms of life produced by biotechnology are those who live on the social, political and economic margins; those, in the words of Scheper-Hughes, 'whose social frailty and all too evident "bioavailability" have proven too tempting to bypass or overlook' (2004: 33).

In addressing what is at stake in contemporary biopolitics, Scheper-Hughes has made the important observation that in the context of organ donation we are essentially concerned with a politics of life:

> the transformation of a person into a 'life' that must be prolonged or saved at any cost has made life into the ultimate commodity fetish. And an insistence on the absolute value of a single human life saved, enhanced and prolonged ends all ethical or moral enquiry and erases the possibility of a global social ethic. (2004: 63)

Scheper-Hughes's point is echoed by Rose, who identifies the biomedical technologies associated with organ transplantation as 'technologies of life' (2007: 17). These technologies are, then, aimed at the goal of maximising bodily functioning for some, albeit at the cost of global imbalance and others' reduced life span. The commerce in human organs makes visible that vitality itself has become a valuable commodity, and one that can be extracted from others. Decisive for Rose, however, is the distinction between a politics of life and a politics of death:

> While biopower, today, certainly has its circuits of exclusion, letting die is not making die. This is not a politics of death, although death suffuses and haunts it, nor even a politics of illness and health; it is a matter of the government of *life*. (2007: 70; italics in original)

Reinforcing his point, Rose insists that current biopolitics should neither be considered a new form of eugenics, nor confused with the explicitly racial politics and ideologies of the mid-twentieth century:

> Our contemporary biopolitics is no less problematic, no less entangled with relations of power and judgements of the differential worth of forms of life, the nature of suffering, and our individual and collective obligations to the future, but it deserves to be analysed on its own terms. (2007: 73)

We are returned here to the difference marked out by Bauman between Agamben's state of exception, which operates according to the principle of making die, and the expansion of capitalism into the trade of body parts, which entails that the medical consumer turns to surplus populations as a source of healthy organs, even if that means letting others die in the fulfilment of market demand.

At first glance, it seems that Ishiguro has committed precisely the conceptual error identified by Rose; namely, he represents and critiques the global organ trade, based in a politics of life, through his depiction of the donation programme, which represents a politics of death. It is instructive here to return to the question of temporality, and to note once more the priority accorded by Ishiguro to the might-have-been. *Never Let Me Go* presents a vision of how biomedicine might have developed had it taken hold in the immediate post-war period, and been informed by the racial laws of eugenics. This is decisively not a portrait of contemporary biotechnologies, and the difference between the two can productively be articulated through Rose's distinction between the politics of life and the politics of death, between letting die and making die. Ishiguro indicates that, in different historical and political circumstances, the instrumentalisation and commodification of the human body that is integral to contemporary bioscience could lend itself to a politics of death.[9] Part of the power of the novel, then, lies in mapping out what might have been, had the breakthroughs in biotechnology taken place a few decades earlier; in Ishiguro's darkened rendering of our own bioeconomy, the deaths that haunt its margins represent state-sanctioned murder rather than collateral damage. At the same time, the dynamics of power and exploitation that are common to the politics of death and the politics of life act as a reminder that, although our own dark trade in organs does not operate according to the state of exception, we are nevertheless implicated in our own version of a biological service economy. Cultural geographer Sarah Atkinson has accordingly diagnosed *Never Let Me Go* as a study in what it means not to care; as in previous chapters, fiction is concerned not with the cultivation of empathy, but rather with our capacity to turn away from others, and to ration or limit the compassion that we extend to them. Atkinson notes that Ishiguro presents the reader with a sliding scale of indifference:

> Once bodies are cast as less valued, as amenable to exploitation to save more valued others, then they are already effectively categorised as lesser humans and the discourse supporting a limited caring about and for those bodies can be easily transformed into the very different justifications underpinning an attitude and practice of uncaring and not caring. (2016: 618)

Yet, while a reflection on not caring undoubtedly forms an important aspect of Ishiguro's novel, it does not capture the full complexity of his sense of the empathetic work of contemporary fiction, which is explored metafictionally in *Never Let Me Go* through the artworks that the clones produce at Hailsham. In the following section, I accordingly ask how we might best read the significance of these strange, and oddly mechanical, aesthetic productions.

Empathy and art

Critic David Palumbo-Liu has rightly noted that organ transplantation provides a compelling narrative device for a writer wishing to explore empathy, observing: 'this phenomenon has provided . . . Ishiguro . . . [with] the vehicle through which to explore radical otherness, the binary of self-other' (2012: 97). The procedure has also proved fertile ground for phenomenologists: the transfer of one person's organ into another's body raises philosophical questions about how the self–other relation is negotiated in and through this lived experience, while the complex interaction between the psychic and the somatic in managing the acceptance of the organ speaks to phenomenology's interest in the embodied self. The two most notable phenomenological explorations of organ donation are by feminist theorist Margaret Shildrick, whose work in this area is based in a long-term interdisciplinary project working with heart-transplant patients, and by French philosopher Jean-Luc Nancy, whose essay *L'Intrus* ('The Intruder', 2002) was based on his own experience of a heart transplant in the early 1990s. Although Nancy and Shildrick both adopt a broadly phenomenological approach, their work tends in opposing directions, and their differing sense of what organ transplantation might mean for relationality is instructive in defining Ishiguro's approach to empathy in *Never Let Me Go*. In what follows, I take my interpretative cue from Palumbo-Liu, who has turned to Nancy, in particular, as a suggestive text to read alongside *Never Let Me Go*.

Shildrick places emphasis on the disruption to the embodied self that is caused by organ transplantation, and that is not sufficiently registered in clinical treatment. In an article published in *The Lancet*, philosophers of science Edgardo Carosella and Thomas Pradeu recognised that 'with the transplant of a *visible* organ, a deep identity split occurs, because one's self image is modified substantially' (2006: 183; my italics), but they failed to register an equivalent response in the recipients of internal organs.[10] Contesting such a view, Shildrick observes the prevalence of ongoing psychological disturbance in heart-transplant patients, and asserts that, from a phenomenological perspective, this reaction is not only a 'predictable' but also a 'meaningful' outcome of the experience (2014: 48). Organ recipients are often resistant to the medical narrative of assimilation and respond instead to their own sense of the organ's irreducible difference. They are, for Shildrick, fundamentally hybrid subjects, and the continuing otherness of the donated organ is registered viscerally through the immunosuppressant drugs upon which organ recipient patients are dependent for the rest of their lives. Central to Shildrick is finding a means to recognise, rather than close down, the hybridity of transplant patients, which would extend beyond the accounts of relationality and self–other relations found in traditional phenomenology to encompass a more radical vision of intercorporeality.

Shildrick is explicitly critical of Nancy's philosophical exploration of organ transplantation because he remains 'indifferent to the identity of his donor and refuses to sentimentalize the experience of otherness within' (2014: 59). It is, however, precisely Nancy's refusal to engage in an imaginative conversation with the other, whose death is the very condition of his own survival, which positions him on a productive intellectual continuum with Ishiguro. Nancy's rejection of relationality with the donor carries a pragmatic dimension, which shades into complicity in the context of the murderous regime represented in *Never Let Me Go*, but both texts speak powerfully – if distinctly – of the ways in which survival is contingent to some degree upon a willingness to look away. Nancy thus strikingly remarks of his own approach to the distribution of available organs:

> I will never ask the question: how does one decide, and who decides, when a single organ is suited to more than one potential graftee? The demand here is known to exceed the supply. . . . From the first, my survival is inscribed in a complex process woven through with strangers and strangeness. (2002: 5)

If Shildrick's stranger represents the donor organ, and the life of the other that it signifies, Nancy's pluralised 'strangers' also encompasses those anonymous clinical figures who arbitrate between one life and another within the global bioeconomy of organ transplantation.

The 'intruder' of Nancy's essay initially seems to refer to the other's organ, which is transplanted into his body in place of his own failing heart. We quickly learn, however, that Nancy's intruder also signifies his original heart, that becomes a stranger within once it ceases to function; the intense medical regimen to which Nancy is subjected; and the multiple, invisible organisms that inhabit his body and are revealed to him through the effects of the immunosuppressant drugs. If he locates an inner self through his experience, it is thus somewhat prosaically composed of innumerable viruses and bacteria. Nancy's identity is, like that of Shildrick's heart transplant patients, fissured and disturbed by the transplant procedure but his is not a hybridity of self and other; it is, rather, an 'I' that has been disrupted by a recognition of the strangeness that already resides within:

> The *intrus* exposes me, excessively. It extrudes, it exports, it expropriates: I am the illness and the medical intervention, I am the cancerous cell and the grafted organ, I am the immuno-depressive agents and their palliatives, I am the bits of wire that hold together my sternum and I am this injection site permanently stitched in below my clavicle,

just as I was already these screws in my hip and this plate in my groin. (2002: 13; italics in original)

Notably, Nancy closes his list with reference to the artificial implant – his already existing hip and joint replacements – to denote his sense of the 'intruder'; his inner being has been exposed to be not only material but also mechanistic: his ailing heart, as well as the anonymous viruses and bacteria, function according to their own systems and laws. It is this vision of an unexpected *in*humanity within that is resonant with Ishiguro's novel.

Tracing the post-war history of organ transplantation, Cooper has observed its development in tandem with the science of prosthetics: '[w]ith the war-driven invention of new materials and later advances in electronics and software, this period witnessed the first large-scale industrial production of prosthetic substitutes for missing organs and bodily functions' (2008: 106). Cooper's list of the most successful innovations includes, alongside Nancy's example of the artificial joint, 'pacemakers, and cardiovascular devices' (2008: 106), indicating that, alongside the implantation of the living organ through transplantation, there have also been important developments in artificial implants to repair the ailing heart. For Cooper, in spite of their apparent dissimilarity, prosthetics and transplantation are bound together by their common vision of the human as machine: 'despite their difference in materiality, both technologies share a mechanistic vision of animation, one that assumes the fundamental equivalence of the organ and the machine' (2008: 106). In what follows, I argue that, for Ishiguro too, transplantation gestures towards and exposes the logics of substitutability and artificiality, a discourse that is heightened and intensified by the figure of the clone. For Ishiguro, the unfamiliar vision of ourselves as oddly mechanical creatures holds the potential for a new mode of empathy. The liminal lives of the clones thus hold up to view the technological, the artificial and the inhuman in us all; aspects of our being that, for Nancy, are unexpectedly revealed through the intervention – or intrusion – of biomedical procedure.

In *Never Let Me Go*, Ishiguro delivers a powerful and well-aimed blow at a proto-Romantic vision of the arts, which is represented as one of the misguided beliefs that the clones develop at Hailsham, and that is revealed to be an illusion in the confrontation of Kathy and Tommy with Madame. At Hailsham, the education of the guardians placed particular emphasis on the creation of artwork, the best of which was removed by Madame on her periodic visits to the institution. The children believed that it was taken to be displayed in Madame's gallery, alongside the best work of former Hailsham students. Neither confirmed nor denied by the guardians, the rumour persists at the Cottages, and takes on heightened significance in the context of conversations about the possibility of deferral. Unable to find any other explanation for the artwork and its periodic selection, the clones develop the conviction that the best work is saved because it reveals or expresses their inner beings. In order to judge an application for deferral, which in the clones' understanding can only be granted on the grounds of true love, the retained artwork is consulted; only in the light of the self that it reveals can a relationship be assessed to be the perfect match required. The extent of the clones' self-deception is revealed when Kathy and Tommy outline their hopes for deferral to Madame and Miss Emily. Madame reveals that their artwork does not, as the clones believe, 'display your *souls*', but rather serves the purpose of '*prov[ing] you had souls at all*' (2005: 248, 255; italics in original). The clones' Romantic (and romantic) interpretation of the value of their art is countered by the instrumentalist agenda of the guardians, who encouraged its production as part of their political campaign, which can most closely be compared to the advocacy of free-range over battery farming. Madame's response not only reveals the failure of the guardians to recognise the clones' humanity; it also returns us to the question of value, and to the conflicting and incompatible criteria by which it is measured, claimed and assessed in the biocapitalist age.

As a writer, Ishiguro might be expected to defend the clones' perspective and to promote the humanising potential of the arts. The clones' viewpoint is, however, fatally compromised by its incapacity to comprehend either the hopelessness of their situation or the full brutality of the donation programme. Ishiguro further distances himself from the Romantic conception of art by allying it to the procedures of organ harvesting: both entail an interest in accessing the human interior, and if the aesthetic encounter with another's inner being is typically accorded positive value, it is reworked in the light of the donation programme into a more predatory process of extraction. Black observes that, if art is fostered at Hailsham, its promise to reveal the soul notably 'prefigures the dismemberment of the students' bodies' (2009: 798). Art thus normalises for the clones a sense that their inner lives are to be given over to others, and it also introduces them to the idea that they are containers of parts that can be extracted. The latter conception takes shape in the children's talk of 'unzipping', which is outlined by Kathy as follows: 'The idea was that when the time came, you'd be able to just unzip a bit of yourself, a kidney or something would slide out, and you'd hand it over' (2005: 86). The act of unzipping strikingly recurs as Tommy opens his bag to reveal his most recent artwork to Madame (2005: 249), indicating that for him as well as for the guardians, his pictures have come to be viewed as another internal resource that can be extracted and exchanged for profit.[11] Tommy's misguided belief is that he can trade this commodity for a few more years of life, while the guardians' miscalculation had been that the artwork could politically justify the institution of Hailsham. Far from revealing a humanising potential, the production and reception of art becomes allied in *Never Let Me Go* to the systems and processes of *de*humanisation. In this respect, Black has rightly noted that '*Never Let Me Go* shares in a pervasive late-twentieth-century cultural scepticism about the viability of empathetic art' (2009: 785).

Yet, Ishiguro does not abandon the notion of empathy altogether in *Never Let Me Go*. The challenge posed by the novel is to relate ourselves to the liminal lives of the clones not by humanising them – this is, after all, the gesture made by Madame and Miss Emily – but rather by recognising the inhuman in ourselves. As in Nancy, we are asked to encounter the artificial intruder within. Black thus observes of the novel:

> *Never Let Me Go* implies that if there is to be any empathetic connection with Ishiguro's protagonists, it will not occur through the consoling liberal realization that they are humans, just like us. It will evolve through the darker realization that art, along with the empathy it provokes, needs to escape the traditional concept of the human. The novel thus calls for a contradiction in terms: an empathetic inhuman aesthetics that embraces the mechanical, commodified, and replicated elements of personhood. (2009: 786)

For Black, the exemplar for such an inhuman – or perhaps more accurately, posthuman – aesthetic is inscribed within the novel itself, in the form of Tommy's drawings. His art represents a series of weird, mechanical creatures that cannot easily be described. Kathy notes that they initially look like the inside of a machine, and are only later recognisable as animal forms: 'The first impression was like one you'd get if you took the back off a radio set . . . and only when you held the page away could you see it was some sort of armadillo, say, or a bird' (2005: 185). The inner self that is depicted by Tommy is thus comprised of mechanical parts: 'tiny canals, weaving tendons, miniature screws and wheels' (2005: 185), which deny the interior spiritual depths promised by Romantic art. Nevertheless, as Kathy examines the pictures, she feels a discernible tenderness towards the creatures portrayed: 'there was something sweet, even vulnerable, about each of them' (2005: 185). It is not hard to recognise a metafictional element in operation here: in representing the clones, Ishiguro, too, has depicted lives that are resistant to being read in terms of psychological depth, but that draw us in through a certain vulnerability that engenders in us a protective concern. If none of the characters in the novel seem able to grasp the significance of Tommy's art, the reader is asked to take a step further, and to begin to conceive of a new empathetic relation in response to the new forms of life produced under biocapitalism; a mode of relationality that reconfigures the very limits and boundaries of the human itself.

For critic Rebecca Walkowitz, it is not Tommy's drawings, but the cassette tapes that surface repeatedly throughout the novel, which offer a model for how the human is reconceptualised within *Never Let Me Go*. As Walkowitz notes, the cassette tape is suggestive not of originality and uniqueness, but of reproducibility; she remarks of the most prominent cassette in the novel, Kathy's recording of the singer Judy Bridgewater:

> As a token, a cassette is one of many copies, perhaps one of thousands. And it is a copy of a copy: the cassette was originally an LP . . . and the LP was originally a recording of the performer Judy Bridgewater's voice; and the voice is an interpretation of the song 'Never Let Me Go' (2007: 227)

The emphasis on repeated reproduction speaks to the condition of the clones, whose status is signalled through the replacement of the surname with a letter that recalls a manufacturer's serial number: Kathy H., Tommy D. *Never Let Me Go* encourages us to see our human lives as more artificial and substitutable than we tend to presume, so that we conform not to the Romantic vision of interior depth but rather to the unoriginality and seriality of the cassette. Particularly telling is Kathy's criticism of Ruth at the Cottages for copying the gestures and intonation that she has seen on the television, a practice that she has in turn picked up from Chrissie and

Rodney, who have been at the Cottages for a longer time. Confronting Ruth, Kathy observes of the habit: '[i]t's not what people really do out there, in normal life, if that's what you were thinking' (2005: 121). Walkowitz rightly notes, however, that Kathy 'seems naïve in her insistence on this point' (2007: 226), given the extent to which we do routinely reproduce – more or less consciously – the physical and verbal phrasings that are mediated to us by popular culture. Kathy's misunderstanding exposes the isolation and insularity of the clones, but it also speaks of our own artificiality; Ishiguro challenges us to recognise in ourselves a characteristic superficiality of being. In so doing, he effectively reverses the traditional aesthetic hierarchy between original and copy, locating value in the latter rather than the former. In representing the liminal lives of the clones, the novel thus articulates a mode of relationality that is succinctly encapsulated by Black: '[t]o be most human . . . is to recognize oneself as inhuman' (2009: 801). I have argued in this section that this is an insight shared by Ishiguro and Nancy, in their respective articulations of the lives that are produced in and through biomedical intervention. It is also the most significant challenge posed to us by the clones; that we confront the difficult reality that we are close to being one of them. Unlike the clones, Ishiguro implies that we are neither cognisant of, nor attuned to, our own inhuman qualities; rather, we cling stubbornly to the outworn myth of our own unique and irreplaceable interiority.

Conclusion

This chapter has focused on Ishiguro's exploration of empathy's limits and potential under the influence of biocapitalism. How, he asks in *Never Let Me Go*, might we relate affectively, imaginatively and critically, to the lives that are produced and circulated in and under the biocapitalist regime? I have argued that Ishiguro's focus is primarily political; he is interested in how biomedicine shapes and regulates the forms of exchange that result from its procedures, inscribing them within capitalist, commodifying and instrumentalist agendas. In his depiction of the donation programme, he represents a politics of death – the programme is based on a state of exception – which draws attention to the waste of human life that haunts the margins of our own bioeconomy, as well as indicating what might have been, had the biomedical revolution taken place a few decades earlier. Ishiguro is also interested in the attenuated and ambivalent modes of feeling that result when affect is placed at the service of the marketplace. In Ishiguro's imagined world, empathy has been entirely co-opted by the biopolitical system that defines and circumscribes the lives of the clones: their feelings for each other are placed at the service of the donation programme by rendering them into conscientious and successful carers. Feelings do circulate in the novel, but they correspond to Ngai's analysis of the minor emotions that are produced under capitalism and they are linked to passivity rather than to rebellion or resistance. An instrumentalist logic extends, too, to the artworks that the clones produce, which are explicitly commodified through the market value invested in them by the students at the Exchanges. This leads Kathy and Tommy to imbue Tommy's artwork with the mistaken hope that it can be exchanged for deferral, only to be confronted with the brutal realisation that they are enmeshed within a system not of exchange but of exploitation. Within this ruthless economy, even their feelings for one another represent an inner resource to be extracted for profit, and this is powerfully symbolised in Ishiguro's refiguring of the Romantic aesthetic, to signify a harvesting of the soul that is analogous to the organ harvesting of the donation programme.

If empathy can retain any meaning or potential at all in the novel, it is through a major reworking of its significance, which disconnects it from its traditional grounding in humanist thought. Ishiguro poses the challenge of an inhuman empathy, which asks us to recognise the mechanical and the artificial in the clones, and then, in turn, to re-envision ourselves in this light. The liminal lives of the clones thus become the vehicle through which Ishiguro redefines the human in the context of biomedicine, pointing – like Nancy – to the strangeness that resides within. Ishiguro's vision of the human, based on surface rather than depth, on the copy rather than the original, also influences the production of the novel itself; reading *Never Let Me Go* is an unsettling experience, because we are asked to respond imaginatively to the superficial banalities of Kathy's narration; a life story that offers us no significant insight or interiority. In his radical rejection of psychological depth within a first-person-narrated novel, Ishiguro refuses to give us the consolation of reader identification; indeed, he positions such an hermeneutic strategy as a misrecognition or denial of the clones' lived experience. *Never Let Me Go* thus draws inventively, if not ingeniously, on the theme of artificially produced life to ask probing questions about the limits of the human, as well as about the ethics of empathetic reading, in the biocapitalist age.

Notes

1. In 2001, a further scandal broke around allegations of organ retention at the Central Manchester and Manchester Children's Hospital University National Health Service Trust. Then Secretary of State for Health, Hazel Blears, asked the Retained Organs Commission to investigate, and their report, published in 2002, concluded that while there was not an exceptional level of retention of children's organs in Manchester, the Trust had nevertheless responded inadequately to public anxiety concerning the issue. Clinical geneticist Ian Ellis noted in *The Lancet* that the Commission also recorded:

   > that the Human Tissue Act of 1961 was unclear, outdated, and not adhered to. It recommended new legislation based on the assumption that explicit consent should be required for the retention of all human material (i.e. organs and tissues, but not cells) except by the coroner or in specified and usually historical circumstances. (2004: 43)

2. I return in the Conclusion to the question of the human–animal relation, and its potential for the medical humanities.
3. Hochschild's work has been particularly influential in the field of nursing; see, for example, Catherine Theodosius (2008). Theodosius challenges the current perception that 'nurses have a lack of compassion ... towards their patients', arguing both that in nursing 'emotional labour is marginalised, creating increasingly stressful environments for patients and nurses alike' and that 'the emotional labour carried out is largely invisible, either because it is misunderstood or because the nature of emotional labour in nursing care has changed and developed alongside nursing work, becoming unrecognisable' (2008: 5–6).
4. For more on the significance of Ruth's mimicry and the discussion of *Daniel Deronda* between Kathy and Ruth, see Anne Whitehead (2011).
5. Cyclosporine is an immunosuppressant drug widely used in organ transplantation to prevent rejection. The drug was approved for use in 1983, and has been instrumental in the rapid growth and routinisation of transplant surgery since then.
6. Rose's evocation of an epochal vision of history resonates with Madame's description of a brave new world of scientific endeavour, a world that advanced both rapidly and unstoppably, and that was conjured at Hailsham as Madame watched Kathy dance to the song, 'Never Let Me Go':

   > I saw a new world coming rapidly. More scientific, more efficient, yes. More cures for the old sicknesses. Very good. But a harsh, cruel world. And I saw a little girl, her eyes tightly closed, holding to her breast the old kind world, one that she knew in her heart could not remain, and she was holding it and pleading, never to let her go. That is what I saw. (2005: 267)

7. In the film version of *Never Let Me Go* (2010, directed by Mark Romanek), the incremental nature of the donations, as well as their debilitating and prematurely ageing effect on the young bodies of Ruth and Tommy, are powerfully visualised.

8. Catherine Waldby and Robert Mitchell argue that the crisis in organ availability has arisen out of the inflated expectations created by regenerative tissue therapies. They note: 'This in turn has put tremendous pressure on "real time" therapies such as organ transplantation, which like blood donation rely on the regenerative capacities of another's body' (2006: 162). For Melinda Cooper, the greatest successes to date in regenerative medicine have been in 'developing structural substitutes such as skin, . . . bone, cartilage and heart valves' (2008: 104), while Gabriele Griffin observes that in 2006: 'Antony Atala et al. reported in *The Lancet* that they had been able to make bladders for patients with end-stage bladder disease using "autologous engineered bladder tissues for reconstruction"' (2009: 649). Although an important step towards organ replacement, Griffin notes that the bladder is nevertheless 'a simple organ in biological terms' (2009: 649).

9. In an observation that supports my reading of Hailsham in terms of the state of exception, Groes and Lewis have remarked of Ishiguro's recent interviews: 'Ishiguro has voiced his concern at the erosion of protections accorded to civilians in recent conflicts and genocides, which suggests that his work is more political than some accounts (including, at times, his own) would suggest' (2011a: 7).

10. The 'visible' organ transplants to which Carosella and Pradeu refer are primarily those of the hand or the face.

11. The students are introduced to an instrumentalised view of art through the Exchanges at Hailsham, which foster in them a sense of their own and others' work (and worth) in terms of commodity value. Kathy thus reflects back on the Exchanges: '[i]f you think about it, being dependent on each other to produce the stuff that might become your private treasures – that's bound to do things to your relationships' (2005: 16).

Conclusion

In this book, I have sought to identify and address some of the limitations and blind spots that the medical humanities could usefully engage with in moving forward as a field of study. I have drawn particular attention to the binarised or dualistic mode of thinking that has characterised the first wave of the medical humanities, setting into opposition the terms 'doctor' and 'patient', 'disease' and 'illness', and 'medicine' and 'humanities', with the expectation that the humanities can help to shift the balance in biomedicine towards the patient's illness experience. While the privileging of the patient voice represents an important critical intervention into contemporary biomedicine, it does not, I argue, go far enough. The medical humanities, I propose, needs a more contextualised, and a more politicised, sense of the patient–practitioner relation, and it could also usefully extend out beyond the clinical to address other medical settings, sites, and domains. More than this, the positioning of the humanities as a 'softening' of biomedicine's 'hard' edges through the production of empathetic feeling not only assumes a subservient role for the arts and humanities, but also limits the more critical, and potentially constitutive, role that these disciplines could play in relation to medical knowledges and practices.

In the preceding chapters, I have examined fictional texts that stage a range of different clinical encounters, retaining the patient–practitioner relation as an important scene for the medical humanities. Departing from the individualising tendencies of mainstream medical humanities, I have emphasised the importance of the historical, geographical, and institutional contexts in which the clinical encounter takes place. I have asked how various modes of positionality, and the related dynamics of power that they entail, inflect the practitioner–patient relation, as well as attending to who, or what,

else might be in the room. I have suggested that empathetic engagement with the patient in the clinical context might be experienced by
its recipient as intrusive or invasive; that it does not lead to an understanding of the 'truth' of her experience; and that it is imbricated as
emotional labour in the discourses and practices of management. Further work might also be carried out in thinking through what would
happen if we reversed the flow of affective feeling, and considered
the potential implications of the patient's empathetic feeling towards
the practitioner.[1] We might also usefully ask more critical questions
of technology's role in relation to the clinical. For Spiro, technology
is positioned in alignment with biomedicine's inhuman tendencies:
'Computed tomographic scans offer no compassion, and magnetic
resonance imaging has no human face. Only men and women are
capable of empathy' (1993c: 14). Yet, twenty-first-century developments in medical technology, as well as new critical engagements with
the digital, can offer a different sense of the potential, as well as the
hazards, of digital technologies and of the diverse forms of relationality and sociality that they enable and produce. I have also extended
my gaze beyond the clinical encounter, thinking variously about the
diagnosis, the brain-imaging scan, the medical laboratory, the transplanted organ, and the literary text itself, as key sites in and through
which medical knowledge is currently circulated, produced and negotiated. The task of opening up different areas of medicine for critical
attention is an important development in the medical humanities and,
undoubtedly, much valuable work remains to be done here.

In challenging the binary thinking of mainstream medical humanities, this book does not seek to instate a further dualism between
first-wave and second-wave medical humanities.[2] The three 'Es' that
I have identified in the Introduction as characterising mainstream
medical humanities – namely Ethics, Experience and Education
– play repeatedly through the chapters of this book, and continue
to constitute an important presence in the field. The categories are,
though, positioned differently in this volume. Not only does ethics
encompass the field of human-rights studies, in addition to medical
ethics and bioethics, but it also orients itself away from closure or
resolution, and towards the open and the inconclusive. Experience
can be that of the patient; in this context, the experience of illness
cannot be separated from broader cultural, social and institutional
dynamics, and neither is it a singular 'truth' that can be accessed by
the practitioner, but rather a dynamic process that is partly constituted in and through the clinical encounter itself. Experience also
pertains to the practitioner, who is not a blank canvas, but brings

her own agency, intentionality and subjectivity to the clinical relation. Education, too, runs in different ways through the pages of this book. For Barker, the medical training encountered in war provides an education in affective detachment, as well as in empathy's limits. For Forna, the training ground of the Sierra-Leonean civil war provides Kai not only with experience in coping with scarce resource, but also with a level of expertise in orthopaedic surgery that positions him as a leader in the field. For Ishiguro, the education of the clones at Hailsham speaks to the neoliberal instrumentalisation of feeling by and for the market economy. Moving away from an emphasis on medical education as the cultivation of empathy, this book thus engages with the limits and the hazards of empathy, as well as with the uneven global economies and social geographies that underpin medical training and migration.

The fourth 'E' of the medical humanities – Empathy – also provides a thread of continuity between the first and second wave of activity in the field, although it is again differently conceptualised in this book. Drawing on phenomenology, I highlight the challenge that empathy itself poses to dualistic thinking, located as it is between subject and object, internal and external, mind and body. More than this, empathy is not something that we *have*, leading to concerns about whether we have enough, and – if not – how we can get more. Instead, it is something that we *do*; it is a located, embodied, performed activity. Feminist affect theory adds to phenomenology's insights the idea of the 'self' not as a stable internal entity that pre-exists the affective encounter, but as dynamically constituted by it. With particular reference to the 'doctor' and 'patient' in the clinical encounter, George Marshall and Claire Hooker have beautifully summarised the implications of this idea for the medical humanities in the following terms: 'instead of looking at stable identities that change because of empathy, we are looking at empathy as a thing that transiently produces these identities in particular ways' (2016: 128). In this book, I have examined the ways in which fictional texts trace out the flows and the sticking points of empathetic feeling that, in circulating between us, gives us both boundary and definition. I have looked at the susceptibility of these affective flows to follow existing routes of privilege and hierarchy, as well as their potential to take surprising new directions. I have also attended to the diverse range of agencies across and between which feeling might flow, that can encompass, variously, the non-human, the material and the conceptual. For Marshall and Hooker, the movement of feeling across human and non-human agents is suggestive of future research into the affective dimensions of the space of the clinical encounter:

> Subjectivities are defined not in isolation, but from within and against the force of these affecting *spaces* and their linguistic, physiological and non-human extensions ... Such an emotional geography can include all that is affected and affects the consultation space including doctors, patient, card, journals, medical language and communities, in short all that becomes enmeshed in the affectivity of the event. (2016: 132; italics in original)

I would add to this list the temporal dimensions of the clinical relation; its unfolding over time, as well in space. The inclusion of the non-human can also extend the clinical relation to animal agents, which are playing an increasing role in treating a number of different health conditions. David Herman (2016) has made a suggestive start in developing a narratological approach to animal–autism stories, and the rich and growing body of work in critical animal studies makes this a particularly productive area of future inquiry.[3]

As well as thinking about empathy as what one *does*, I have also asked: who does the work of empathy? Framing empathy in the context of critical debates on the commercialisation of feeling, I have indicated that the medical humanities should be cognisant of the neoliberalisation of empathy into management discourses and practices. This calls attention to the ways in which empathy can be harnessed into agendas of compliance, as well as opening up the problem of affective disconnection produced when emotional labour is introduced into the world of work. I have examined how the work of empathy is valued, and whether this is differentially assessed according to who is performing the labour, as well as attending to the social, economic and cultural status of those who deliver care. If care work is increasingly drawing in and on the non-human – animals, but also artificial intelligence – we might appropriately question the future implications in terms of the value and status accorded to this form of labour. I have also indicated that the economic geography of service labour is one that broadly maps on to global north and south, following existing hierarchies of privilege and power. Future work might, however, look more closely at the distribution and constitution of service-labour networks. In the context of cross-border reproductive care, social scientist Bronwyn Parry has recently challenged the prevailing neoliberal paradigm, arguing against the assumption that the movement of exchange is 'largely unidirectional and characterised by a dynamic of provision in which "the rest" services "the West"' (2015: 32). A more nuanced and sensitive account of the politics and practices of service labour would thus situate it more fully within its social and cultural contexts, as well as differentiate between diverse health domains and practices.

If this volume has maintained a commitment to the activity of literary reading as central to the medical humanities, it has turned away from the notion of the text as productive either of empathy or of the 'truth' of another's experience. I have emphasised, instead, contemporary fiction's own engagement with, and scepticism of, empathy's boundaries, limits and aesthetics. Departing from interpretative strategies based in feeling 'for' or 'with' individual characters, I have examined the ways in which novels trace out how empathy flows between characters, as well as where it sticks, and how this in turn influences the formation of identities, subjectivities and cultures. I have highlighted, in particular, the genre of the 'phenomenological' or 'syndrome' novel, which engages with the complexity of lived experience not only in its embodied materiality, but also in the density of its imagined physical, social and cultural environment. Another key aspect of this fictional form is its effect of estrangement or defamiliarisation, whether in its representation of cognitive damage and dysfunction as rendering us strangers to ourselves, or in its insistence that we will always and necessarily exceed diagnostic and neo-corporate definitions of who we are. Cognitive estrangement is also central to another literary genre examined in this book, namely the science-fiction novel. Literary critics Gavin Miller and Anna McFarlane have recently argued that its temporality 'opens up a critical engagement with the hegemonic narrative of medical advance and progress', while the similarities of the fictional world that it depicts to our own reality enables 'a new perspective on technological innovations, and their material, social, and political implications'. For them, '[s]cience fiction's critical engagement with the dominant technoscientific imaginary must be given due recognition' (2016: 215), not only because of its disruptive potential, but also because the widespread popularity of the genre can engage new audiences with the medical humanities. While recognising the value of such an approach, my own emphasis has been on the diversity of fictional modes and genres that can contribute to the medical humanities, and I have deliberately ranged across novels that are realist and speculative, historical and futuristic, young-adult and adult, first-person and third-person, and that encompass a wide spectrum of engagement with the 'medical'.

The final binary of the medical humanities that this book critiques centres on the notion of the 'human' itself. Mainstream medical humanities has set the 'humanising' potential of the humanities against the cold technologies of biomedicine. I have asked what it looks like if we reverse this duality, thinking about what the humanities might tell us about emotional distance, and the inhuman. I have examined contemporary fiction's fascination with the instability and fragility of the notion of the 'human', which is represented not as a fixed, stable and knowable category, but as a volatile entity that is complexly entangled with the animal, the digital and the inanimate. I question how the understanding of empathy as an attribute that one has or lacks might be implicated in marking out and policing the boundaries of the human. If only humans have, or are capable of, empathy, what are the implications for those diagnosed with empathy 'deficit' disorders? How might we name and articulate our subjective inter-relations with animals, or with the forms of life produced by the new technologies of biomedicine? These questions matter because they define who, or what, comes to matter. This book has therefore also probed the intersection of the 'human' and the 'citizen'; it is the latter status that recognises and formalises the former category and the human rights that are attendant upon it – not least, that of access to health care. I have examined the imbrication of medicine in the neoliberal and capitalist economic structures that have produced life itself as a marketable commodity, and that expose the vulnerability and exposure – what Judith Butler (2004) has aptly termed the 'precariousness' – of human life to a lack of political recognition and justice. In moving forward, I suggest, the medical humanities should retain the 'human' as central to its concerns, but engage more fully with the instability and the dynamism of the term, which is currently mobilising significant critical and cultural debate about how, where and with what effects the term is produced, and also open out to a recognition of diversity, difference and alterity.

Where, then, does all of this leave the medical humanities? What of the field's original intentions to rebalance medicine towards empathy, to prioritise patient experience, and to critique the increasingly bureaucratic and impersonal structures and systems of biomedicine? This book has made clear that there is no straightforward or transparent link between the generation of empathy and the achievement of more equitable and compassionate systems of care. In the eloquent words of Carolyn Pedwell: 'empathetic engagement can distance as much as it connects, exclude as much as it humanises, fix as much as it transforms and oppress as much as it frees' (2014: 190). The medical humanities should, then, engage with empathy in a mode that is cognisant of its problems, as well as of its promise, and that is attentive to the ways in which it can reinforce as well as overcome existing power differentials. In so doing, scholars and practitioners in the field can draw on the humanities as a resource that enables a complex, critical engagement with questions of diversity, distance and difference. I have also pointed to empathy as a powerful affective force that shapes us and connects us to one another, as well as to other agencies and objects, in multiple, mobile and unpredictable ways. It speaks to our entangled and embodied relations with each other, and ultimately also with ourselves. By fostering attunement to a critically sensitive and dynamically performative model of empathy, I propose, the medical humanities can move forward in its own new, surprising and unexpected directions, as well as remaining grounded in – albeit differently oriented towards – the founding ethical commitments of the field.

Notes

1. Anne Karpf has suggested, in response to this proposed direction of study, the relevance of public support for the junior doctors' strikes of 2016, relating to a dispute over contracts between the British Medical Association and the National Health Service in England.
2. Josie Billington (2017) has raised this point in relation to the critical medical humanities.
3. Feminist theorist Donna Haraway (2003, 2008) provides a strong critical underpinning for the project of thinking through human–animal relations. See also Lorraine Daston and Gregg Mitman (2005); Lori Gruen (2015); and Kari Weil (2012).

Bibliography

Agamben, Giorgio (1998), *Homo Sacer: Sovereign Power and Bare Life*, trans. Daniel Heller-Roazan, Stanford: Stanford University Press.

Ahmed, Sara (2004), *The Cultural Politics of Emotion*, Edinburgh: Edinburgh University Press.

— (2006), *Queer Phenomenology: Orientations, Objects, Others*, Durham, NC and London: Duke University Press.

— (2010), *The Promise of Happiness*, Durham, NC and London: Duke University Press.

Akbar, Arifa (2010), 'Wartime Loves and Betrayals: Aminatta Forna's New Novel Casts a Fresh Light on Old Wounds', *The Independent*, 2 April, <http://www.independent.co.uk/arts-entertainment/books/features/wartime-loves-and-betrayals-aminatta-fornas-new-novel-casts-a-fresh-light-on-old-war-wounds-1933458.html> (last accessed 14 December 2016).

Alderson, David (2011), '*Saturday*'s Enlightenment', in Rachael Gilmour and Bill Schwarz (eds), *End of Empire and the English Novel Since 1945*, Manchester: Manchester University Press, pp. 118–237.

Andrews, Lindsey and Jonathan M. Metzl (2016), 'Reading the Image of Race: Neurocriminology, Medical Imaging Technologies and Literary Intervention', in Anne Whitehead and Angela Woods (eds), *The Edinburgh Companion to the Critical Medical Humanities*, pp. 242–59.

Arnold, Matthew (1971 [1869]), *Culture and Anarchy: An Essay in Political and Social Criticism*, ed. Ian Gregor, The Library of Literature, vol. 17, Indianapolis: Bobbs Merrill.

— (1964 [1882]), 'Literature and Science', in Noel Annan (ed.), *Matthew Arnold: Selected Essays*, London, New York and Toronto: Oxford University Press, pp. 208–32.

Atkinson, Sarah (2016), 'Care, Kidneys and Clones: The Distance of Space, Time and Imagination', in Anne Whitehead and Angela Woods (eds), *Edinburgh Companion to the Critical Medical Humanities*, pp. 611–26.

Avery, Simon (2011), 'Forming a New Political Aesthetic: The Enabling Body in Pat Barker's *Life Class*', in Pat Wheeler (ed.), *Re-reading Pat Barker*, Newcastle upon Tyne: Cambridge Scholars, pp. 131–50.

Banville, John (2005), 'A Day In the Life', *New York Review of Books*, 26 May, <http://www.nybooks.com/articles/2005/05/26/a-day-in-the-life> (last accessed 6 November 2016).

Barad, Karen (2007), *Meeting the Universe Halfway: Quantum Physics and the Entanglement of Matter and Meaning*, Durham, NC and London: Duke University Press.

Barker, Pat (1996), *The Regeneration Trilogy*, London: Viking.

— (2004), *Double Vision*, London: Hamish Hamilton.

— (2007), *Life Class*, London: Hamish Hamilton.

— (2012), *Toby's Room*, London: Hamish Hamilton.

Baron-Cohen, Simon (1995), *Mindblindness: An Essay on Autism and Theory of Mind*, Cambridge, MA: MIT Press.

— (2000), 'The Cognitive Neuroscience of Autism: Evolutionary Approaches', in M. S. Gazzaniga (ed.), *The New Cognitive Neurosciences*, 2nd edn, Cambridge, MA: MIT Press, pp. 1249–58.

— (2003), *The Essential Difference: Male and Female Brains and the Truth About Autism*, New York: Basic Books.

— (2008), *Autism and Asperger Syndrome*, Oxford: Oxford University Press.

— (2011), *Zero Degrees of Empathy: A New Theory of Human Cruelty*, London: Penguin.

Baron-Cohen, Simon, Alan M. Leslie and Uta Frith (1985) 'Does the Autistic Child Have a "Theory of Mind"?' *Cognition* 21: 37–46.

Batson, C. Daniel (1991), *The Altruism Question: Toward a Social-Psychological Answer*, Hillsdale, NJ: Erlbaum.

— (1998), 'Altruism and Prosocial Behaviour', in D. T. Gilbert, S. T. Fiske and G. Lindsey (eds), *The Handbook of Social Psychology*, vol. 2, New York: McGraw-Hill, pp. 282–316.

Bauman, Zygmunt (2004), *Wasted Lives: Modernity and its Outcasts*, Cambridge: Polity.

Bazalgette, Peter (2017), *The Empathy Instinct: How to Create a More Civil Society*, London: Hodder & Stoughton.

Belling, Catherine (2012), 'A Happy Doctor's Escape from Narrative: Reflection in *Saturday*', *Medical Humanities* 38.1: 2–6.

Berger, James (2008), 'Alterity and Autism: Mark Haddon's *Curious Incident* in the Neurological Spectrum', in Mark Osteen (ed.), *Autism and Representation*, pp. 271–86.

Berlant, Lauren (1998), 'Poor Eliza', *American Literature* 70.3: 635–68.

— ed. (2004a), *Compassion: The Culture and Politics of an Emotion*, Abingdon: Routledge.

— (2004b), 'Introduction: Compassion (and Withholding)', in Lauren Berlant (ed.), *Compassion: The Culture and Politics of an Emotion*, pp. 1–14.

— (2008), *The Female Complaint: The Unfinished Business of Sentimentality in American Culture*, Durham, NC and London: Duke University Press.

— (2011), *Cruel Optimism*, Durham, NC and London: Duke University Press.

Billington, Josie (2017), 'Book Review: The Edinburgh Companion to the Critical Medical Humanities', *BMJ Blogs*, 17 January, <https://blogs.bmj.com/medical-humanities/2017/01/17/book-review-the-edinburgh-companion-to-the-critical-medical-humanities> (accessed 20 January 2017)

Bishop, Jeffrey (2008), 'Rejecting Medical Humanism: Medical Humanities and the Metaphysics of Medicine', *Journal of Medical Humanities* 29: 15–25.

Black, Shameem (2009), 'Ishiguro's Inhuman Aesthetics', *Modern Fiction Studies* 55.4: 785–807.

Bloom, Paul (2017), *Against Empathy: The Case for Rational Compassion*, London: Bodley Head.

Bourke, Joanna (1996), *Dismembering the Male: Men's Bodies, Britain and the Great War*, London: Reaktion.

Boxall, Peter (2013), *Twenty-First Century Fiction: An Introduction*, Cambridge: Cambridge University Press.

Bradby, Hannah (2016), 'Medical Migration and the Global Politics of Equality', in Anne Whitehead and Angela Woods (eds), *The Edinburgh Companion to the Critical Medical Humanities*, pp. 491–507.

Brockman, John (2002), *The Next Fifty Years: Science and the First Half of the Twenty-First Century*, New York: Vintage.

Burdett, Carolyn (2011), 'Is Empathy the End of Sentimentality?' *Journal of Victorian Culture* 16.2: 259–74.

Burke, Lucy (2016), 'On (Not) Caring: Tracing the Meanings of Care in the Imaginative Literature of the "Alzheimer's Epidemic"', in Anne Whitehead and Angela Woods (eds), *The Edinburgh Companion to the Critical Medical Humanities*, pp. 596–610.

Burks-Abbott, Gyasi (2008), 'Mark Haddon's Popularity and Other Curious Incidents in My Life as an Autistic', in Mark Osteen (ed.), *Autism and Representation*, pp. 289–96.

Burn, Stephen J. (2013), 'Mapping the Syndrome Novel', in T. J. Lustig and James Peacock (eds), *Diseases and Disorders in Contemporary Fiction*, pp. 35–52.

Butler, Judith (2004), *Precarious Life: The Powers of Mourning and Violence*, New York: Verso.

Campo, Rafael (1997), *The Desire to Heal: A Doctor's Education in Empathy, Identity, and Poetry*, New York and London: W. W. Norton.

Carden-Coyne, Ana (2007), 'Ungrateful Bodies: Rehabilitation, Resistance and Disabled American Veterans of the First World War', *European Review of History* 14.4: 543–65.

— (2008), '"Painful Bodies and Brutal Women": Remedial Massage, Gender Relations and Cultural Agency in Military Hospitals', *Journal of War and Culture Studies* 1.2: 139–58.

Carosella, Edguardo and Thomas Pradeu (2006), 'Transplantation and Identity: A dangerous split?' *The Lancet* 368: 183–4.

Chambers, Emma (2009), 'Fragmented Identities: Reading Subjectivity in Henry Tonks' Surgical Portraits', *Art History* 32.2: 578–607.

Charon, Rita (2006), *Narrative Medicine: Honoring the Stories of Illness*, Oxford and New York: Oxford University Press.

Churchland, Patricia (2011), *Braintrust: What Neuroscience Tells Us About Morality*, Princeton and London: Princeton University Press.

Collini, Stefan (1988), *Arnold*, Oxford: Oxford University Press.

— (1998), 'Introduction', in C. P. Snow, *The Two Cultures*, Cambridge: Cambridge University Press, pp. ix–lxxiii.

Cooper, Melinda (2008), *Life as Surplus: Biotechnology and Capitalism in the Neoliberal Era*, Seattle and London: University of Washington Press.

Coplan, Amy and Peter Goldie (2011), 'Introduction', in Amy Coplan and Peter Goldie (eds), *Empathy: Philosophical and Psychological Perspectives*, Oxford: Oxford University Press, pp. ix–xlvii.

Craps, Stef (2013), *Postcolonial Witnessing: Trauma Out of Bounds*, Basingstoke: Palgrave.

Currie, Mark (2013), *The Unexpected: Narrative Temporality and the Philosophy of Surprise*, Edinburgh: Edinburgh University Press.

Cvetkovich, Ann (2003), *An Archive of Feelings: Trauma, Sexuality, and Lesbian Public Cultures*, Durham, NC and London: Duke University Press.

Dames, Nicholas (2007), *The Physiology of the Novel: Reading, Neural Science, and the Form of Victorian Fiction*, Oxford and New York: Oxford University Press.

Dancer, Thom (2012), 'Towards a Modest Criticism: Ian McEwan's *Saturday*', *Novel* 45.2: 202–20.

Das, Santanu (2005), *Touch and Intimacy in the First World War*, Cambridge: Cambridge University Press.

Daston, Lorraine and Gregg Mitman (eds) (2005), *Thinking with Animals: New Perspectives on Anthropomorphism*, New York: Columbia University Press.

Day, Sophie (2016), 'Waiting and the Architecture of Care', in Veena Das and Clara Han (eds), *Living and Dying in the Contemporary World: A Compendium*, Oakland: University of California Press, pp. 167–84.

de Waal, Frans (2005), *Our Inner Ape*, New York: Riverhead Books.

— (2009), *The Age of Empathy: Nature's Lessons for Kinder Society*, Toronto: McClelland and Stewart Ltd.

Diedrich, Lisa (2007), *Treatments: Language, Politics and the Culture of Illness*, Minneapolis: University of Minnesota Press.

Dowd, Siobhan (2007), *The London Eye Mystery*, Oxford: David Fickling.

Ellis, Ian (2004), 'Beyond Organ Retention: The New Human Tissue Bill', *The Lancet* 364: 42–3.

Evans, Martyn (2016), 'Medical Humanities and the Place of Wonder', in Anne Whitehead and Angela Woods (eds), *The Edinburgh Companion to the Critical Medical Humanities*, pp. 339–55.

Falconer, Rachel (2008), *The Crossover Novel: Contemporary Children's Literature and Its Adult Readership*, Abingdon: Routledge.

Fitzgerald, Des and Felicity Callard (2016), 'Entangling the Medical Humanities', in Anne Whitehead and Angela Woods (eds), *The Edinburgh Companion to the Critical Medical Humanities*, pp. 35–49.

Fludernik, Monika (1996), *Towards a 'Natural' Narratology*, London and New York: Routledge.

Fluet, Lisa (2007), 'Immaterial Labours: Ishiguro, Class and Affect', *Novel: A Forum on Fiction* 40.3: 265–88.

Forna, Aminatta (2002), *The Devil That Danced on the Water*, London: HarperCollins.

— (2006), *Ancestor Stones*, London: Bloomsbury.

— (2010), *The Memory of Love*, London: Bloomsbury.

— (2013), *The Hired Man*, London: Bloomsbury.

— (2014), 'Ebola: Amid the World's Hysteria the Real Heroes Are Forgotten', *Guardian*, 20 August, <https://www.guardian.com/commentisfree/2014/aug/20/ebola-western-hysteria-health-workers-risking-lives> (last accessed 14 December 2016).

— (2015), 'Aminatta Forna: Don't Judge a Book by its Author', *Guardian*, 13 February, <https://www.guardian.com/books/2015/feb/13/aminatta-forna-dont-judge-book-by-cover> (last accessed 14 December 2016).

Frank, Arthur W. (1995), *The Wounded Storyteller: Body, Illness, and Ethics*, Chicago: Chicago University Press.

Frith, Uta (2003), *Autism: Explaining the Enigma*, Oxford: Blackwell.

Gallagher, Shaun (2001), 'The Practice of Mind: Theory, Simulation or Interaction', *Journal of Consciousness Studies* 8.5–7: 83–108.

Gallagher, Shaun and Dan Zahavi (2012), *The Phenomenological Mind*, 2nd edn, Abingdon: Routledge.

Garden, Rebecca Elizabeth (2007), 'The Problem of Empathy: Medicine and the Humanities', *New Literary History* 38.3: 551–67.

Goldberg, Elizabeth Swanson and Alexandra Schultheis Moore (2012), 'Introduction: Human Rights and Literature: The Development of an Interdiscipline', in Elizabeth Swanson Goldberg, Elizabeth Swanson and Alexandra Schultheis Moore (eds), *Theoretical Perspectives on Human Rights and Literature*, Abingdon: Routledge, pp. 3–16.

Goldman, Alvin I. (2006), *Simulating Minds: The Philosophy, Psychology, and Neuroscience of Mindreading*, Oxford: Oxford University Press.

Gottschall, Jonathan and David Sloan Wilson (eds) (2005), *The Literary Animal: Evolution and the Nature of Narrative*, Evanston: Northwestern University Press.

Grandin, Temple (2006), *Thinking in Pictures and Other Reports from My Life with Autism*, London: Bloomsbury.

— and Catherine Johnson (2006), *Animals in Translation: The Woman Who Thinks Like a Cow*, London: Bloomsbury.

Griffin, Gabriele (2009), 'Science and the Cultural Imaginary: The Case of Kazuo Ishiguro's *Never Let Me Go*', *Textual Practice* 23.4: 645–63.

Groes, Sebastian and Barry Lewis (eds) (2011a), 'Introduction: "It's good manners, really" – Kazuo Ishiguro and the Ethics of Empathy', in Sebastian Groes and Barry Lewis (eds), *Kazuo Ishiguro: New Critical Visions of the Novels*, pp. 1–12.

— (2011b), *Kazuo Ishiguro: New Critical Visions of the Novels*, Basingstoke: Palgrave Macmillan.

Gruen, Lori (2015), *Entangled Empathy: An Alternative Ethic for Our Relationships with Animals*, New York: Lantern Books.

Hacking, Ian (1999), *The Social Construction of What?* Cambridge, MA and London: Harvard University Press.

— (2009), 'Autistic Autobiography', *Philosophical Transactions of the Royal Society: Biological Sciences* 364.1522: 1467–73.

Haddon, Mark (2003), *The Curious Incident of the Dog in the Night-Time*, London: Vintage.

Hadley, Elaine (2005), 'On a Darkling Plain: Victorian Liberalism and the Fantasy of Agency', *Victorian Studies* 48.1: 92–102.

Hallett, Christine (2009), *Containing Trauma: Nursing Work in the First World War*, Manchester: Manchester University Press.

Halpern, Jodi (2001), *From Detached Concern to Empathy: Humanizing Medical Practice*, Oxford and New York: Oxford University Press.

Hammond, Meghan Marie (2014), *Empathy and the Psychology of Literary Modernism*, Edinburgh: Edinburgh University Press.

Haraway, Donna (2003), *The Companion Species Manifesto: Dogs, People, and Significant Otherness*, Chicago: Prickly Paradigm Press.

— (2008), *When Species Meet*, Minneapolis: University of Minnesota Press.

Head, Dominic (2002), *The Cambridge Introduction to Modern British Fiction, 1950–2000*, Cambridge: Cambridge University Press.

— (2007), *Ian McEwan*, Manchester: Manchester University Press.

Hemmings, Clare (2005), 'Invoking Affect', *Cultural Studies* 19.5: 548–67.

— (2011), *Why Stories Matter: The Political Grammar of Feminist Theory*, Durham, NC and London: Duke University Press.

Herman, David (2002), *Story Logic: Problems and Possibilities of Narrative*, Lincoln and London: University of Nebraska Press.

— (ed.) (2011), *The Emergence of Mind: Representations of Consciousness in Narrative Discourse in English*, Lincoln and London: University of Nebraska Press.

— (2016), 'Trans-Species Entanglements: Animal Assistants in Narratives about Autism', in Anne Whitehead and Angela Woods (eds), *The Edinburgh Companion to the Critical Medical Humanities*, pp. 463–80.

Hertz, Neil (2004), 'Poor Hetty', in Lauren Berlant (ed.), *Compassion: The Culture and Politics of an Emotion*, pp. 87–104.

Hester, Rebecca J. (2016), 'Culture in Medicine: An Argument Against Competence', in Anne Whitehead and Angela Woods (eds), *The Edinburgh Companion to the Critical Medical Humanities*, pp. 541–58.

Higonnet, Margaret (2002), 'Authenticity and Art in Trauma Narratives of World War I', *Modernism/Modernity* 9.1: 91–107.

Hochschild, Arlie Russell (2012 [1983]), *The Managed Heart: Commercialization of Human Feeling*, updated with a new preface, Berkeley and London: University of California Press.

Holloway, Karla F. C. (2011), *Private Bodies, Public Texts: Race, Gender, and a Cultural Bioethics*, Durham, NC and London: Duke University Press.

Hooker, Claire and Estelle Noonan (2011), 'Medical Humanities as Expressive of Western Culture', *Medical Humanities* 37: 79–84.

Horton, Emily (2014), 'Reassessing the Two-Culture Debate: Popular Science in Ian McEwan's *The Child in Time* and *Enduring Love*', *Modern Fiction Studies* 59.4: 683–712.

Houston, Rab and Uta Frith (2000), *Autism in History: The Case of Hugh Blair of Borgue*, Oxford: Blackwell.

Hsieh, Lili (2006), 'The Other Side of the Picture: The Politics of Affect in Virginia Woolf's *Three Guineas*', *Journal of Narrative Theory* 36.1: 20–52.

Hume, David (1978 [1739]), *A Treatise of Human Nature*, ed. L. A Selby-Bigge, Oxford: Clarendon Press.

Humm, Maggie (2003), 'Memory, Photography and Modernism: The "Dead Bodies and Ruined Houses" of Virginia Woolf's *Three Guineas*', *Signs* 28.2: 645–63.

Hunt, Lynn (2007), *Inventing Human Rights: A History*, New York and London: W. W. Norton.

Iacobini, Marco (2008), *Mirroring People: The Science of Empathy and How We Connect With Others*, New York: Picador.

Illouz, Eva (2007), *Cold Intimacies: The Making of Emotional Capitalism*, Cambridge: Polity.

Ishiguro, Kazuo (2005), *Never Let Me Go*, London: Faber.

Jaggi, Maya (2013), 'Aminatta Forna: A Life in Writing', *Guardian*, 3 May, <http://www.theguardian.com/books/2013/may/03/aminatta-forna-a-life-in-books> (last accessed 14 December 2016).

Jamison, Leslie (2014), *The Empathy Exams: Essays*, London: Granta.

Jurecic, Ann (2011), 'Empathy and the Critic', *College English* 74.1: 10–27.

Keen, Suzanne (2007) *Empathy and the Novel*, Oxford: Oxford University Press.

Kentikelenis, Alexander, Lawrence King, Martin McKee and David Stuckler (2014) 'The International Monetary Fund and the Ebola Outbreak', *The Lancet*, December 22, <http://dx.doi..org/10.1016/S2214-109X (14)70377-8> (accessed 20 January 2017).

Kittay, Eva Feder (2001), 'When Caring Is Just and Justice Is Caring: Justice and Mental Retardation', *Public Culture* 13.3: 557–79.

Kleffel, Rick (2005), 'Interview with Kazuo Ishiguro', *Interzone* 198 (May/June): 62–3.

Kleinman, Arthur (1988), *The Illness Narratives: Suffering, Healing, and the Human Condition*, New York: Basic Books.

Knights, David and Emma Surman (2008), 'Editorial: Addressing the Gender Gap in Studies of Emotion', *Gender, Work and Organization* 15.1: 1–8.

Kramnick, Jonathan (2012), 'Literary Studies and Science: A Reply to My Critics', *Critical Inquiry* 38.2: 431–60.

Krishnan, Madhu (2015), 'Affect, Empathy, and Engagement: Reading African Conflict in the Global Marketplace', *Journal of Commonwealth Literature*, pp. 1–19, <http://journals.sagepub.com/doi/pdf/10.1177/0021989415596011> (accessed 5 April 2017).

Leavis, F. R. (1972a [1966]), 'Luddites? Or, There Is Only One Culture', in F. R. Leavis, *Nor Shall My Sword*, pp. 75–100.

— (1972b), *Nor Shall My Sword: Discourses on Pluralism, Compassion and Social Hope*, London: Chatto and Windus.

— (1972c [1962]), 'Two Cultures? The Significance of Lord Snow', in F. R. Leavis, *Nor Shall My Sword*, pp. 39–74.

Lipps, Theodor (1966 [1897]), *Raumästhetik und geometrische-optische*, Amsterdam: E. J. Bonset.

Lochner, Liani (2011), '"This is what we're supposed to be doing, isn't it?": Scientific Discourse in Kazuo Ishiguro's *Never Let Me Go*', in Sebastian Groes and Barry Lewis (eds), *Kazuo Ishiguro: New Critical Visions of the Novels*, pp. 225–35.

Longden, Eleanor, Philip Davis, Josie Billington, Sofia Lampropoulou, Grace Farrington, Fiona Magee, Erin Walsh and Rhiannon Corcoran (2015), 'Shared Reading: Assessing the Intrinsic Value of a Literature-based Health Intervention', *Medical Humanities* 41: 113–20.

Lustig, T. J. and James Peacock (eds) (2013), *Diseases and Disorders in Contemporary Fiction: The Syndrome Syndrome*, Abingdon: Routledge.

McEwan, Ian (2001), 'Only Love and Then Oblivion: Love Was All They Had to Set Against Their Murderers', *Guardian*, 15 September, <http://www.theguardian.com/world/2001/sep/15/september11.politicsphiloso-phyandsociety2> (last accessed 03/11/2016).

— (2005a [2001]), 'Literature, Science, and Human Nature', in Jonathan Gottschall and David Sloan Wilson (eds), *The Literary Animal*, pp. 5–19.

— (2005b) *Saturday*, London: Jonathan Cape.

McKechnie, Claire (2014), 'Anxieties of Communication: The Limits of Narrative in the Medical Humanities', *Medical Humanities*, May 28: 1–6.

Makkreel, Rudolf (1996), 'How Is Empathy Related to Understanding?' in T. Nenon and L. Embree (eds), *Issues in Husserl's Ideas II*, The Hague: Kluwer Academic Publishers, pp. 199–212.

Malabou, Catherine (2012), *The New Wounded: From Neurosis to Brain Damage*, trans. Steven Miller, New York: Fordham University Press.

Marcus, Laura (2009), 'Ian McEwan's Modernist Time: *Atonement* and *Saturday*', in Sebastian Groes (ed.), *Ian McEwan: Contemporary Critical Perspectives*, London and New York: Continuum, pp. 83–98.

Marshall, George Robert Ellison and Claire Hooker (2016), 'Empathy and Affect: What Can Empathied Bodies Do?', *Medical Humanities* 42: 128–34.

Metzl, Jonathan M. (2009), *The Protest Psychosis: How Schizophrenia Became a Black Disease*, Boston: Beacon Press.

Miller, Gavin and Anna McFarlane (2016), 'Science Fiction and the Medical Humanities', *Medical Humanities* 42: 213–18.

Moran, Joe (2010), *Interdisciplinarity: New Critical Idiom*, Abingdon: Routledge.

Morrison, Toni (1987), *Beloved*, London: Vintage.

Mukhopadhyay, Tito Rajarshi (2000), *Beyond the Silence: My Life, the World and Autism*, London: National Autistic Society.

Murray, Stuart (2006), 'Autism and the Contemporary Sentimental: Fiction and the Narrative Fascination of the Present', *Literature and Medicine* 25.1: 24–45.

— (2008), *Representing Autism: Culture, Narrative, Fascination*, Liverpool: Liverpool University Press.

— (2012), *Autism*, Abingdon: Routledge.

— (2016), 'Afterword: Health, Care Citizens', in Anne Whitehead and Angela Woods (eds), *The Edinburgh Companion to the Critical Medical Humanities*, pp. 627–32.

Nadesan, Majia Holmer (2005), *Constructing Autism: Unravelling the "Truth" and Understanding the Social*, Abingdon: Routledge.

Nancy, Jean-Luc (2002), *L'Intrus*, trans. Susan Hanson, Ann Arbor: Michigan State University Press.

Ngai, Sianne (2005), *Ugly Feelings*, Cambridge, MA and London: Harvard University Press.

Norridge, Zoe (2012), 'Sex as Synecdoche: Intimate Languages of Violence in Chimamanda Ngozi Adichie's *Half of a Yellow Sun* and Aminatta Forna's *The Memory of Love*', *Research in African Literatures* 43.2: 18–39.

— (2013), *Perceiving Pain in African Literature*, Basingstoke: Palgrave Macmillan.

— (2014), 'Ways of Knowing Civil War: Human Rights and the Traction of Complicity in Aminatta Forna's *The Hired Man*', *Critical Quarterly* 56.4: 99–113.

Nussbaum, Martha C. (1997), *Cultivating Humanity: A Classical Defense of Reform in Liberal Education*, Cambridge, MA: Harvard University Press.

— (2010), *Not For Profit: Why Democracy Needs The Humanities*, Princeton and Oxford: Princeton University Press.

Obama, Barack (2007), 'Pres. Barack Obama: Literacy and Empathy', <http://www.youtube.com/watch?v=LGHbbJ5xz3.g> (last accessed 7 October 2016).

Osteen, Mark, ed. (2008a), *Autism and Representation*, Abingdon: Routledge.

— (2008b), 'Autism and Representation: A Comprehensive Introduction', in Mark Osteen (ed.), *Autism and Representation*, pp. 1–47.

Palmer, Alan (2008), *Fictional Minds*, Lincoln and London: University of Nebraska Press.

Palumbo-Liu, David (2012), *The Deliverance of Others: Reading Literature in a Global Age*, Durham, NC and London: Duke University Press.

Parry, Bronwyn (2015), 'Narratives of Neoliberalism: "Clinical Labour" in Context', *Medical Humanities* 41: 32–7.

Pedwell, Carolyn (2014), *Affective Relations: The Transnational Politics of Empathy*, Basingstoke: Palgrave Macmillan.

Pedwell, Carolyn and Anne Whitehead (2012), 'Introduction: Affecting Feminism: Questions of Feeling in Feminist Theory', *Feminist Theory* 13.2: 115–29.

Pick, Daniel (1993), *War Machine: The Rationalization of Slaughter in the Modern Age*, New Haven, CT: Yale University Press.

Potter, Rachel and Lyndsey Stonebridge (2014), 'Writing and Rights', *Critical Quarterly* 56.4: 1–16.

Preston, Stephanie and Frans de Waal (2002), 'Empathy: Its Ultimate and Proximate Bases', *Behavioural Brain Sciences* 25.1: 1–20.

Raghuram, Parvati (2009), 'Caring about "Brain Drain" Migration in a Postcolonial World', *Geoforum* 40: 25–33.

Rajan, Kaushik Sunder (2006), *Biocapital: The Constitution of Pregenomic Life*, Durham, NC and London: Duke University Press.

Ratcliffe, Matthew (2012), 'Phenomenology as a Form of Empathy', *Inquiry* 55.5: 473–95.

Rejali, Darius (2007), *Torture and Democracy*, Princeton: Princeton University Press.

Remnick, David (2010), *The Bridge: The Life and Rise of Barack Obama*, New York: Alfred A. Knopf.

Resene, Michelle (2016), 'A "Curious Incident": Representations of Autism in Children's Detective Fiction', *The Lion and the Unicorn* 40.1: 81–99.

Rose, Nikolas (2007), *The Politics of Life Itself: Biomedicine, Power, and Subjectivity in the Twenty-First Century*, Princeton and Oxford: Princeton University Press.

Rose, Nikolas and Joelle M. Abi-Rached (2013), *Neuro: The New Brain Sciences and the Management of the Mind*, Princeton: Princeton University Press.

Salisbury, Laura (2010), 'Narration and Neurology: Ian McEwan's Mother Tongue', *Textual Practice* 24.5: 883–912.

— (2016), 'Aphasic Modernism: Languages for Illness from a Confusion of Tongues', in Anne Whitehead and Angela Woods (eds), *The Edinburgh Companion to the Critical Medical Humanities*, pp. 444–62.

Savarese, Ralph James and Lisa Zunshine (2014), 'The Critic as Neurocosmopolite; Or, What Cognitive Approaches to Literature Can Learn from Disability Studies', *Narrative* 22.1: 17–44.

Schaffer, Kay and Sidonie Smith (2004), *Human Rights and Narrated Lives: The Ethics of Recognition*, New York: Palgrave.

Scheper-Hughes, Nancy (2004), 'Parts Unknown: Undercover Ethnography of the Organ-trafficking Underworld', *Ethnography* 5.1: 29–73.

Shildrick, Margaret (2014), 'Visceral Phenomenology: Organ Transplantation, Identity, and Bioethics', in Kristian Zeiler and Lisa Folkmarson Käll (eds), *Feminist Phenomenology and Medicine*, New York: SUNY Press, pp. 47–59.

Skloot, Rebecca (2010), *The Immortal Life of Henrietta Lacks*, London: Pan.

Slaughter, Joseph R. (2007), *Human Rights, Inc.: The World Novel, Narrative Form, and International Law*, New York: Fordham University Press.

— (2014), 'The Enchantment of Human Rights; or, What Difference Does Humanitarian Indifference Make?', *Critical Quarterly* 56.4: 46–66.

Smajdor, Anna (2013), 'Reification and Compassion in Medicine: A Tale of Two Systems', *Clinical Ethics* 8.4: 111–18.

Small, Helen (2013), *The Value of the Humanities*, Oxford: Oxford University Press.

Smith, Adam (1976 [1759]), *The Theory of Moral Sentiments*, ed. D. D. Rafael and A. L. Macfie, Vol. I, Glasgow Edition of the Works and Correspondence of Adam Smith, Oxford and New York: Oxford University Press.

Snow, C. P. (1998 [1959]), *The Two Cultures*, with an Introduction by Stefan Collini, Cambridge: Cambridge University Press.

Sontag, Susan (2003), *Regarding the Pain of Others*, New York: Farrar, Straus, and Giroux.

Spelman, Elizabeth V. (1997), *Fruits of Sorrow: Framing Our Attention to Suffering*, Boston, MA: Beacon Press.

Spiro, Howard, Mary G. McCrea Curnen, Enid Peschel and Deborah St James (eds) (1993a), *Empathy and the Practice of Medicine: Beyond Pills and the Scalpel*, New Haven, CT: Yale University Press.

— (1993b), 'Empathy: An Introduction', in Howard Spiro et al. (eds), *Empathy and the Practice of Medicine*, pp. 1–6.

— (1993c), 'What Is Empathy and Can It Be Taught?', in Howard Spiro et al. (eds), *Empathy and the Practice of Medicine*, pp. 7–14.

Squier, Susan Merrill (2004), *Liminal Lives: Imagining the Human at the Frontiers of Biomedicine*, Durham, NC and London: Duke University Press.

Stein, Edith (1989 [1917]), On the Problem of Empathy, trans. Waltraut Stein, 3rd rev. edn, Washington, DC: ICS Publications.

Stevenson, Sheryl (2008), 'M(O)thering and Autism: Maternal Rhetorics of Self-Revision', in Mark Osteen (ed.), *Autism and Representation*, pp. 197–211.

Stowe, Harriet Beecher (2004 [1852]), *Uncle Tom's Cabin, or Life Among the Lowly*, Fairfield, IA: First World Library.

Swan, Elaine (2008), '"You Make Me Feel Like a Woman": Therapeutic Cultures and the Contagion of Femininity', *Gender, Work and Organization* 15.1: 88–107.

Theodosius, Catherine (2008), *Emotional Labour in Health Care: The Unmanaged Heart of Nursing*, London and New York: Routledge.

Thrailkill, Jane F. (2011), 'Ian McEwan's Neurological Novel', *Poetics Today* 32.1: 171–201.

Todman, Dan (2007), *The Great War: Myth and Memory*, London: Bloomsbury Academic.

Tolan, Fiona (2010), '"Painting While Rome Burns": Ethics and Aesthetics in Pat Barker's *Life Class* and Zadie Smith's *On Beauty*', *Tulsa Studies in Women's Literature* 29.2: 375–93.

Viney, Will (2016), 'Getting the Measure of Twins', in Anne Whitehead and Angela Woods (eds), *The Edinburgh Companion to the Critical Medical Humanities*, pp. 104–19.

Vischer, Robert (1994 [1873]), 'On the Optical Sense of Form: A Contribution to Aesthetics', in *Empathy, Form and Space: Problems in German Aesthetics*, trans. Harry Frances Mallgrave and Eleftherios Ikonamou, Los Angeles: Getty Research Institute, pp. 89–123.

Waldby, Catherine (2002), 'Biomedicine, Tissue Transfer, and Intercorporeality', *Feminist Theory* 3.3: 239–54.

Waldby, Catherine and Robert Mitchell (2006), *Tissue Economies: Blood, Organs, and Cell Lines in Late Capitalism*, Durham NC and London: Duke University Press.

Walkowitz, Rebecca L. (2007), 'Unimaginable Largeness: Kazuo Ishiguro, Translation, and the New World Literature', *Novel: A Forum on Fiction* 40.3: 216–39.

Waugh, Patricia (1997), 'The New Prometheans: Literature, Criticism, and Science in the Modern and Postmodern Condition', *European Journal of English Studies* 1.2: 139–64.

— (2011), 'Kazuo Ishiguro's not-too-late modernism', in Sebastian Groes and Barry Lewis (eds), *Kazuo Ishiguro: New Critical Visions of the Novels*, pp. 13–30.

— (2013), 'The Naturalistic Turn, the Syndrome, and the Rise of the Phenomenological Novel', in T. J. Lustig and James Peacock (eds), *Diseases and Disorders in Contemporary Fiction*, pp. 17–34.

— (2016), 'Afterword: Evidence and Experiment', in Anne Whitehead and Angela Woods (eds), *The Edinburgh Companion to the Critical Medical Humanities*, pp. 153–60.

Weil, Kari (2012), *Thinking Animals: Why Animal Studies Now?* New York: Columbia University Press.

Whitehead, Anne (2011), 'Writing with Care: Kazuo Ishiguro's *Never Let Me Go*', *Contemporary Literature* 52.1: 54–83.

— (2014), 'The Medical Humanities: A Literary Perspective', in Victoria Bates, Alan Bleakley and Sam Goodman (eds), *Medicine, Health and the Arts: Approaches to the Medical Humanities*, London and New York: Routledge, pp. 107–27.

— (2015), 'War and Beauty: The Act of Unmasking in Pat Barker's *Toby's Room* and Louisa Young's *My Dear, I Wanted to Tell You*', in Corrine

Saunders, Jane Macnaughton and David Fuller (eds), *The Recovery of Beauty: Arts, Culture, Medicine*, Basingstoke: Palgrave, pp. 217–34.

Whitehead, Anne and Angela Woods, with Sarah Atkinson, Jane Macnaughton and Jennifer Richards (eds) (2016), *The Edinburgh Companion to the Critical Medical Humanities*, Edinburgh: Edinburgh University Press.

Whitehead, Anne and Angela Woods (2016), 'Introduction', in Anne Whitehead and Angela Woods (eds), *The Edinburgh Companion to the Critical Medical Humanities*, pp. 1–31.

Williams, Carolyn (2004), 'Moving Pictures: George Eliot and Melodrama', in Lauren Berlant (ed.), *Compassion: The Culture and Politics of an Emotion*, pp. 105–44.

Wilson, Elizabeth A. (2004), *Psychosomatic: Feminism and the Neurological Body*, Durham, NC and London: Duke University Press.

— (2015), *Gut Feminism*, Durham, NC and London: Duke University Press.

Wilson, E. O. (2005), 'Foreword from the Scientific Side', in Jonathan Gottschall and David Sloan Wilson (eds), *The Literary Animal*, pp. vii–xi.

Wimmer, Heinz and Josef Perner (1983), 'Beliefs about Beliefs: Representation and Constraining Function of Wrong Beliefs in Young Children's Understanding of Deception', *Cognition* 13.1: 103–28.

Winning, Jo (2016), 'Afterword: The Body and the Senses', in Anne Whitehead and Angela Woods (eds), *The Edinburgh Companion to the Critical Medical Humanities*, pp. 325–38.

Wooden, Shannon R. (2011), 'Narrative Medicine in the Literature Classroom: Ethical Pedagogy and Mark Haddon's *The Curious Incident of the Dog in the Night-Time*', *Literature and Medicine* 29.2: 274–96.

Woods, Angela (2011), 'The Limits of Narrative: Provocations for the Medical Humanities', *Medical Humanities* 37: 73–8.

Woodward, Kathleen (2004), 'Calculating Compassion', in Lauren Berlant (ed.), *Compassion: The Culture and Politics of an Emotion*, pp. 59–86.

Woolf, Virginia (1977 [1938]), *Three Guineas*, London: Hogarth Press.

Yergeau, Melanie (2013) 'Clinically Significant Disturbance: On Theorists Who Theorise Theory of Mind', *Disability Studies Quarterly* 33.4, <http://dsq-sds.org/article/view/3876/3405> (accessed 5 April 2017).

Young, Louisa (2011), *My Dear, I Wanted to Tell You*, London: HarperCollins.

Zahavi, Dan (2014), 'Empathy and Other-directed Intentionality', *Topoi* 33: 129–42.

Zahavi, Dan and Josef Parnas (2003), 'Conceptual Problems in Infantile Autism Research: Why Cognitive Science Needs Phenomenology', *Journal of Consciousness Studies* 10.9–10: 53–7.

Zunshine, Lisa (2003), 'Theory of Mind and Experimental Representations of Consciousness', *Narrative* 11.3: 270–91.

— (2006), *Why We Read Fiction: Theory of Mind and the Novel*, Columbus: Ohio State University Press.

Index